D1615891

HOW THE DRUG WAR RUINS AMERICAN LIVES

HOW THE DRUG WAR RUINS AMERICAN LIVES

ARTHUR BENAVIE

 PRAEGER™

An Imprint of ABC-CLIO, LLC
Santa Barbara, California • Denver, Colorado

Library of Congress Cataloging-in-Publication Data

Names: Benavie, Arthur, author.
Title: How the drug war ruins American lives / Arthur Benavie.
Description: Santa Barbara : Praeger, 2016. | Includes bibliographical
    references and index.
Identifiers: LCCN 2015043642 | ISBN 9781440850110 (print : alk. paper) |
    ISBN 9781440850127 (ebook)
Subjects: LCSH: Drug control—United States. | Drug legalization—United
    States. | Drug testing—United States. | Social problems—United States.
Classification: LCC HV5825 .B436 2016 | DDC 363.450973—dc23
LC record available at http://lccn.loc.gov/2015043642

ISBN: 978-1-4408-5011-0
EISBN: 978-1-4408-5012-7

20 19 18 17   2 3 4 5

This book is also available on the World Wide Web as an eBook.
Visit www.abc-clio.com for details.

Praeger
An Imprint of ABC-CLIO, LLC

ABC-CLIO, LLC
130 Cremona Drive, P.O. Box 1911
Santa Barbara, California 93116-1911

This book is printed on acid-free paper (∞)

Manufactured in the United States of America

To my wife, Marcy,
with all my love.

Contents

Acknowledgments

For several years I have conducted a seminar on the drug war for students who are in their first year at the University of North Carolina at Chapel Hill. Their insights and compassion have been a joy and an inspiration to me and have boosted my optimism about the future of our country. They have made an indelible contribution to this book.

I wish to express my appreciation to Judge James P. Gray who read portions of an earlier version of the manuscript and shared with me his knowledge and enthusiasm for the project.

I am grateful to a number of people with whom I have discussed this project and who gave me their advice: Daryl V. Atkinson, Ethan Nadelmann, Jeffrey A. Miron, Pat Oglesby, Jessica Smith, Richard B. Whisnant, and two Chapel Hill police officers.

I am deeply indebted to two knowledgeable, anonymous reviewers who read an earlier version of the manuscript and provided many constructive suggestions on both substance and style. They went far beyond the usual duties of a reviewer. Whoever you are, thank you!

My profound thanks to my editor, Jessica Gribble, for her support and encouragement.

Finally, and most of all, I owe a debt of gratitude to my wife, Marcy Lansman, who spent many weeks working on the manuscript with me. To the extent that the book is lucid and well-organized she deserves much of the credit.

Introduction

In August 2008, Terrance L. Mosley, an African American man, was seated in the passenger seat of a parked car. A police officer searched the car allegedly because it had duplicate license plates and was parked facing traffic. The officer found two bags of marijuana in the car totaling about two pounds. Mosley said he was just getting a ride and vehemently denied that he knew about the marijuana. The driver pleaded guilty and received probation; but Mosley was sentenced as a habitual offender because of 12-year-old convictions for nonviolent drug offenses. His only two priors were for possession with intent to distribute cocaine when he was 17 and for distribution of cocaine when he was 18. Because of these three crimes, Mosley was sentenced to life in prison. He had been a special education student and has an eighth-grade education. He is the father of five children and his fiancée visits him regularly.[1]

It's unlikely that you've heard about this tragedy because similar stories are so common they're rarely covered by the media, but it exemplifies how millions of nonviolent U.S. citizens have had their lives ruined by our national obsession with drugs. We have become a country where the merest contact with illicit drugs—or even an unfounded accusation by an officer or an informant—can cause people to lose their job, their property, and even their freedom. The upsurge in drug arrests and incarcerations that began in the 1980s was a backlash against the cultural upheavals of the 1960s, a decade characterized by protests against the Vietnam War, civil rights demonstrations, riots, homicides, and a soaring use of illicit drugs.

President Richard Nixon envisioned a war on drugs as an ideal strategy to deal with what was widely perceived as a breakdown of law and order. Nixon told his chief of staff H. R. Haldeman, "You have to face the fact that the whole problem is really the blacks. The key is to devise a system that recognizes this without appearing to."[2] The president's White House counsel, John Ehrlichman, explained the rationale for a drug war this way,

> The Nixon White House . . . had two enemies: the antiwar Left, and black people . . . We knew we couldn't make it illegal to be either against the war or [the] black(s). But by getting the public to associate the hippies with marijuana and blacks with heroin, and then criminalizing both heavily, we could disrupt those communities. We could arrest their leaders, raid their homes, break up their meetings, and vilify them night after night on the evening news. Did we know we were lying about the drugs? Of course we did.[3]

But Nixon was faced with a major obstacle in expanding the war: The federal government had little authority over street crimes. That function belonged to state and local police, who were overwhelmed with violent crimes and had little incentive to go after nonviolent drug law offenders.

By the 1980s, many were blaming illicit drugs for just about everything that went wrong with the country. Respected national figures were vying with each other in demonizing drug users and sellers and recommending medieval punishments, with scarcely any publicly expressed dissents:

> "If you are a casual drug user, you are an accomplice to murder," said Nancy Reagan.[4]
>
> Los Angeles police chief Daryl Gates testified before the Senate Judiciary Committee in 1990 that casual drug users "ought to be taken out and shot . . . We're in a war, and even casual drug use is treason."[5]

In this hysterical and vengeful atmosphere, overwhelming bipartisan pressure developed for the federal government to assume a major role in cracking down on state and local drug crimes. In the 1980s, Congress and the states responded by enacting laws authorizing law enforcement to profit from the war on drugs, laws that are still with us today. This legislation introduced a corrupting element into our criminal justice system by allowing police and prosecutors to earn revenue by arresting drug law violators and confiscating their property.[6]

As Founding Father George Mason warned in the debates in the Federal Convention of 1787: "When the same man, or set of men, holds the sword and the purse, there is an end to Liberty."[7] Our law enforcement is holding both the sword and the purse.

The theme of this book is that the escalation of the war on drugs has eroded our human and property rights. Parts I through V explore the several interrelated ways in which the drug war has inflicted these damages. Part VI looks at the question I am most frequently asked, "Is the drug war coming to an end?" Part VII contains a summary, and also assesses the evidence on whether the war on drugs has had any benefits that could weigh against its costs to our society.

Here is a brief overview of the seven parts of the book:

Part I explains how policing for profit works and describes how it has caused a variety of assaults on our civil liberties, assaults that did not even exist prior to the 1980s: the mass incarceration of nonviolent drug law violators, SWAT teams violently breaking into homes hunting for illicit drugs, suspicionless drug sweeps of pedestrians and travelers, and government confiscation of property without clear proof of guilt.

Part II focuses on how racism infects every aspect of the war on drugs. The well-known racial disparity in drug arrests and incarcerations is no accident; it's rooted in the nature of the war. The reason? Law enforcement cannot begin to arrest all those who commit drug offenses (a nonviolent crime); they routinely arrest less than 5 percent of the perpetrators. So police have enormous discretion as to where they send their troops to fight the war. Given the widespread stereotype of blacks and Latinos as drug traffickers, even the least prejudiced officers are prone to target people of color. Moreover, law enforcement is unlikely to be punished for even the most blatant racial disparities in arrests and incarcerations because the U.S. Supreme Court has made it practically impossible to win a lawsuit challenging racial injustice.

Part III describes the damage to our civil liberties resulting from the increase in undercover police and criminal informants that are necessitated by the escalation of the drug war. Because drug crimes involve willing transactors, police rarely receive reports about these illegal and hidden transactions. Consequently, officers must go undercover to solve these crimes, where they require help from informants in order to navigate the criminal underworld. Undercover police are prime targets for bribes from wealthy drug cartels and some are corrupted by these temptations. Officers who operate undercover for more than a short time face serious psychological as well as physical dangers; they constitute one of the rarely mentioned casualties of the war on drugs. Criminal informants (a.k.a. snitches) are notorious liars, willing to say to anything that might persuade prosecutors to shorten their sentences. As a result of their false testimony, many innocent people have been imprisoned.

In addition, innumerable people have had their residences invaded by SWAT teams because of false information from snitches.

Part IV describes how the escalation in the drug war has condemned millions of nonviolent and otherwise law-abiding Americans to a lifetime of struggling with barriers to full citizenship. After completing the sentence mandated by a judge, anyone convicted of a drug law violation is caught in a maze of additional penalties, such as obstacles to employment, housing, welfare, education benefits, driver's licenses, and voting rights. These penalties, which are outside the traditional sentencing framework, are called "invisible punishments." Three invisible punishments target drug law violators. Those convicted of a drug offense, no matter how minor, will be denied federal welfare benefits for the rest of their life. No other crime carries such a draconian punishment, not even rape or murder. Suspensions of federal education benefits and driver's licenses are the other invisible punishments that single out drug law violators.

Part V looks at how the escalation of the war has led to the emergence of nationwide, random drug testing of employees as well as of high school students, an invasion of privacy that did not exist prior to the 1980s. Self-serving propaganda by law enforcement officials that marijuana is not only a hazardous substance but is a gateway to hard drugs has played a role in frightening many Americans into supporting drug testing.[8] Drug czar John Walters, for example, has referred to marijuana as a "poison."[9] Contrary to the views of the American public, the U.S. Supreme Court, and government officials, major empirical studies, such as those by the U.S. Department of Education and the University of Michigan, have failed to find evidence that random testing is effective at diminishing illicit drug use or affecting attitudes toward the risks involved in consuming these substances.

Part VI looks at the question of whether the drug war is ending. Recent events suggest the war may have reached a turning point. A majority of Americans now approve the legalization of marijuana. The federal government has conditionally acquiesced to the drug's legalization in several states. The former U.S. Attorney General Eric Holder has inveighed against the harsh sentences imposed on low-level, nonviolent drug offenders. Surprisingly, Holder even attempted in January 2015 to diminish some of the revenue state and federal police get from the drug war.[10] These evolving attitudes by the American public and the federal government are good news for those who want to end the war. But there are also contrary forces, influential groups that benefit from the drug war, such as law enforcement, government agencies, and numerous corporations. One way to get an idea of how powerful the groups are that profit from the war is to compare the attitudes and statements of Barack Obama about drug policy before and after he became president. He has undergone such a dramatic transformation from anti–drug war to pro–drug war that it's hard to avoid the conclusion that once he assumed the presidency he succumbed to pressure from groups that benefited from the war. After all, Obama's administration, Holder's rhetoric notwithstanding, still adamantly opposes the legalization of marijuana and continues to classify it as a Schedule I drug, the same class as heroin, LSD, and ecstasy, which signifies it has no accepted medical use and has a high potential for abuse.[11]

Part VII contains a summary of the main arguments of the book. It also explores the question of whether the drug war has produced the results laid out in its statement of its goals, namely, to diminish the consumption of illicit drugs, reduce drug abuse, and curtail violence around illegal drug markets.

Read on!

Part I

Policing for Profit

CHAPTER 1

The License to Steal

People are shocked, even incredulous, when I tell them the government can legally confiscate their property without even charging them with a crime or proving that a law has been broken. Or, even worse, that law enforcement, both state and federal, are motivated to seize property because they profit from it.

Yet, it's true. While the drug war is almost 100 years old,[1] a seismic change occurred in the 1980s: The war dramatically escalated. The federal government had finally found a way to gain control over street crime: policing for profit.

In 1982, President Ronald Reagan, with overwhelming bipartisan support, signed an executive order declaring war on illicit drug transactions.[2] He announced that "drugs already reach deeply into our social structure, so we must mobilize all our forces to stop the flow of drugs into this country."[3] The president likened this planned mobilization to the bloody Battle of Verdun in World War I and affirmed his administration's "unshakeable" determination to "end the drug menace."[4] He issued a national security directive stating that illegal drugs were a threat to U.S. "national security."[5]

Civil Asset Forfeiture

Implementing the president's war plan, a federal law was passed in 1984, the Comprehensive Crime Control Act, which created the Assets Forfeiture Fund, into which the U.S. attorney general was to deposit the proceeds from forfeitures to be used by the Department of Justice and other law enforcement agencies.[6] (A "forfeiture" is a property taken by the government without compensation.) Consequently, from 1984 on, federal law enforcement agencies have been authorized to spend the proceeds from forfeitures with scarcely any oversight, giving them a financial incentive to generate forfeiture funds. (Prior to 1984, forfeiture proceeds were deposited with the Treasury to be spent as Congress decided.)

Here's how this 1984 forfeiture law works.[7] It's a civil law, not a criminal law, and the charge is initiated against the property, not its owner. Civil forfeiture is based on the bizarre fiction that it's the property that has violated the drug law and must be judged guilty or innocent. (I know this sounds crazy. But it really is the law!)

Before the suspected property can be turned over to a court for judgment, it has first to be taken control of ("seized") by law enforcement. To justify seizure, it's usually only necessary that the police have "probable cause" ("enough facts to support a reasonable belief") that the property violated the drug laws.[8] But, probable cause is often based on hearsay, circumstantial evidence, rumor, gossip, or a tip from an anonymous informant who is cooperating with prosecutors to get a lighter sentence and/or money.[9] Probable cause is an easy standard to meet, and judges rarely disagree with officers who make that call.[10] Once state or local police have seized suspected property—which is contested by less than 20 percent of owners[11]—they can request an authorized federal agency, such as the FBI or the Drug Enforcement Administration (DEA), to "adopt" the seizure for possible forfeiture. Once adopted, the property becomes subject to federal, not state, law.[12] The case then goes to a federal court, usually to a judge, to decide whether the property is guilty. If found guilty—and not challenged in court by the owner[13]—the property is permanently confiscated by the federal government, where the 1984 law has authorized the U.S. attorney general to share the forfeiture proceeds "equitably" with state and local law enforcement.[14] Under "equitable sharing" the police department that turned the seizure over to the federal agency receives up to 80 percent of the value of the forfeiture and the Department of Justice and other federal law enforcement agencies receive the rest.[15]

Compared to a person charged with a crime, property tried in court has severely limited constitutional protections.[16] The Bill of Rights applies mostly to criminal defendants, not to property. A main difference is the standard required to establish guilt: In most federal civil forfeiture cases, the standard is a "preponderance of evidence"—namely, whether it's "more likely than not" that the property is guilty—clearly a much lower standard than "beyond a reasonable doubt," which is required for a criminal conviction.[17] With the "more likely than not" standard used in civil forfeiture cases, innocent owners are faced with a significant probability that their property could be incorrectly deemed guilty. Civil forfeiture is favored over criminal forfeiture by law enforcement: It's much quicker and easier, and it's profitable.[18]

Equitable sharing often gives state and local law enforcement a better deal than abiding by the forfeiture laws of their own states, where forfeiture money might be allocated to other needs, such as education or health care. Consequently, equitable sharing has motivated many departments to bypass their own state laws.[19] Research has found that "when state laws make forfeiture more difficult and less rewarding, law enforcement instead takes advantage of easier and more generous federal forfeiture laws through equitable sharing."[20] State officials protest that police circumvent their own state laws, but they appear helpless to do anything about it. For example, when Missouri passed a law that forfeiture proceeds should be deposited in an education fund, law enforcement bypassed it by increasing their access to equitable distribution.[21] North Carolina is the only state that does not allow civil asset forfeiture; it only permits criminal forfeiture. So, the state and local police routinely bypass North Carolina state law by utilizing equitable sharing.[22] Florida does not allow the seizure of real property, but federal law does, so the equitable sharing program allows Florida police to benefit from those seizures.[23]

Equitable sharing provides still another benefit for law enforcement. As mentioned above, prior to 1984, forfeitures by the federal government had to be deposited in the U.S. Treasury's General Fund, where expenditures were subject to authorization by Congress. The same was true for the states. By contrast, starting in 1984, money from civil forfeitures was liberated from congressional or state legislative oversight as to how the money was acquired or spent. The Department of Justice, as well as many state law enforcement agencies, could now affect the size of their budgets by how aggressively they elected to pursue forfeitures. They also acquired almost unfettered freedom as to how they spent that money. Many states do not even require police to report on how much forfeiture money is raised or how it is used.[24]

Given this lack of oversight, there's a temptation for police to misuse forfeiture money, and there are many examples. A sheriff in Camden County, Georgia, used the money from property confiscated over the years to purchase a sports car, a boat, and gas for his employees' personal cars, as well as to establish a scholarship in his name at his college.[25] A police department in Lakewood, Colorado, used the

$1.5 million in forfeiture funds received from the federal government for the following law enforcement purposes: "$1,235 on the chief's Christmas party, $208 on a new aquarium, $2,100 on a buffet for policemen who worked on Labor Day, $720 on amusement park tickets, and $32,375 on banquets."[26]

The conflict of interest inherent in civil asset forfeitures is obvious and dangerous. Even a federal official responsible for the civil forfeiture program has spoken of the attractiveness and dangers of forfeiture money: Michael F. Zeldin, director of the Justice Department's Asset Forfeiture Office under President George H. W. Bush said, "The desire to deposit money into the asset forfeiture fund became the reason for [the] being of forfeiture, eclipsing in certain measure the desire to effect fair enforcement of the laws."[27]

Fed by the proceeds from civil forfeitures, the Justice Department's forfeiture fund soared from $27 million in 1985, to $1 billion in 1996, and to more than $3 billion in 2008, with almost all the money doled out each year to federal and local law enforcement.[28] A 2014 study by the *Washington Post* analyzed Justice Department records of civil forfeiture cash seizures. The *Post* found that since 9/11 police had, without search warrants or indictments, made 62,000 cash seizures on highways and elsewhere, totaling $2.5 billion, with none of the people ever charged with a crime. About $1.7 billion was distributed to state and local police departments under the equitable sharing program, with $800 million given to the U.S. Justice Department and shared with Homeland Security and other federal agencies. Given the cost of legal action against the government, only one-sixth of the seizures were legally challenged, with 41 percent of those who challenged—4,455—getting money back. The appeals process took over a year in 40 percent of the cases, with those who got cash back often required to sign an agreement that they would not sue police over the seizure.[29]

Many police departments have become dependent on forfeiture money. Criminologist John Worrall, who surveyed 770 police executives, found that 40 percent of the respondents admitted that civil forfeiture is "necessary as a budget supplement."[30] Criminal justice professors Mitchell Miller and Lance Selva reported observing many "cases where the operational goal was profit rather than the incarceration of drug offenders."[31]

One of my students in a seminar on the drug war at the University of North Carolina at Chapel Hill interviewed a police officer in 2010 who had served on the narcotics squad. The student reported: "I asked him if his department had ever been involved in a forfeiture case where the feds adopted the case and gave them back 80% of the seized funds." He immediately answered, "Of course, they do it as often as they can."[32] The officer shocked the student, and me, by telling him—and repeating to me—that the police "took a tax man with them on drug busts, so that unpaid taxes could be calculated and added to the value of the assets they seized." The explanation for this is that when acquiring illegal drugs, you must purchase a tax stamp in North Carolina, one of 20 states that taxes illegal substances.[33] For example, the North Carolina stamp for marijuana costs $3.50 per gram; and, for cocaine, $50 per gram. Buying the stamp does not cause the purchase to be legal; it only means that you are fulfilling your obligation to pay taxes![34] As *The Economist* explains: "Locked in a vault within the North Carolina Department of Revenue is a lickable bit of Kafka: a government-issued stamp that is expected to remain un-purchased, but which users of illegal goods must, by law, affix to substances they are not allowed to possess."[35]

State and local police and prosecutors are not alone in being addicted to civil forfeiture money. The U.S. Department of Justice is too. Consider this remarkable warning by an attorney general of the United States, which was sent to all U.S. attorneys: "We must significantly increase forfeiture production to reach our budget target. Failure to achieve the $470 million projection would expose the Department's forfeiture program to criticism and undermine confidence in our budget predictions. Every effort must be made to increase forfeiture income in the three remaining months of fiscal year 1990."[36]

In 2000, a source from the U.S. Department of Justice told *Frontline* that police keep the value of forfeitures low enough so that attorneys would advise their clients that a challenge would not be worth it. It's ironic that a war that is supposed to be targeting drug kingpins often winds up confiscating property of so little value that it doesn't make sense to try to get it back.[37] Studies have found that taking assets from people with modest income has been going on for some time. In 1992, prosecutors in California conducted over 6,000 forfeitures, with 94 percent involving seizures of $5,000 or less.[38] In 1991, reporters from the *Pittsburgh Press* conducted a 10-month study reviewing 25,000 seizures made by the federal Drug Enforcement Administration. They found that 80 percent of the people whose property was confiscated were never charged with a crime and that "most of the seized items weren't the luxurious playthings of drug barons, but modest homes and simple cars and hard earned savings of ordinary people."[39]

On January 16, 2015, Attorney General Holder, as he was preparing to leave office, made the shocking decision to discontinue a portion of the 40-year-old equitable sharing program: He ruled that state and local police can no longer seize suspected property and have it adopted by federal law enforcement, with both sharing in the proceeds resulting from a forfeiture.[40] Holder's new policy is certain to generate controversy; it will affect law enforcement budgets in almost every state, as well as the budget of federal law enforcement. Since 2001, some 7,600 of the country's police departments and task forces have participated in equitable sharing, which has accounted for 20 percent or more of their annual budgets in many cases.[41]

There are, however, major loopholes in Holder's ruling. It grants an exemption for joint task forces, that is, where state and/or local police are partnered with federal authorities, with the proceeds from a forfeiture shared according to their respective seizure efforts.[42] This exception is significant because there are hundreds of federally subsidized regional and multijurisdictional drug task forces made up of local officers who are often deputized as federal agents.[43] Holder's new policy also makes an exception for "seizure warrants issued by federal courts," which authorize federal law enforcement to pursue civil asset forfeitures.[44] As a result of these exceptions to the new ruling, police and prosecutors—federal, state, and local—can continue profiting from equitable sharing. In fact, using Department of Justice data, it appears that Holder's ruling prevents less than 6 percent of civil forfeitures over all levels of government.[45]

According to attorney David Smith, an expert on forfeiture law, "The loophole . . . where officials can secure a federal seizure warrant—could easily be exploited by federal prosecutors to circumvent Holder's intent. I have little faith in the federal judges to look at these requests with much scrutiny. The prosecutors can say just about anything to get what they want, and there's usually no record of what's actually said at the hearings." Smith also argues that because of a "lack of accountability in the Department of Justice" there would be "no consequences when federal prosecutors violate the rules or break the law."[46]

Clearly, law enforcement will be motivated to restore the financial status quo by reversing Holder's ruling, as well as by efforts to expand joint task forces. Police and sheriffs immediately began criticizing the new policy, arguing that depriving law enforcement of funds from civil asset forfeitures would damage efforts to fight crime, terrorism, and drug smuggling.[47] As Bill Johnson, the executive director of the National Association of Police Organizations, put it, "There is some grave concern about the possible loss of significant funding while local police and state police are being asked to do more and more each year."[48] "It seems like a continual barrage against police," said John W. Thompson, interim executive director of the National Sheriffs' Association, "I'm not saying there's no wrongdoing, but there is wrongdoing in everything."[49]

Holder's new policy does not alter civil forfeiture laws at the state level.[50] Police and prosecutors in many states will still be able to profit from seizing property and turning it over to a state court. The financial advantages and disadvantages of using state forfeiture law versus equitable distribution differ from state to state (see footnote).[51] It's a safe bet that Holder's new rule will galvanize many state police departments to replace as much as they can of the lost equitable sharing money with state forfeiture money.

Federal Grants That Reward Drug Busting

Civil forfeiture is not the only way law enforcement profits from the drug war. State and local law enforcement are rewarded with federal grant money for the number of drug busts.[52] In the Anti-Drug Abuse Act of 1988, Congress created a grant named after Edward Byrne, a narcotics officer killed by a drug dealer.[53] An investigation in 2001 by *Madison Capital Times* revealed that the size of Byrne grants was based almost entirely on the number of drug arrests.[54] The study estimated that for each drug arrest, a local police department would receive $153. Radley Balko reported that by the mid-1990s, the grant programs that Congress started in 1988 "had pushed police departments across the country to prioritize drug crimes over other investigations. When applying for grants, departments are rewarded with funding on the basis of statistics such as the number of overall [drug] arrests, the number of warrants served, and the number of drug seizures."[55] As a result, while drug arrests in the United States in 1984 were estimated to be 6.1 percent of total arrests, this measure of the intensity of drug enforcement steadily grew; and, by 2010, it had reached 12.5 percent.[56] The sociologist Harry Levine points out that Byrne grant money "targets low-income people and people of color" even though the government claims it goes toward arresting high-level traffickers.[57]

Federal grants have also created hundreds of multiregional and multijurisdictional antidrug task forces. Because they rely on federal money and asset forfeiture proceeds, these task forces have little if any dependence on local, elected sheriffs or police chiefs. This lack of oversight has contributed to botched raids, scandals, and tragedies, such as those in Tulia and Hearne, Texas, where dozens of people, mostly poor and black, were falsely raided, arrested, and imprisoned for alleged drug offenses.[58]

Federal grants to local law enforcement held steady at around $1 billion a year from 1996 to 2001, but starting in 2002 they began to decrease, reaching $170 million in 2008. In the presidential campaign of 2008, Barack Obama criticized President George W. Bush and the Republicans for cutting these grants, saying they "had been critical to creating the anti-gang and anti-drug task forces our communities need."[59] Obama's 2009 American Recovery and Reinvestment Act boosted the Byrne grants by $2 billion to be spread over the next four years.[60]

It will be difficult to stop law enforcement from profiting from the drug war. Police and prosecutors have become a powerful national lobby with the goal of protecting this source of income. The lobby successfully blocked a measure that would have diminished their revenue from the equitable sharing program. Educators and others who were losing revenue to law enforcement lobbied to change the federal law. They inserted a provision into the Anti-Drug Abuse Act of 1988 that required the U.S. attorney general to guarantee that equitable sharing money would not go to law enforcement if that violated state law, where forfeiture money was often allocated to education or some other non–law enforcement purpose.[61] This change would have prevented state and local police from getting more money from equitable sharing than they could get from their own state. The law enforcement lobby immediately sprang into action to repeal the offending provision. Congress heard testimony from law enforcement agencies all across the country, including the U.S. Attorney General Joseph W. Dean who argued that if there were no equitable sharing, there would be no forfeitures: "The irony is that if local and state law enforcement agencies cannot share, the assets will in all likelihood not be seized and forfeited. Thus, no one wins but the drug trafficker. If this financial sharing stops, we will kill the goose that laid the golden egg."[62]

A U.S. attorney from eastern North Carolina actually suggested that if equitable distribution [sharing] were abolished, the police would focus less on drug arrests and more on criminal convictions: "Drug agents would have much less incentive to follow through on the assets potentially held by drug traffickers, since there would be no reward for such efforts and would concentrate their time and resources on the criminal prosecution."[63]

The law enforcement lobby succeeded in 1988 in defeating the education agencies and others who were being damaged by the equitable sharing program. The offending provision was repealed, and the repeal was hidden in a Defense Appropriations bill.[64] A financial threat to law enforcement emerged again in the Civil Asset Forfeiture Reform Act of 2000, in which a key change was ending the sharing of the seizure proceeds between federal agencies and state and local police. Again the lobby was successful in getting this feature cut from the bill because of vigorous opposition from police and prosecutors.[65]

Former House Judiciary Committee Chairman Henry Hyde, who more than anyone has spearheaded reforming the drug laws said, "The financial considerations involved in the present . . . [equitable sharing] system mean unyielding opposition from law enforcement officials at all levels to any change in the law."[66] He also pointed out that "Even moderate forfeiture reforms have been officially opposed by the U.S. Department of Justice, the National Association of Attorneys General and the National District Attorneys Association."[67] It's not surprising that organizations would oppose changes that diminish their income. But the emotion in the district attorneys' opposition suggests how important confiscations are to them. As Hyde put it: "Indeed, if you listen to the police and prosecutorial rhetoric loosed in response to proposed forfeiture reform, you would think that the end of the world was at hand."[68]

Law enforcement has taken full advantage of their authorization to profit from nonviolent drug law violations. Following the passage of the laws in the 1980s on civil asset forfeiture and federal grants, arrests, incarcerations, and SWAT raids soared:

- Annual drug arrests increased from 0.6 million in 1980 to 1.5 million in 2013;[69]
- Incarcerations for nonviolent drug law violators increased from 41,000 in 1980 to over 500,000 in 2011;[70] and
- SWAT raids jumped from 3,000 a year in the early 1980s (mostly for riots and hostage-rescuing) to over 60,000 a year today (mostly violent break-ins searching for drugs).[71]

So far, I've examined the laws that authorize police and prosecutors to profit from equitable sharing and drug arrests. But, how does law enforcement make use of this authorization? How do police actually get profits from the drug war? They do so in four different ways, which are explored in the following chapters, namely, by traffic stops (Chapter 2); confiscating houses (Chapter 3); SWAT team raids (Chapter 4); and random drug sweeps (Chapter 5).

CHAPTER 2

Traffic Stops

Traffic stops made in search of drugs are a popular revenue source for law enforcement. Anyone driving with a significant amount of cash is a tempting target. Believe it or not, police can determine that the cash is drug money and permanently confiscate it, even if they find no drugs. The courts accepted this reasoning in the case of Emiliano Gonzalez: In 2003, a Nebraska trooper stopped Mr. Gonzalez for speeding. The officer asked to search the car and discovered $124,700 in cash in the back seat, but no drugs.[1] Gonzalez explained that he had pooled the cash from family and friends to buy a refrigerated truck in Chicago, but when he got there the truck had already been sold. He was on his way home when he was stopped. The trooper seized the cash pursuant to federal forfeiture law by alleging that it was involved in a drug-trafficking offense. The trial court found Gonzalez's story plausible and denied the forfeiture. But the Eighth Circuit Court of Appeals reversed this decision in 2006 and ruled that the government had established a "substantial connection" between the money and a drug crime. The Eighth Circuit wrote, "We have adopted the common sense view that bundling and concealment of large amounts of currency, combined with other suspicious circumstances, supports a connection between money and drug trafficking."[2] (The suspicious circumstances cited referred to the fact that a canine sniff had alerted to residue on the currency. Studies have shown that there is widespread contamination of our currency by cocaine.)[3]

Police have profited from this ruling. Between 2006 and 2008, law enforcement officials in Tenaha, Texas, stopped more than 140 out-of-state drivers, mostly black, and arrested them.[4] The police justified these actions claiming the stretch where the arrests were made was a major drug route between Shreveport, Louisiana, and Houston, Texas. Once arrested, the officers took the people to jail, and the prosecutor threatened to file charges unless they signed statements giving up their valuables. Here are the experiences of some of the victims:

Jennifer Boatright and her husband gave the Tenaha police more than $6,000 after the DA threatened to charge them with money laundering and put their two children in foster care. Boatright said, "If it's the money you want, you can take it, if that's what it takes to keep my children with me."[5]

Roderick Daniels was pulled over in Tenaha for driving 37 in a 35-mph zone. The officers found $8,500 on him, which he planned to use to buy a car. The prosecutor threatened to charge him with money laundering if he didn't turn over the money. He said, "To be honest, I was five, six hundred miles from home. I was petrified."[6]

Amanee Busbee, from Maryland, was on her way to Houston to purchase a restaurant. She was with her child, her fiancé, and her business partner. Busbee claimed the Tenaha police threatened to put her son in child protective services if she refused to tell them what they wanted to hear.

David Guillory, who represented eight plaintiffs in Tenaha, said that of the 40 motorists he contacted 39 were African American. He estimated that the officials had seized a total value of $3 million in the two-year period. The DA used the money for a popcorn machine, candy, catering services, a youth baseball team, as well as for contributions to a church and a Chamber of Commerce.[7] None of the plaintiffs had been arrested for violating the drug laws. While the officials denied any wrongdoing, they were forced to return some of the money, including Boatright's. No penalties were imposed on law enforcement.[8]

If police take from motorists a few thousand dollars, or their cell phones, or their jewelry, or even their cars, they usually decide not to challenge it in court for many reasons: They'll need to hire a lawyer; they may be hundreds of miles from home and will have to show up in court at a later date; they may be afraid the DA will decide to bring criminal charges against them; or the burden will be on them to prove they are innocent. So, it's no wonder that more than 80 percent of people who have their property seized never try to get it back.[9]

In January 2009, Anthony Smelley, a 22-year-old college student, was stopped by police in Putnam County, Indiana, at 3:00 in the morning, allegedly for an unsafe lane change and a partly obscured license plate.[10] When asked for a driver's license, he said he had lost it in a recent car accident. The police asked him to come out of the car, and in patting him down they discovered $17,500 worth of cash, contradicting his initial statement that he wasn't carrying much money. He claimed that it was part of a settlement of $50,000 he had received from the accident and that the money he was carrying was for the purpose of buying a car from his aunt.

A record check showed that as a teenager he had been arrested but not convicted for drug possession. At that point the officers called in a dog to sniff the car, which yielded indications that narcotics might be present. Under Indiana's forfeiture law, the police seized the cash, even though a search of the car revealed no drugs. Because there was no other evidence, no criminal charges were filed, and Smelley produced a letter verifying that the cash was a settlement from the accident. Putnam County initiated legal proceedings to confiscate the money permanently on the bizarre rationale that he was going to use the cash to buy drugs at some future time! Thirteen months later, Putnam County Circuit Court Special Judge David Polk ruled that while the behavior of the police was legal, the county would have to return Smelley's money because no drugs were found and there was no other evidence of illegal activity. Under Indiana law, he will not be reimbursed for his lost interest, court costs, attorney's fees, or time.[11]

Law enforcement have also developed a profitable practice called the "reverse sting," where police, posing as dealers, sell illegal drugs to consumers and then arrest them, instead of seizing and destroying the drugs from traffickers.[12] One officer involved in sting operations said, "This strategy was preferred by every agency and department with which I was associated because it allowed agents to gauge potential profit before investing a great deal of time and effort."[13] Dan Garner, an undercover narcotics agent in California said, "You see that there's big money out there, you want to seize the big money for your department. For our unit, the sign of whether you were doing good or poorly was how much money you seized."[14] Patrick Murphy, former police commissioner of New York City, defended the reverse sting in testimony to Congress in 1993. He stated that the police had "a financial incentive to impose roadblocks on the southbound lane of I-95 which carry the cash to buy drugs, rather than the northbound lanes, which carry the drugs. After all, seized cash will end up forfeited to the police dept., while seized drugs can only be destroyed."[15]

CHAPTER 3

Houses Arrested

It was March 2004, and Leon Williams, 46, was finally moving into his dream home in Fredericksburg, Virginia, after selling his home in Caroline County.[1] He had already spent $1,000 on a new carpet and was busy building a fence for his dogs. Moments before closing on his new home, he received a call from the Fredericksburg Circuit Court informing him that the house had been seized by the state police as a "drug house" and was now surrounded by crime scene tape. "And just like that," he said, "I've got no place to live."[2]

Leon Williams never imagined he would have a problem with the seller, Barbara Beck, the ex-wife of a judge and the former sister-in-law of the city's mayor.[3] When he bid on Barbara Beck's house in 2004, he had no idea it had been raided the previous summer by state police. The raid was part of an investigation into a large-scale marijuana-trafficking operation. Two confidential informants told police that Barbara Beck's son John was one of the major suppliers and that he had used his mother's house to grow and store marijuana. What led to Leon Williams's loss of his house was the arrest of John Beck just as the closing was about to take place. After John's arrest, the police seized his mother's house under the state's civil asset forfeiture law. Leon Williams was out thousands of dollars in moving costs and processing fees; he subsequently found a new home and said he hopes "nothing falls through this time." Barbara Beck was never charged with a crime, most likely because confiscating her house would have been far more difficult for the government if she had been.[4]

Innocent Owner Defense

Until 2000, owners could lose property suspected of drug law violations even if they were innocent. The law did not contain an innocent owner defense. The lack of such a defense led to outrageous Supreme Court decisions, such as *Calero-Toledo* (1974), where the Court permitted the forfeiture of a $19,800 yacht because one marijuana cigarette was left there by a renter, even though all parties acknowledged the owner had no knowledge that the property was being used in violation of the law.[5] In *Bennis v. Michigan* (1996), the Court upheld the forfeiture of an automobile owned by Bennis and her husband based on the husband's conviction of consorting with a prostitute. Even though Bennis had no knowledge that her husband had used the car in violation of Michigan's laws, the Court ruled that she could not use an innocent owner defense because it was not constitutionally required.[6]

The media as well as jurists strongly condemned the lack of an innocent owner defense. Justice Clarence Thomas in one of his dissenting opinions argued that "improperly used, forfeiture could become more like a roulette wheel employed to raise revenue from innocent but hapless owners whose property is unforeseeably misused."[7]

A *Chicago Tribune* editorial asked, "Can the government now seize a hotel or a football stadium merely because the owners failed to prevent illegal acts that they didn't condone and knew nothing about? Can it confiscate your house because, while you were out for the evening, your teenager was caught smoking dope on the patio? It's hard to see why not."[8]

As a result of the storm of criticism, Congress passed and President Clinton signed the Civil Asset Forfeiture Reform Act of 2000 (CAFRA), where an innocent owner can avoid federal forfeiture by proving lack of either knowledge or consent, as long as there was no negligence in discovering and trying to prevent the illegal use of the property. This reform law also raised the standard the Department of Justice has to meet to establish that the property is guilty from probable cause to the current standard of a preponderance of evidence (more likely than not). CAFRA did not include Treasury agencies, which can still use probable cause, the lowest standard required to establish guilt in civil forfeitures.[9]

Unfortunately, the burden in a civil forfeiture case still rests on the owner, who is presumed guilty until he can prove his innocence. Also, CAFRA applies only to federal law; it was not extended to the states, which with only a few exceptions follow the federal government in requiring the owner to prove innocence.[10]

Not only is the property owner assumed guilty, it could take a year or more before getting a hearing in a state court. In 2009, the Supreme Court, in *Alvarez v. Smith*, heard oral arguments on the issue of an unreasonably long delay.[11] Six petitioners were challenging Illinois's civil asset forfeiture law. Each had automobiles or other property seized by police on suspicion the property had been violating drug laws. None of the petitioners were charged with a crime. Under Illinois's law, the government can delay a preliminary hearing on a seizure of less than $20,000 for up to six months, and property can be held for more than a year before it's returned. In addition, the state can use hearsay evidence and only needs to show probable cause to permanently confiscate seized property. On the other hand, the owner is not only presumed guilty but has a greater burden than the government, namely, of having to prove innocence by a preponderance of evidence.

The federal appeals court ruled that the six were entitled to a prompt hearing.[12] The case then went to the Supreme Court, which decided 8–1 to avoid any decision, ruling that the case was moot, because the police had by then returned all seized property.[13] In effect, the Supreme Court upheld the power of states to seize property on grounds of suspicion and hold it for over a year.[14]

The main failure of CAFRA was that it did little to diminish the ability of police to profit from seizing property.[15] A judge can still find property guilty of violating drug laws by the slim standard of "more likely than not." The money earned by state and local law enforcement agencies from the equitable sharing program continues to flourish, earning more than $433 million in 2014.[16] This does not include the millions of unaccounted-for profits that police earned from forfeitures in their own states.[17] The Assets Forfeiture Fund of the U.S. Department of Justice also soared post-CAFRA: Total deposits rose from $407 million in 2001 to $1.9 billion in 2013.[18] From 2001 through 2010, the U.S. Department of Justice confiscated 3,706 residences yielding $677 million of deposits into the Department's Assets Forfeiture Fund.[19]

Where did the bizarre idea of civil asset forfeiture come from, and is there any justification for it? How can an inanimate object, like your car or your house, violate the law? Ironically, confiscations of "guilty" property by British authorities was a key grievance that led to the American Revolution. The Writs of Assistance allowed customs officers to seize and forfeit suspected contraband and to retain part of the proceeds. The colonists were outraged at how this law produced corrupt officials.[20]

The U.S. Department of Justice proudly points to the antiquity of this doctrine, stating that it has "survived for thousands of years."[21] The director of the Office for Civil Asset Forfeiture argues that this "ancient legal procedure is proving to be dramatically effective in attacking modern crime."[22] Justice William J. Brennan, who wrote the notorious Pearson Yacht decision, justified it by tracing civil forfeiture all the way back to the Bible (Exodus 21:28): "If an ox gore a man or a woman, that they die: then the ox shall be surely stoned, and his flesh shall not be eaten." But the Court's logic is flawed. There is a fundamental difference between the confiscation of an inanimate object for the benefit of the government and the execution of a dangerous ox, whose death not only safeguards the community, but does not benefit any particular human beings, because its meat cannot be eaten.

U.S. civil forfeiture law stems from the English medieval law of "deodand" (given to God), where inanimate as well as animate objects could be punished. Under that law, any object causing the death of a person could be confiscated and its value forfeited to the king. The practice was ended in the mid-nineteenth century. Lord Campbell commented that it was a "wonder that a law so extremely absurd and inconvenient should have remained in force [so long]."[23] The United States adopted civil forfeiture but not the deodand. The earliest cases involved the forfeiture of ships violating navigation laws, because the owners were located overseas and not subject to the jurisdiction of the courts. It was later used to combat the slave trade and piracy and to confiscate property during the Civil War and alcohol Prohibition.[24] But since the 1980s, civil asset forfeiture exploded as a profitable weapon of the American government in its war on drugs.[25]

What's puzzling is the strong support of the U.S. Supreme Court for civil asset forfeiture as well as for the equitable sharing program. It's no secret that these laws motivate the government to confiscate property with scanty evidence and no criminal charges; that they encourage the circumvention of state laws by state and local police; and that they authorize law enforcement to raise and spend money with no meaningful congressional or legislative oversight. According to the constitutional historian Leonard W. Levy, the Supreme Court has consistently failed to "seriously scrutinize the injury to property rights."[26]

Here is the Supreme Court's rationale for supporting civil asset forfeiture: "The Government has a pecuniary interest in forfeiture that goes beyond merely separating a criminal from his ill-gotten gains; that legitimate interest extends to recovering all forfeitable assets, for such assets are deposited in a Fund that supports law-enforcement efforts in a variety of important and useful ways. The sums of money that can be raised for law-enforcement activities this way are substantial, and the

Government's interest in using the profits of crime to fund these activities should not be discounted."[27]

Following are a couple of post-CAFRA examples of how the government's "pecuniary interest in forfeiture" succeeds in "separating a criminal from his ill-gotten gains."

In 2009, a 56-year-old nurse, Mara Lynn Williams, was fighting to stop federal prosecutors from seizing her house and 40 acres in Chilton County, Alabama.[28] She was diagnosed with breast cancer in 2003, which spread to her liver, lungs, and bone, but the cancer appears to be in remission. Her husband used marijuana for chronic pain after several surgeries. Criminal charges were brought against him, and while the jury was deliberating he committed suicide. She knew her husband was using marijuana but claimed she did not know he was growing it on their farm. She was not charged with a crime; but, according to Tommie Brown Hardwick, the asset forfeiture coordinator, it's standard procedure for the U.S. attorney's office to seize property that they believe has been used to commit a crime. Hardwick said that her "[husband's] death, which ended the criminal case, had no effect on the ongoing civil case. The bottom line is, we don't want people to benefit from criminal activity."[29]

Mrs. William's attorney, David Karn, said that the government would have to show that she herself was involved in illegal drug activity; otherwise she is protected by the "innocent spouse" rule. (Alabama is one of only a half-dozen states where a property owner is innocent until proven guilty.) But, he added that a civil forfeiture case "is an uphill battle from any landowner's perspective."[30] In April 2010, a compromise was reached in court: The property was not confiscated, but the $18,400 that the government had already seized would be kept permanently.[31]

Russel and Patricia Caswell have owned and operated a motel in Tewksbury, Massachusetts, for over 30 years. In 2011, the U.S. Drug Enforcement Agency and the Tewksbury Police Department invoked probable cause to seize the entire property, worth over a million dollars, because in 1994 guests were arrested more than once for violating the drug laws.[32] Since 1994, Caswell Motel had rented more than 125,000 rooms. Until the papers were filed in federal court to seize the motel, no one from the police department had suggested that the Caswells failed to do all they could to protect their property from illegal drug activity. In response to an increase in drug violations in Tewksbury, the Caswells installed security cameras, reported suspicious activities to the police, and, upon request, made available to law enforcement all guest records.

The state did not claim the Caswells were guilty of any crime; they simply pointed out that the federal civil forfeiture law gave them the authority to take the property. The couple was now faced with the daunting task of going up against the U.S. attorney in a federal court to prove that they were innocent. Had they lost, the local police would have gotten as much as 80 percent of the motel's value and the Department of Justice the rest. In a major victory for property rights, a federal court in Massachusetts in January 2013 dismissed the civil forfeiture action against the Caswells. As Darpana Sheth, an attorney for the Institute of Justice said: "Civil forfeiture is a draconian power that is too easily abused. This case epitomizes what an aggressive U.S. attorney wielding these laws can do to a small property owner like Russ Caswell."[33]

CHAPTER 4

SWAT Raids

Until the 1980s, police paramilitary units known as SWAT (Special Weapons and Tactics) teams were used rarely, and only for threats to public safety like terrorism, civil riots, or hostage situations.[1] The escalation of the drug war brought about the proliferation of SWAT teams. According to a survey by the criminologist Peter Kraska, 90 percent of cities with a population of 50,000 or more had at least one paramilitary police unit by 1997.[2] By 2005, 80 percent of towns between 25,000 and 50,000 people had their own SWAT team, up from 25.6 percent in 1984.[3]

Congress supported this militarization of law enforcement by authorizing the transfer of surplus military equipment from the Department of Defense to state and local police departments. As retired police chief of New Haven, Connecticut, Nick Pastore told *The New York Times*, "I was offered tanks, bazookas, anything I wanted. I turned it all down because it feeds a mind-set that you're not a police officer serving a community, you're a soldier at war."[4] Pastore's reaction was unusual. Many police departments across the country found this Pentagon give-away to be irresistible. They used federal grants to purchase battle garb to start SWAT teams.

SWAT teams are very different from our image of the friendly cop on the beat. These police units are equipped with submachine guns, automatic shotguns, M16s, sniper rifles, percussion grenades, stinger grenades, tear gas, battering rams, C4 plastic explosives, and, in many cities, military-armored personnel carriers.[5] Typically SWAT officers wear "black or urban camouflage 'battle dress uniforms (BDUs),' laced-up combat boots, full body armor, Kevlar helmets, and sometimes goggles with 'ninja' style hoods."[6] Once police acquire all this gear and the training that goes with it, they're eager to use it. As Sheriff Rick Fullmer, of Marquette County, Wisconsin, explained when he disbanded the county's SWAT team, "Quite frankly, they get excited about dressing up in black and doing that kind of thing. This is ridiculous. All we're going to end up doing is getting people hurt."[7]

As a result of the federal antidrug grants and the civil asset forfeiture law, it has become profitable for police to deploy SWAT teams for routine drug investigations.[8] The result has been frequent invasions of homes by heavily armed police units dressed like commandos. Raids too often target the residences of innocent people or of nonviolent drug offenders who may be guilty of nothing more than a misdemeanor.

An investigation of SWAT teams by *Capital Times* of Wisconsin reported, "To sell local governments on the need for SWAT teams, police officials usually talk about preparedness for terrorist incidents or barricaded hostage situations. But once trained, SWAT personnel are most commonly used to serve drug warrants and make drug arrests. The federal war provides targeted incentives for stepped-up police activity, handing out money on the basis of the number of arrests scored."[9] Every year the Wisconsin Office of Justice Assistance distributes millions of federal dollars to the state's drug task forces, who routinely work together with SWAT teams. Twenty percent of this money is available as an award for drug sales arrests.[10] *Capital Times* estimated the profits from these arrests. For example, The Milwaukee County drug task forces lost an estimated $40,000 of funding from 1999 to 2000 because their drug arrests dropped by 2,122; during the same period, Jackson County SWAT teams boosted their drug arrests from 13 to 57 increasing their estimated funding by $6,783. On the average in Wisconsin, each drug sales arrest earned a task force an estimated $153.[11]

According to Peter Kraska, the number of SWAT raids grew from about 3,000 a year in the early 1980s to 30,000 in 1995 and 40,000 in 2001; and, in 2011, he estimated that the raids exceed 60,000 a year.[12] The ACLU, in a study using data from 2011 and 2012, estimated that 62 percent of the SWAT raids involved a search for drugs and that "SWAT teams either forced (or probably forced) entry into a person's home using a battering ram or other breaching device 65 percent of the time."[13] The study also found that "the SWAT teams studied were much more likely to force entry in drug search cases than in other scenarios. When [a] SWAT [team] was deployed to search a home for drugs, the squad forced entry in more than 60 percent of incidents. In contrast, when SWAT was deployed for a reason other than searching a home for drugs, the squad forced entry in fewer than 40 percent of cases."[14]

"Entries" are frequently botched because anonymous informants are usually the source of tips for the police. In one study in the Raleigh-Durham area, 87 percent of SWAT break-ins were triggered by snitches.[15] Here is how Police Chief Philip Hardiman of Harvey, Illinois, explained a mistaken raid: "We make out search warrants when we get information from drug informants. Sometimes they give us incorrect information, and warrants are made out for one house when we're really looking for the house next door. I think that's what happened here. That happens from time to time in any police department."[16] New York's Police Chief Raymond Kelly admitted that 10 percent or more of the 450 no-knock drug raids a month in New York were served on the wrong address, but he then hedged his estimate by conceding that his department did not keep a careful account of cases that went wrong.[17] Kraska reports that at least 780 cases of flawed SWAT raids reached the appellate court level between 1989 and 2001; prior to the 1980s such cases were nonexistent.[18]

Police have no problem getting a search warrant, even on the word of anonymous informants. In many cases SWAT teams don't even bother to get a warrant, especially if they're breaking into the homes of minorities and the poor. Law enforcement defends these methods, arguing that overwhelming force, along with shock and surprise, are crucial to minimize the destruction of evidence and to reduce the danger to themselves.[19] The U.S. Supreme Court has supported these methods. In 1995, the Court ruled that police do not have to knock and announce themselves if they have a reasonable suspicion that doing so would expose them to danger or lead to the destruction of evidence.[20] In 2006, the Court further strengthened the hand of law enforcement by ruling that drugs seized in a home can be admitted as evidence in a trial even if the police failed to knock and announce their presence.[21]

Given this latitude by the courts, it's not surprising that SWAT raids are often unannounced. They are usually carried out late at night or just before dawn. When the break-ins are violent; doors are broken open with a battering ram or blown down with explosives; flash-bang grenades are tossed into the house to shock and stun; and the police point their guns and rifles at everyone inside.[22] Too often the raids have resulted in injuries and deaths to residents as well as police officers, and many homes have been wrongly targeted.[23]

A remarkable interactive national map of mistaken SWAT raids has been created by Radley Balko in conjunction with his 2006 study,

"Overkill: The Rise of Paramilitary Police Raids."[24] The map is available at http://www.cato.org/raidmap. It shows hundreds of raids that went wrong, divided into six categories symbolized by different color balloons:

- death of an innocent,
- death or injury of a police officer,
- death of a nonviolent offender,
- raid on an innocent suspect,
- unnecessary raids on doctors and sick people, and
- other examples of botched police break-ins.

Clicking on a balloon reveals the story of the raid from one or more newspaper accounts.

Studying the stories of these SWAT break-ins, I was appalled by the profusion of wrong addresses as well as the gratuitous cruelty exhibited by some officers. Here are a few typical examples of raids on mistaken residences in which SWAT members were not held accountable for behavior that seemed excessively brutal.

In November 2002, a San Antonio, Texas, SWAT team stormed an apartment occupied by three Hispanic men. It was the wrong address. The men claimed they were repeatedly "kicked and punched" and one of them was taken to the hospital with a cut on his face and a bruised head. As Vincent Huerta put it, "The way they entered, I never thought it could be police." All three thought they were being robbed. The police blamed the mistaken address on the darkness and "a cluster of look-alike buildings," even though their search warrant stated they had staked out the residence for two days.[25]

In June 2006, in Elyria, Ohio, around 6:00 a.m., 57-year-old Jerry Agee heard a loud banging on his front door and a voice yelling, "We're coming in!" Police broke down his front door with a battering ram, yelled at him to hit the ground, and burst in with guns pointing at him. He was making breakfast before going to work. His girlfriend was just getting out of the shower, and they ordered her to come out with her hands up. Agee said, "She was naked and they didn't even let her put nothing on. I was mad because I felt like she was being violated." Police placed both Agee and his girlfriend in handcuffs and waited several minutes before giving her a blanket to cover herself. Some eight police officer spent 20 minutes searching through drawers, closets, and the refrigerator. Even after the police admitted they had the wrong address they continued their search for 10 minutes, Agee said. Finally, they left with no apology.[26]

One feature of these SWAT raids that was especially shocking to me was that homeowners who defended themselves against what they reasonably believed was a break-in by robbers were charged with assault with a deadly weapon if they injured an officer. In cases where an officer had been killed during a raid, residents were charged with a capital offense, and some received a death sentence. Reading these cases, it seems clear to me that residents—many of whom had been asleep—had been terrified and panicked by the raid and really believed criminals were breaking into their home. They could easily have failed to hear or believe a police announcement, assuming one had been made. Confronted with an invasion of their home, reaching for a weapon to defend themselves and their family seemed like a natural first reaction.[27]

Here are a few cases where members of a SWAT team have been injured or killed by a resident during a break-in:

In 2002, in Brunswick County, North Carolina, a SWAT team dressed in camouflage raided the trailer of 25-year-old Paul Pelham. An informant claimed Pelham had bought crack from him. Awakened at night to the sound of flash-bang grenades. Pelham thought the police were intruders. Grabbing his gun, he shot Deputy Steven Lanier, permanently disabling him. He in turn was shot numerous times by the police but was not killed. The officers claimed they had announced themselves, but neighbors testified they heard no announcement. Pelham was acquitted of the charge of selling crack but was convicted of assault with a deadly weapon with intent to kill and inflicting serious injury, in addition to drug charges. He was sentenced to 19 to 26 years in prison.[28]

In 2006, a SWAT team conducted a no-knock drug raid at 1:30 a.m. on a residence in Macon, Georgia. The residents Antwon Dawayne Fair, 26, and Damon Antwon Jolly, 25, shot and killed Deputy Joseph Whitehead. Sheriff Jerry Modena told the *Macon Telegraph* that once the suspects realized the raid was by police and not gang members, they immediately surrendered. In spite of that evidence, the prosecutors charged five of the residents with murder, including one who was not even present during the raid. Jolly and Fair, the two who fired their weapons, faced the death penalty.[29] In November 2010, the Georgia Supreme Court ruled 5–2 that Fair and Jolly were eligible for the death penalty if found guilty of killing Deputy Joseph Whitehead.[30] In June 2012, Fair pleaded guilty and received a life sentence.[31] In November 2012, Damon Jolly also pleaded guilty and, in a plea agreement, was sentenced to life in prison with the possibility of parole after 14 years.[32]

These examples of SWAT raids give you an idea of how terrifying they are and how dangerous to both residents and police. For additional cases see Radley Balko's seminal 2006 study "Overkill: The Rise of Paramilitary Police Raids in America" and the comprehensive 2014 study "War Comes Home" by the ACLU.

Here are some YouTube videos of SWAT raids:[33]

http://www.youtube.com/watch?v=6rDOPcCxHOI&feature=related

Fresno, California, May 21, 2009: incredible video of mistaken raids that terrified children, women, and an elderly couple. The dispatcher misdirected all three raids!

http://www.youtube.com/watch?v=Ng6mfpZ2kR4

Columbia, Missouri, May 27, 2011: searching for marijuana. Two dogs killed.

http://www.youtube.com/watch?v=6b-67q0vlCw

Columbia, Missouri, May 5, 2010: searching for marijuana.

http://www.youtube.com/watch?v=cSfOBPlY2n0

Utah, September 16, 2010: SWAT team kills an apparently unarmed man on a drug raid.

CHAPTER 5

Random Drug Sweeps

Policing for profit has been enthusiastically supported by the U.S. Supreme Court as well as by Congress. By the 1980s, the Court—in the words of Justice John Paul Stevens—had become "a loyal foot soldier" in the war on drugs.[1] Over the next 20 years, the Court issued a series of rulings that contributed to the escalation of the war by strengthening the hand of legislators, police, and prosecutors.[2]

The Court has declared drug trafficking to be "as serious and violent as the crime of felony murder."[3] Given this view, it's not surprising that the Court upheld the following harsh mandatory minimum sentences for nonviolent drug law violators: a first offense for possession with intent to sell the following amounts of drugs will result in a mandated sentence of five years in a federal prison without the possibility of parole—5 grams of crack cocaine (currently 28 grams); 500 grams of powder cocaine; 100 grams of heroin; 1 gram of LSD; 5 grams of methamphetamine.[4] These sentences are doubled if there is a previous felony drug conviction. One consequence of these mandatory minimums is that the average prison sentence for selling illicit drugs is often longer than the sentence for many violent crimes. For example, the median prison sentence in U.S. District Courts for drug trafficking is 60 months, while for assault it's 27 months and for manslaughter 37 months.[5]

In 1982, the Supreme Court, declaring that the length of prison sentences for felonies was "purely a matter of legislative prerogative," upheld the constitutionality of a 40-year prison sentence imposed on a Virginia man for possession with intent to distribute nine ounces of marijuana.[6] The Court, by a vote of 6–3, reversed rulings by two lower federal courts that the sentence was so harsh in proportion to the crime as to violate the Eighth Amendment's prohibition against cruel and unusual punishment.[7] In 1991, the Court upheld a life sentence for a man with no previous convictions who attempted to sell 23 ounces of crack cocaine.[8] As Michelle Alexander points out, "A life sentence for a first-time drug offense is unheard of in the rest of the developed world."[9] In the U.K., a conviction for selling a kilogram of heroin yields a prison sentence of six months, compared to a mandatory 10-year sentence in the United States.[10]

Prior to the 1980s, the law, as set forth by the U.S. Supreme Court, was that a search warrant could not be obtained by an anonymous tip unless the informant had demonstrable knowledge of the facts and there was independent corroboration.[11] This law was designed to protect against warrants being issued on the basis of rumors and lies. In rulings in 1983 (*Illinois v. Gates*) and 1990 (*Alabama v. White*), the Court dramatically reduced this protection as a result of drug cases, holding that an anonymous tip along with "sufficient indicia of reliability" was enough to provide reasonable suspicion for a search warrant.[12]

To strengthen law enforcement, the Reagan administration lobbied for an elimination of the "exclusionary rule"—which states that if a police officer violated a suspect's Fourth Amendment rights during a search, any evidence obtained could not be used in court. The judiciary had created the exclusionary rule to bolster the right guaranteed by the Fourth Amendment of the Constitution that people remain free of "unreasonable searches and seizures."[13] The Supreme Court obliged the administration in *US v. Leon* (1984),[14] ruling that if a magistrate mistakenly issued a warrant without probable cause and the police relied on the warrant "in good faith," the evidence could still be admitted at trial.[15] Because proving bad faith is impossible barring an admission by the officer, it seems that the Court's ruling, as Radley Balko put it, is "an instruction manual for police to use to get around the Fourth Amendment."[16]

By 1985, the Supreme Court was confronted with a new and expanding type of drug enforcement investigation. Police were conducting random sweeps of buses and trains in search of drugs. In August 1985, Terrance Bostick, a 28-year-old African American was traveling by Greyhound bus on his way from Miami to Atlanta, a 19-hour trip. He was asleep in the back of the bus when he was awakened to find two police officers standing over him.[17] They were wearing green jackets bearing the insignia of the Broward County Sheriff's Office and were displaying their badges. One held a gun in a plastic pouch. The officers were "working the bus" looking for anyone carrying illegal drugs. They requested

Bostick's consent to search his baggage. Virtually everyone agrees to such a request. (One officer reported he had obtained consent to search some 3,000 bags without being refused once.[18]) Bostick consented even though he had a pound of cocaine in his bag. When prosecutors charged him with drug possession, he challenged the conduct of the police. Bostick's case went to the Florida Supreme Court, which was so outraged over the behavior of the police that it compared their method to those used in totalitarian states, declaring, "This is not Hitler's Berlin, nor Stalin's Moscow, nor is it white supremacist South Africa."[19] The Florida court found the police behavior in violation of the Fourth Amendment. It ruled that Bostick had been unreasonably "seized" because he was not under suspicion and that the police had him trapped in the back of the bus so he was not free to leave.[20]

The U.S. Supreme Court reversed the Florida court, ruling that the proper test for an "unreasonable seizure" in the absence of suspicion was not whether Bostick felt free to leave but whether a "reasonable passenger would feel free to decline the officers' requests or otherwise terminate the encounter";[21] that is, refuse to answer questions and inform the police they could not search his luggage. The consequence of *Florida v. Bostick* (1991) was that police were freed to engage in suspicionless, dragnet-like drug searches of anyone on buses, trains, and planes. As long as they received permission, they were not violating the Fourth Amendment.

Justice Thurgood Marshall, joined by Justices Harry Blackmun and John Paul Stevens, dissented, stating: "it was one of the primary aims of the Fourth Amendment to protect citizens from the tyranny of being singled out for search and seizure without particularized suspicion . . . The law-enforcement technique with which we are confronted in this case—the suspicionless police sweep of buses in intrastate or interstate travel—bears all of the indicia of coercion and unjustified intrusion."[22]

Not surprisingly, the Supreme Court's conception of a "reasonable person" has been strongly criticized. David Cole, a law professor at the Georgetown University Law Center, commented that "the Supreme Court's 'reasonable person' has a lot more mettle than the average Joe."[23] As Bostick's lawyer stated, "No 'reasonable person' would agree to a search of a bag that contained a pound of cocaine if he really believed he was free to say no without adverse consequences."[24] Law professor Tracey Maclin argued that the Court "ignores the real world that police officers and black men live in.[25] . . . The realities of the street . . . make challenging an officer's authority out of the question for a black man."[26] More generally, Maclin states that it's "common sense" that "the average, reasonable individual . . . will not feel free to walk away from a typical police confrontation . . . Most of us do not have the chutzpah or stupidity to tell a police officer to 'get lost' after he has stopped us and asked for identification . . . Practically every constitutional scholar who has considered the issue has agreed that the average, reasonable person will not feel free to leave a law enforcement official who has approached and addressed questions to them."[27]

So police have the constitutional right to carry out suspicionless searches for drugs on buses and trains as long as it is a "consent search"; that is, as long as they have the consent of the person being searched. Can they do the same for people driving down the street? The Supreme Court said yes. It's called a "pretext stop"—that is, a traffic stop that can be nothing more than an excuse to fish for illegal drugs. Police can always find a justifiable pretext to stop a car because of some traffic violation.[28] The Supreme Court ruled in *Whren v. United States* (1996) that as long as the stop is legal, a suspicionless consent search of a car to look for illegal drugs does not violate the Fourth Amendment.[29] Because people can legally say no to a random consent search, why not require police to inform people that they have that right? The Supreme Court answered that question in the following case.

In 1996, Robin D. Robinette was caught speeding on an interstate north of Dayton, Ohio.[30] After pulling him over, the officer ran a computer check that indicated he had no previous violations. The officer then issued a verbal warning to Robinette and returned his license. At that point, the officer asked, "One question before you get gone [sic]: are you carrying any illegal contraband in your car? Any weapons of any kind, drugs, anything like that?" The answer was no, after which the officer asked permission to search the car. Robinette testified that he "automatically" consented, and the officer discovered a small amount of marijuana and a pill that was methamphetamine. His conviction was overturned by the Supreme Court of Ohio that ruled that the officer had extended a legitimate traffic stop and used a lengthy detention as a way of coercing Robinette to consent to a search. The Ohio court also adopted a "bright-line rule" requiring officers to inform drivers they are free to leave before requesting consent to search.[31] The U.S. Supreme Court struck down the Ohio court's bright-line rule in *Ohio v. Robinette* (1996), ruling that it was "unrealistic"[32] to require police officers to always inform detainees they are free to go before a consent to search may be deemed voluntary.[33] The Court's rationale was that consent searches are necessary for law enforcement because they "may be the only means of obtaining important and reliable evidence."[34]

In sum, these Supreme Court rulings have given law enforcement a constitutional license to stop any car they wish for any reason and search for drugs as long as they have the driver's permission. In addition, police are not required to inform drivers that they have the right to refuse.

The federal government has made good use of this authority. It funded a program in 1984 called "Operation Pipeline" with the goal of stopping drivers across the nation in the search for illegal drugs.[35] After the 1996 *Whren* ruling (legalizing the suspicionless consent searches of drivers), state and local police participation in Operation Pipeline escalated. As one officer trainee was told by his DEA instructor, "After *Whren*, the game was over. We won."[36] Operation Pipeline has trained hundreds of state and local law enforcement agencies on how to convert a traffic stop into a drug investigation by requesting consent or manufacturing reasonable suspicion. As of 2000, the DEA had trained approximately 27,000 officers in Operation Pipeline tactics; these officers, in turn, trained many others.[37] State and local law enforcement agencies make huge profits from the national dragnet. Taking advantage of the equitable sharing program, they receive up to 80 percent of the value of seized cars and cash, with the rest going to the DEA. Thousands of innocent people have been stopped and intimidated into having their vehicle searched—and possibly torn apart—in the hunt for illegal drugs.[38] As one California Highway Patrol officer said in a deposition taken by the ACLU, "It's sheer numbers . . . You kiss a lot of frogs before you find a prince."[39] In a study of more than 6,000 traffic stops in Texas, 99 percent of the drivers were found to have no illegal drugs.[40]

The DEA maintains that they do not train police to use racial profiling, but a battery of lawsuits against police departments using Operation Pipeline suggests otherwise. For example, an ACLU lawsuit against the California Highway Patrol revealed that Hispanics were three times more likely and blacks twice as likely as whites to be stopped. Internal documents revealed how New Jersey troopers were trained to target blacks and Hispanics and how management blocked an investigation by the Department of Justice while the DEA praised the success of the officers.[41]

Pipeline officers are taught to check cars for several "indicators" that are supposedly used by drug couriers, such as air fresheners, attorney business cards, atlases, prepaid phone cards, and rented cars.[42] Police are trained to have drivers get out of their cars and to ask them a series of questions, such as where they come from, what their travel plans are, and whether they have ever been arrested. Finally, they are trained to ask something like, "You don't mind if I search your car then, do you?" Drivers rarely refuse.[43] If they do, Pipeline-trained police often bring in drug-sniffing dogs. The Supreme Court ruled in 1983 that a canine sniff of baggage in an airport is not a "search" within the meaning of the Fourth Amendment, and thus it does not require a search warrant.[44] Since that ruling, dog sniffs have been upheld by lower courts outside of airports.[45] The issue of drug-detection dogs found its way to the Supreme Court in a case involving Roy Caballes. The case provides a good example of a Pipeline stop.

In 1998, Illinois State Trooper Gillette stopped Caballes for driving 71 miles per hour in a 65 mile-per-hour zone on Interstate 80.[46] Trooper Graham, a member of the Illinois State Police Drug Interdiction Team, heard over the police radio that Caballes had been stopped; although Gillette did not ask for help, Graham drove to the scene with a drug-detection dog. Meanwhile, with Caballes in the backseat of the patrol car, Gillette informed him he had been speeding and requested his license, car registration, and proof of insurance. After checking the validity of the documents and making sure no warrants were outstanding, Gillette informed Caballes he was going to write a warning ticket. He then proceeded to ask Caballes a series of questions, such as where he was going, why he was wearing a suit, whether he had ever been arrested. Finally, he asked whether he could search the car. Surprisingly, Caballes refused. While Gillette was writing the ticket, trooper Graham arrived with a drug-detection dog and began walking the dog around the car. The dog alerted at Caballes's trunk, giving the troopers what they thought was the probable cause they needed to justify searching the trunk. They found marijuana.

Caballes was convicted of a narcotics offense and sentenced to 12 years in prison. The case went to the Illinois Supreme Court, which considered whether it was reasonable under the Fourth Amendment for a drug-detection dog to sniff a vehicle during a legitimate traffic stop when there was no reasonable suspicion of illicit drugs. The Illinois Court voided Caballes's conviction arguing that the use of a drug-sniffing dog unjustifiably expanded a routine traffic stop into a drug investigation. The U.S. Supreme Court reversed the Illinois Court, ruling in *Illinois v. Caballes* (2005) that "a dog sniff conducted during a concededly lawful traffic stop that reveals no information other than the location of a substance that no individual has any right to possess does not violate the Fourth Amendment."[47] The Court reaffirmed and strengthened this opinion in *Florida v. Harris* (2013) ruling 9–0 that a drug-detection dog's alert to the exterior of a vehicle provides an officer with probable cause to conduct a warrantless search of the interior of the vehicle.[48]

The Supreme Court revisited the issue of dog sniffs during a lawful traffic stop in 2015.[49] Justice Ginsburg delivered the opinion of the Court stating, "We hold that a police stop exceeding the time needed to handle the matter for which the stop was made violates the Constitution's shield against unreasonable seizures." Whether this ruling will have any effect on the police use of dog sniffs in traffic stops is an open question.[50]

Using dogs to conduct drug searches loads the dice in favor of a positive result. Drug-detection dogs are trained to respond to cocaine as well as other drugs. But scientific investigations have consistently found that between 30 and 97 percent of U.S. currency in circulation is contaminated with cocaine. A 2009 study from the American Chemical Society found cocaine on 90 percent of 234 banknotes from 18 cities.[51] Even former U.S. Supreme Court Justice David Souter has referred to "the pervasive contamination of currency by cocaine."[52] In spite of this evidence, dog sniffs are still routinely used to establish probable cause in random consent searches for drugs.

Nondrug Crimes Are Neglected

There is substantial evidence that the drug war has diminished police efforts to go after nondrug crimes such as robbery, burglary, and even manslaughter. Drug enforcement is profitable for police, but they receive no financial benefit in catching burglars, rapists, or murderers. Time spent on arresting, convicting, and imprisoning nonviolent drug law violators is time not spent on catching dangerous criminals.

As Judge James P. Gray observed, "Our courts are so crowded with drug cases that other defendants, including rapists and murderers, can get away with lenient plea bargains because prosecutors lack the time and resources to prosecute them more fully."[53]

According to the former Los Angeles Deputy Chief of Police Stephen Downing, "The availability of huge federal anti-drug grants incentivizes departments to pay for SWAT team armor and weapons, and leads our police officers to abandon real crime victims in our communities in favor of ratcheting up their drug arrest stats."[54]

A study by the *Los Angeles Times* found that only 47 percent of the murders in Los Angeles County were prosecuted in the early 1990s compared with 80 percent in the late 1960s.[55] In Chicago, the percentage of homicides solved by police in 1991 was 70 percent, but by 2008 and 2009, it was down to less than 40 percent.[56]

There are also rigorous empirical studies showing that the surge in the war on drugs has been responsible for increases in other types of crime, including robbery, burglary, larceny, motor vehicle thefts, property crimes, violence, and even homicide.[57] These results are consistent with the incentive for police to reallocate their efforts from nondrug to drug crimes. But there are additional possible explanations for these results as well:[58]

- People found guilty of illicit drug possession often lose their jobs and their welfare benefits, motivating them to commit property crime and possibly even violent crimes;
- An increase in arrests for illicit drug sales could lead to violence between rival drug cartels;[59] and
- Prisons overcrowded with nonviolent drug violators serving mandatory minimum sentences have less room for those convicted of violent crimes.[60]

Part II

RACIAL INJUSTICE

CHAPTER 6

Shutting the Courthouse Door

R ecall that in *Whren* the Supreme Court allowed random consent searches of cars for illicit drugs as long as the stop was legal. But suppose the majority of drivers stopped are black, as in fact is the case? Doesn't a significant racial disparity in traffic stops violate the protections of the Fourth Amendment? Here's how Justice Scalia, speaking for the Supreme Court in *Whren*, responded to that question: "We of course agree . . . that the Constitution prohibits selective enforcement of the law based on considerations such as race. But the constitutional basis for objecting to intentionally discriminatory application of laws is the Equal Protection Clause [of the Fourteenth Amendment], not the Fourth Amendment."[1] In other words, as far as the Fourth Amendment is concerned, an officer's intention is irrelevant as long as the traffic stop itself is legal; if the lion's share of stops happen to consist of blacks and Hispanics, take it up with the Fourteenth Amendment.[2]

The Supreme Court's seminal Fourteenth Amendment decision concerning protection for racial minorities occurred in *McCleskey v. Kemp* in 1987. Warren McCleskey, a black man, was convicted of the murder of a white police officer in the superior court of Fulton County, Georgia.[3] McCleskey faced the death penalty. Represented by the NAACP, he challenged the sentence on the grounds that Georgia's death penalty system was racially biased and therefore violated the equal protection clause of the Fourteenth Amendment.

In support of his challenge, the NAACP offered an exhaustive study of some 2,000 murder cases in Georgia in the 1970s, named the Baldus study after its lead author professor David Baldus.[4] The researchers, after controlling for relevant nonracial variables, found that defendants charged with killing whites were 4.3 times more likely to get the death penalty than those charged with killing blacks. The Baldus study concluded that black defendants such as McCleskey, who killed whites, had the greatest likelihood of receiving the death sentence.

The Supreme Court accepted the statistical evidence that there were significant racial disparities in sentencing outcomes but ruled that disproportionate racial impact is not sufficient to establish a violation of the equal protection clause of the Fourteenth Amendment. What is required is proof that there was conscious racial bias in McCleskey's individual case. That is, McCleskey would have had to show that his prosecutor or jury imposed the death penalty for racial reasons.[5] This ruling has been critical in drug law cases.

At the end of its opinion, the Court revealed its concern with accepting racially disproportionate impact per se as a violation of equal protection: "If we accepted McCleskey's claim that racial bias has impermissibly tainted the capital sentencing decision, we could soon be faced with similar claims as to other types of penalty."[6] In his dissent, Justice William J. Brennan Jr. remarked that the Court's rationale for the ruling "seems to suggest a fear of too much justice."[7] The Court has affirmed the principle many times that disproportionately damaging racial minorities does not violate equal protection unless there is proof of discriminatory intent.[8]

Sentencing is one stage in the criminal justice process, prosecution is another. Since the introduction of mandatory minimum sentences in 1986, there has been a shift of power from judges to prosecutors. When an officer makes an arrest based on probable cause that a person has committed a crime, he does not decide what the formal charge will be or whether there will even be a charge. That decision rests with the prosecutor, who has almost unlimited discretion to determine whether a person will face criminal charges and, if so, what they will be. Suppose, for example, an individual is arrested for possessing cocaine. The prosecutor could decide to dismiss the case, even if there were sufficient evidence to convict. No judge or lawyer could challenge such a decision; in fact, few would even know about the dismissal, because decisions are usually made in the privacy of the prosecutor's office. If the prosecutor decides to bring charges, there is a great deal of discretion as to what the charge will be: It could be simple possession, possession with intent to distribute, or trafficking. The differences in penalties are enormous: anywhere from a maximum of one year in jail to a mandatory sentence of 10 years in prison or more.[9]

As Professor Angela Davis observed: "The prosecutor now essentially controls the criminal justice system."[10] If a prosecutor is charging defendants differently based on race, would that conduct violate equal protection and result in dismissal of the tainted cases? The correct answer seems obvious, and indeed in 1886 the Supreme Court unanimously answered yes to the question, dismissing a case where there was evidence of racial bias by the prosecutor.[11]

As for current law, the critical case is *U.S. v. Armstrong* (1996). In 1992, a drug task force of federal and state agents raided a motel in Los Angeles and arrested Christopher Lee Armstrong and four of his companions. They were indicted in federal court for conspiracy to distribute more than 50 grams of crack cocaine. All the men were black.[12] The public defenders assigned to Armstrong's case by prosecutors were federal, not state. These attorneys noted that of the 53 crack cases assigned to them during the preceding three years, 48 defendants were black, 5 Hispanic, and none white. They knew that many whites had been tried on crack cocaine charges, but whites had been sent by prosecutors to the California state court system, where the penalties were much less severe than in the federal system.

As a result of these observations, Armstrong's defenders suspected that blacks were systematically being sent to the federal system, while whites were being routed to the more lenient state system. The federal government's own data supported the lawyers' suspicion. Of 2,400 people charged with federal crack violations over a three-year period, all but 11 were black, and none were white. In addition, the U.S. Sentencing Commission reported in 1995 that two-thirds of all crack users were white.[13] If the public defenders' suspicions were confirmed, the prosecutorial conduct was racially biased, which would violate the equal protection clause of the Fourteenth Amendment and require the case to be dismissed. But suspicions are not evidence. The information as to what the prosecutors were doing was under their control. So the lawyers requested permission to conduct "discovery" (that is, a search) of the prosecutors' files to determine whether there was evidence of deliberate discrimination. The District Court found the evidence sufficient to justify discovery, but the prosecutors refused to open their files and appealed the issue all the way to the U.S. Supreme Court. The Court in an 8–1 decision reversed the District Court, stating that Armstrong's evidence "failed to show that the [federal] Government declined to prosecute similarly situated suspects of other races."[14] The Supreme Court refused to accept the defense attorneys' sworn statements that white defendants had systematically been prosecuted for crack cocaine violations in state court, calling this information "hearsay."[15] The federal government's own evidence was also rejected.

As a result of *U.S. v. Armstrong*, a defendant who maintains he has been discriminated against by a district attorney faces a catch-22. He must first present evidence of deliberate racial discrimination by the prosecutor before he can gain access to the best—and usually the only—evidence of discrimination, which resides in the files and documents of the prosecutor.[16] Barring a public admission of racial prejudice by the prosecutor, defendants face an insurmountable barrier to obtain discovery. According to Michelle Alexander, "Immunizing prosecutors from claims of racial bias . . . has created an atmosphere in which conscious and unconscious biases are allowed to flourish."[17]

As we have seen, the Supreme Court has made it virtually impossible to challenge racial discrimination by using either the Fourth Amendment or the Fourteenth Amendment. There is, however, a remaining avenue available in the criminal justice system: Title VI of the Civil Rights Act of 1964, which prohibits federally funded programs from discriminating on the basis of race. It employs a "disparate impact test" for discrimination; that is, if the program has a racially discriminatory impact, and cannot be justified as a law enforcement necessity, it would be unlawful. Proving discriminatory intent was not necessary.[18] Title VI sounds like a promising way to combat racial discrimination because nearly all law enforcement agencies receive funds from the federal government to fight the drug war.

Unfortunately, the Supreme Court eliminated the right of people who claim racial discrimination to sue under the Civil Rights Act. In *Alexander v. Sandoval* (2001), the Supreme Court ruled that neither an individual nor a private organization, like the ACLU, can file a lawsuit claiming that a government-funded program violates Title VI. Only the federal government has the right to do so. The Court further held that to win a racial discrimination suit under Title VI it is necessary to prove intentional bias. Disproportionate impact is not sufficient.[19] (The Court does not apply this standard in gender discrimination cases, even though the statutory language is identical.[20])

The 2001 *Sandoval* ruling closed off the last remaining avenue for challenging racial discrimination in the criminal justice system. The decision has virtually eliminated lawsuits alleging racial profiling in drug law enforcement because most of those suits were brought pursuant to Title VI of the Civil Rights Act of 1964.[21]

CHAPTER 7

Racial Disparities

All that you've read so far reveals that the drug war disproportionately affects racial minorities, especially African Americans. Why
this disparity? It's clear that our country has made great strides toward
color blindness in the past 50 years. Expressions of racial bigotry have
become widely considered intolerable. Politicians rarely endorse policies
that are transparently racially biased and routinely condemn discrimination against blacks and Hispanics. In fact, even a remark seen as racially
bigoted can seriously damage a public figure.

Even as early as the 1980s, surveys showed that 90 percent of Americans believed that black and white children should attend the same
schools; 71 percent endorsed the idea that blacks had the right to live in
white neighborhoods; 80 percent said they could support a black president; and 66 percent opposed laws that would prevent intermarriage.[1]
This support for racial justice has increased since the 1980s. According
to a 2004 study of racial attitudes, "Regardless of whether one regards
these shifts in racial opinion as shifts in genuine sentiments or merely
shifts in what sentiments the public is willing to express, it is clear that
many people have learned to control the expression of (race-based) prejudice and stereotypes. They have learned to act in a more color-blind
manner, proclaiming that race matters little and that everyone should be
treated equally and respected as individual human beings."[2] Neverthe-
less, in a 2012 Associated Press Survey of Racial Attitudes, 7 percent of
the sample said they would not vote for Barack Obama because he was
black, and 5 percent refused to answer the question.[3] Explicit racism
may be on the decline, but it's clearly still alive and explains some of the
disproportionate impact of the drug war on racial minorities.

But as we'll see, a critical additional factor in causing racial disparities in the war on drugs is the implicit (or unconscious) racial bias against blacks in almost all of us. Abundant research shows that African Americans are widely stereotyped as drug felons.[4] This stereotype is fed by the disproportionate representation of blacks in prison because of their rate of committing violent crimes. An investigation by Alfred Blumstein found that blacks constituted over 50 percent of the arrests for homicide and armed robbery and almost 50 percent for rape.[5] He concluded that, except for drug and property crimes, differential black rates of incarceration are explained almost entirely by differential rates of violent offenses.[6]

When it comes to nonviolent drug violations, however, arrests and incarcerations of African Americans are out of all proportion to their offenses. From the 1980s on, the lion's share of all imprisonments were a result of nonviolent crimes, especially drug offenses: From 1985 to 2000, only 16 percent of sentenced felony offenders had been convicted of a violent crime; while 84 percent were convicted of nonviolent drug or property crimes. As Marc Mauer sums it up: "A general law enforcement emphasis on drug-related policing in communities of color has resulted in African-Americans being prosecuted for drug offenses far out of proportion to the degree that they use or sell drugs. White admissions to prison for nonviolent drug offenses increased by a factor of seven between 1983 and 1998, while African American admissions increased 26-fold."[7] These numbers stand in stark contrast to use rates of illegal drug use by blacks versus whites, which involve only slight differences: 7.7 percent of blacks used illicit drugs in the previous month, compared to 6.6 percent of whites.[8]

Currently, African Americans constitute 14 percent of drug users, yet constitute 33.9 percent of those arrested for a drug offenses and 53 percent of those sentenced to prison for a nonviolent drug offense.[9] According to a National Survey on Drug Use and Health, only one-third of crack cocaine users in the United States were African American. On the other hand, the U.S. Sentencing Commission reported that blacks constituted more than 80 percent, and whites less than 8 percent, of the defendants sentenced to prison under the federal crack cocaine laws.[10]

It's impossible to rationalize the stunning levels of black overrepresentation in prison for nonviolent drug offenses by their higher commission of these crimes.[11]

So how can we explain it?

Law enforcement has little choice but to attempt to arrest someone charged with a violent crime.[12] The family and friends of those killed or injured demand it—not to mention a frightened public. Police can't decide to apprehend one suspected rapist or murderer and not another. The situation is vastly different with nonviolent drug law offenses. More than 15 percent of Americans are estimated to violate these laws each year, but, even with financial incentives, police arrest only about 6 percent of drug law violators.[13] Currently, for example, there are around 1.5 million arrests a year for illicit drug users, but there are some 25 million Americans aged 12 or older who have used illicit drugs during the month prior to the survey.[14] So 94 percent of those who commit drug crimes escape arrest every year. Obviously, law enforcement can't arrest 25 million people every year for violating drug laws. The flip side of this impossibility is that police have enormous discretion as to where they send their troops in the war on drugs. How do they decide? Because police stereotype blacks as drug felons—evidence examined in the following chapter—they will be motivated to target blacks. If, in addition, our laws fail to penalize law enforcement for racial discrimination, then we should not be surprised to find African Americans disproportionately punished for nonviolent drug offenses. Unfortunately, as we saw in the previous chapter, Supreme Court rulings have largely immunized police and prosecutors from lawsuits challenging racial injustice.

It's conventional wisdom among law enforcement that focusing on low-income, inner-city communities is the most productive way to combat illegal drug activity. Consequently, police go hunting in poor, largely African American communities rather than in the mostly white middle-class neighborhoods. Street sweeps, and rounding everyone up for questioning and searches, are common, as are aggressive and often warrantless drug searches in public housing projects.

Here is how one agent from the Bureau of Alcohol, Tobacco, and Firearms explained the rationale for a Washington, D.C., street sweep: "This is definitely not a method you'd want to use in Georgetown or out in the suburbs. But in a neighborhood like this we knew the probability was great that one out of every ten people we detained, at least six or seven would be in some kind of trouble with the law. That was our thinking. It was that kind of neighborhood."[15] President Obama's drug czar, Gil Kerlikowske, when he was Seattle's police chief, justified the tactics of his department this way: "In the condos, there could be as much cocaine use as in certain street corners of downtown, but often it's more difficult—if not impossible—to get."[16]

A former prosecutor explained the strategy this way: "It's a lot easier to go out to the 'hood, so to speak. And pick somebody than to put your resources in an undercover [operation in a] community where there are potentially politically powerful people."[17]

CHAPTER 8

Police Bias in Seattle

It may be politically easier to target illegal drug activity in inner-city neighborhoods, but is it really the most effective way for police to conduct the war on drugs? Police departments frequently argue that targeting inner-city areas is the most efficient strategy to enforce the drug laws. Here is the reasoning typically employed by law enforcement in support of the strategy: Poor, inner-city communities have relatively little access to private space for illegal drug activity, so they tend to commit crimes on the streets. Therefore, to effectively enforce the drug laws, police need to focus on outdoor markets where drug crimes are disproportionately concentrated. Racial disparity in drug arrests is just an unfortunate consequence.[1] In other words, the disproportionate impact of the drug war on blacks is not a result of racist police tactics, it's simply a result of police going where most drug crimes take place.

Consider the strategy of the Seattle Police Department (SPD) in the period 1999–2001. The department focused much more on crack cocaine than on other illegal drugs, arresting 2,018 crack dealers during this period, but only 138 sellers of methamphetamine, ecstasy, and powder cocaine combined.[2] They concentrated on busting street dealers instead of those in indoor drug venues. The police justified this policy by asserting that outdoor markets were the source of the majority of community complaints; that crack markets were especially rife with violent crime; that crack constituted one of the greatest dangers to health; and that the most productive hunting grounds for catching drug dealers were open-air crack markets.

As Richard Gil Kerlikowske, the Chief of SPD during this period—and formerly the drug czar under President Obama—explained, "You go where the information takes you and you go where the complaints and problems are most visible and where you're going to be able to prosecute those cases."[3] He also stated, "In the condos, there could be as much cocaine use as in certain street corners of downtown, but often it's more difficult—if not impossible—to get . . . There are less complaints and less overdoses. We end up going to the hot spots . . . Enforcement on the street needs less resources; it's less dangerous to police personnel than going into a house undercover."[4]

The Assistant Chief John Diaz added, "We are targeting certain neighborhoods that are experiencing serious problems with drug dealing and violence. Yes, but it was at the request of the neighborhood. Resources are based on calls for service. Some of the wealthier areas get less police service."[5] Kris Nyrop, executive director of Street Outreach Services in Seattle, stated that street-level enforcement is as easy as "shooting fish in a barrel."[6] Jerry Adams, manager of the Investigative Support Unit, High Intensity Drug Trafficking Area, reported, "If you take all of the arrests by SPD and look at the race of the informants, I would bet close to a paycheck that 85 percent or more of the informants are black. It's the path of least resistance—the investigations are driven by informants. The informants are addicts. So the strategy is driven by drug addicts for whom it is okay to snitch on someone to get out of a beef."[7] He pointed out that most of the confidential informants come from the streets rather than the indoor drug market. These are people who have been arrested for drug selling and can "work off" their case by becoming snitches for the police.[8]

This elaborate rationale of the Seattle Police Department was subjected to rigorous empirical testing in 2005 and 2006 by a team of sociologists from the University of Washington.[9] Here are their findings:

- Did the majority of citizen complaints result from the open-air drug activity? No. Citizens were much more likely to complain about suspected drug activity in indoor residences (63 percent) than in outdoor markets (10 percent). In fact, the precinct with the least complaints involved the most drug arrests.[10]
- Were crack cocaine markets characterized by violent crime? No. There was no "significant level of violence associated with crack."[11] The outdoor crack markets were "significantly 'over policed' relative to [violent and property] crime rates."[12]
- Was crack more dangerous for health than the other drugs? No. The office of the King County Medical Examiner found that 402 overdose deaths involved heroin and other opiates, while 213 overdose deaths

involved cocaine, which could have been snorted, smoked, or injected. Furthermore, the public health dangers of intravenous drug use are "arguably far greater" than those resulting from smoking crack.[13] As Ron Jackson, director of Evergreen Treatment Services, remarked, "It's White guys in their thirties who are dying [from heroin], but it's black guys who are going to jail."[14]

- Was law enforcement more productive in focusing on outdoor drug markets than on indoor venues? No. The researchers found that buy-bust operations targeting street dealers yielded an average of 33 cents seized per officer hour, compared to $749 seized per officer hour spent on search warrant arrests for indoor venues. So, even though indoor arrests required more police hours per arrest, it was more than worth it.[15]

In sum, the rationale espoused by the Seattle Police Department for focusing on crack cocaine and outdoor drug markets over the period of 1999 to 2001 did not stand up to rigorous empirical scrutiny. The drug arrests were not a response to citizen complaints; they were not related to violent criminal activity; they were not motivated by public health concerns; and, finally, they were relatively unproductive in terms of both seized drugs and weapons.

By concentrating almost three-quarters of the drug arrests in open-air markets, the police were contributing to the overrepresentation of blacks, because blacks were more likely than whites to be arrested outdoors. Even more important as a contributor to racial disparity was the focus on crack possession arrests: 75 percent of the arrests were for crack possession, while the main users of crack by far were blacks.[16]

Even in areas where white drug users and sellers predominated, the majority of those arrested were black. For example, the researchers found that "although our observations indicated that 3 percent of those purchasing drugs in the Capitol Hill area were black, 20.5 percent of those arrested for possession in that area were black."[17]

The study concluded: "The racial disparity is difficult to explain in race-neutral terms . . . Although it is difficult to rule out racial animus in Seattle's anti-drug efforts, we believe that . . . [these] practices are more likely to reflect implicit racial bias: [namely] the unconscious impact of race on official perceptions of who and what constitutes Seattle's drug problem."[18]

The investigators mentioned two observations that reinforced their conviction that implicit racism played a major role in the disproportionate arrest of blacks:

- The officers responsible for a predominantly white area reported that very few heroin sales occurred on the streets. Yet the researchers observed numerous heroin sales taking place in that area in a very short period of time, and the vast majority of users and dealers were white.[19]
- Officers interviewed about the downtown drug market failed to mention an active market for illegal prescription drugs that consisted mostly of white consumers and sellers.[20]

While this investigation applies only to Seattle, the researchers' interpretation of the role of race is consistent with the consensus view of social psychologists: Voluminous research over many decades has consistently found that implicit (unconscious) racial bias is widespread and shapes our perceptions of crime-related problems. Implicit bias exists even among those of us who do not explicitly (consciously) harbor prejudiced views.[21] These stereotypes can lead to discriminatory actions that we are not aware of. Here are a few examples of studies that reveal implicit bias:

- In one study, a video game contained photographs of blacks and whites holding either a gun or some other object. In an attempt to tap implicit racial bias, participants were told to shoot the target as quickly as possible if they thought they saw a gun. The shooters were more likely to mistake a black person as armed when he was not and more likely to see a white person as unarmed when he was in fact armed. Interestingly, black participants exhibited the same shooter bias as whites.[22]
- In a 1995 survey, people were asked to close their eyes, imagine a drug user, and describe the person they saw. Ninety-five percent of the respondents described a black male. The result was startling because only 15 percent of drug users were black at the time.[23]
- Two studies examined unconscious racial stereotypes using police and probation officers as participants. They read two hypothetical crime reports. In one, a 12-year-old boy with no record was accused by a store manager of stealing $40 worth of toys, which he denied. In another, a 15-year-old boy allegedly assaulted a 16-year-old peer, and witnesses were unsure as to whether the assault was provoked. The race of the boys was unstated. Participants were divided into two groups: One read the reports without racial priming, while the other was primed subliminally, with words associated with blacks. The primed participants reported more negative traits, more culpability, and greater expected recidivism than the unprimed

participants. They also endorsed harsher punishments than the unprimed group.[24]

- Another study, which involved both black and white participants, compared implicit versus explicit preferences for white versus black faces. Not surprisingly, whites explicitly preferred white faces over black faces, but their implicit preference for white over black was even greater than their explicit preference. As for black participants, they explicitly preferred black faces over white but implicitly revealed a small preference for white over black.[25]

In sum, psychological research has confirmed repeatedly that racial bias in arrests and incarcerations is no accident. This bias is rooted in both conscious and unconscious stereotypes, even among people who believe they are free of racial prejudice. These studies warn us that racial injustice may seriously infect our criminal justice system, especially in the case of drug law violations where law enforcement personnel have enormous discretion as to where they search and whom they arrest.

Citizens of color are not only frequently stopped and frisked by police in inner-city neighborhoods, but they are also disproportionately targeted in bus terminals, airports, and train stations and on highways. In theory, the police use drug-courier profiles to select suspects. But, according to Professor David A. Harris in his study of racial profiling, "no one has any statistics on the success rate of drug-courier profiles that would show us how effective this technique really is."[26] In fact, it seems impossible to get any measure of how successful these profiles are in catching law breakers because they describe *any* pattern of appearance or behavior you could dream up—and many are self-contradictory: Law Professor David Cole, in his study of racial injustice, presents a list of 47 drug-courier profiles that have been used by federal agents.[27] Here are a few pertaining to plane passengers:[28]

- arrived late at night
- arrived early in the morning
- arrived in the afternoon
- one of the first to deplane
- one of the last to deplane
- deplaned in the middle

(You get the idea.)

Some DEA agents have even testified in court that they explicitly take race into account. The agency has admitted that it trains police to use race as "one of many factors" when considering whether to search a vehicle.[29] A DEA drug profile listed categories to watch out for, which included black males aged 25 to 50 years of age.[30] A review of federal court decisions based on drug-courier profiles from January 1, 1990, to August 2, 1995, found that of 63 cases where race was known, only 3 were not minorities: 34 were blacks, 25 were Hispanics, 1 was Asian, and 3 were whites.[31]

CHAPTER 9

Police Bias in New York

Inner-city black and Hispanic youths are frequently stopped, questioned, and frisked, often by paramilitary-type police units.[1] The policy of the New York Police Department (NYPD) is a prime example. The department's tactics recently have been both rigorously investigated and the subject of lawsuits challenging their constitutionality.

In the 1990s, the NYPD initiated a stop-and-frisk program as part of a zero-tolerance approach to policing. The idea was to bear down on minor crimes as a way of preventing serious crimes, despite controversy as to whether this so-called Broken Windows strategy is effective.[2] Between 2004 and 2009, New York police officers stopped 2.8 million residents and visitors, restraining their freedom, if only temporarily; over 50 percent of people stopped were African Americans, 30 percent were Latinos, while only 10 percent were whites.[3] In 2011, black and Hispanic men, between the ages of 14 and 24, constituted 41.6 percent of the stops, though they were only 4.7 percent of the population.[4] Under New York law, possession of a small amount of marijuana is a misdemeanor only if it is in public view, but black and Hispanic men frequently complain that the police search their pockets so they can manufacture an offense by claiming the drug was in plain view.[5]

In 2012, Judge Shira Scheindlin of the Federal District Court granted class-action status to a lawsuit that accused the NYPD of using race as a basis for stops and frisks (*Floyd v. the City of New York*).[6] The question posed by the lawsuit was whether the stops and frisks comply with the Constitution. According to a 1968 ruling by the U.S. Supreme Court, the law regarding when a police officer is allowed to frisk is clear: They can legally do so only if they have a reasonable suspicion, based on articulable facts, not just a hunch, that the person is armed and dangerous.[7]

The 2012 lawsuit employed a detailed investigation by the criminologist Jeffrey Fagan on the stop-and-frisk policy of the NYPD. He conducted a comprehensive statistical analysis using six years of the NYPD's own data. Fagan's major conclusion is that the NYPD's stop-and-frisk program is not about crime; it's about race.

Here are some of the findings of the Fagan report:[8]

- The majority of stops occur in black and Latino neighborhoods, even after controlling for such factors as crime rates and social conditions.
- Blacks and Hispanics were the most likely to be stopped even in neighborhoods that were mostly white.
- Over the past six years, nearly 150,000 stops were unconstitutional, lacking any legal justification.
- The vague term "furtive movements" was the sole justification cited in nearly half of all documented stops.
- In more than half the documented stops, the justification cited was "high crime area" as an "additional circumstance," even in precincts where the crime rates were lower than average.
- Arrests occurred in 4 percent of the stops, an arrest rate lower than at random check points.
- The rates of weapons and contraband seizures were 0.12 percent for weapons and 1.8 percent for illegal drugs. These rates were also lower than seizure rates at random stops.
- Compared to whites accused of the same crime, blacks and Latinos were more likely to be treated violently and were more likely to be arrested than issued a summons.

At the trial, Inspector Kenneth C. Lehr, commanding officer of the 67th Precinct, was asked by Judge Scheindlin whether he was "concerned" that only 4 percent of police stops resulted in a summons or an arrest, and he answered "yes." When further asked whether he "worried" that the stops might be unlawful, he responded with another "yes."[9]

Plaintiffs introduced sworn testimony by New York State Senator Eric Adams, who had retired after 20 years in the NYPD. Adams claimed that in a meeting in July 2010, Police Commissioner Raymond Kelly told him that the NYPD targets young black and Hispanic men because "it wants to instill the belief in members of these two populations that they could be stopped and frisked every time they leave their homes so that they are less likely to carry weapons."[10] Commissioner Kelly denied this, maintaining that the stops are based on reasonable suspicion. "At the meeting, I did discuss my view that stops serve as a deterrent to criminal activity, which includes the criminal possession of a weapon," said Kelly.[11]

Pedro Serrano, a Bronx police officer, testified at the trial that police supervisors had instituted quotas that pressured officers to stop people unlawfully, especially blacks and Hispanics. Serrano, as a Hispanic man in the Bronx, had himself been stopped many times. He said he was worried about doing something illegal as an officer, so he started taping interactions with his supervisors. One recording played in court was of a conversation with his commanding officer, Deputy Inspector Christopher McCormack, who said that to suppress violent crime it was necessary to stop, question, and, if necessary, frisk "the right people at the right time [in] the right location." Serrano pressed the Inspector about what he meant by "the right people." McCormack said police needed to stop the people creating "the most problems . . . the problem was, what, male blacks. And I told you at roll call, and I have no problem telling you this, male blacks 14 to 20, 21."[12]

The trial court also heard from Officer Adhyl Polanco of the 41st Precinct, who had taped proceedings at the station house. He testified that officers were subject to a quota system that required "20 summonses and one arrest per month."[13]

John Eterno, a retired police captain and chairman of the criminal justice department at Molloy College on Long Island, has stated publicly that the NYPD has a "quota system" for stops: "Quotas exist," he said in May 2012. "Anyone who tells you any different is a liar. They occur and right now they are stringent about it, particularly with the young cops."[14] According to The New York Times, "Some former police officers . . . are increasingly vocal in their complaints about commanders forcing officers to make as many stops and to write as many summonses as possible."[15]

One part of the NYPD's stop-and-frisk program, called Operation Clean Halls, allows police to patrol thousands of private apartment buildings across New York City. In March 2012, another class-action lawsuit was granted by Judge Scheindlin, this one on behalf of residents of the buildings enrolled in this program (Ligon v. City of New York).[16] The suit claimed that Operation Clean Halls engaged in suspicionless police stops and arrests, primarily targeting blacks and Latinos.

Here are a few examples of the cases presented at the trial:

On May 3, 2011, after finishing the day's work as a security guard, Charles Bradley, a 51-year-old African American resident of the Bronx, went to visit his fiancée, Lisa Rappa, who lived in a Clean Halls building.[17] Bradley, who had formerly lived with Rappa, possessed keys to her apartment, but as a result of a disagreement, he had returned the keys. He was let into the building by a friend who knew about his relationship with Rappa. He went up to her apartment and knocked. When she did not answer, Bradley left the building and waited outside. As he was standing on the sidewalk, a police van approached, an officer called him over and asked what he was doing here. He explained that he had a date with Rappa and that he worked as a security guard. The officer responded by suggesting Bradley was acting "like a fucking animal."[18] He searched Bradley's pockets, handcuffed him, and placed him in the van where there were two other officers. They asked Bradley, "When was the last time you saw a gun? When was the last time you got high? When was the last time you bought some drugs?" and they took him to the station house. He was stripped and searched "in inappropriate areas."[19] For two hours he waited in a cell with other arrestees. He was fingerprinted and given a date to appear in court on a criminal charge of trespassing. Bradley's arrest was justified by the police on the grounds that he was in a "drug prone location" with "a lot of robberies [and] a lot of shootings" in the area.[20] Later, Bradley's attorney gave the DA's office a notarized letter from Rappa, stating that Bradley had been visiting her. Bradley eventually received paperwork stating that "the People of New York declined to prosecute."[21] Judge Scheindlin found that the testimony from Bradley was "credible"; she also determined that the officer's version of what happened—which differed from Bradley's—"contained numerous self-serving errors" and statements that were "false."[22]

In the evening of March 26, 2011, Abdullah Turner, a 24-year-old African American, was on his way to a party with a friend, Anginette Trinidad.[23] Just before arriving at the party, Trinidad said she had to return a sweater to a friend in the next building, a Clean Halls building. Turner remained outside, and while waiting he called another friend on his cell phone. While he was talking, someone snatched the phone out of his hand. As he turned around, he saw three police officers. The one holding his phone questioned him about what he was doing there and whether he lived there. After he explained, the officer asked for identification and Turner gave him his driver's license. He was questioned as to whether he knew anybody in the building and said no, at which point the officer asked him to stand against the wall. Eventually, Trinidad emerged from the building and verified Turner's story. The officer then informed Turner that the building Trinidad had entered was enrolled in

Operation Clean Halls and that he (Turner) was therefore trespassing and would be taken to jail. Turner asked how he could be trespassing when he was outside the building. He was then handcuffed and driven to the precinct, spent several hours waiting, and was transferred to central booking, where he spent several more hours. The arresting officer claimed that Turner had admitted he was in the Clean Halls building for the purpose of buying marijuana. He arrested Turner based on "the fact that he had no lawful reason to be in the building and that he knowingly was there to buy marijuana."[24] The next day a judge released Turner, but he was required to go to court eight to ten times before his charges were finally dismissed. Judge Scheindlin concluded: "I find that Turner's behavior provided no grounds for suspicion of trespass or any other crime."[25]

The judge pointed out that the humiliating sequence of events in these examples is typical and that in some cases the stops escalated into an arrest, "with all the indignities, inconveniences, and serious risks that follow from an arrest even when the charges are quickly dropped."[26] Arrests create a criminal record that can haunt a person for years to come.[27] Judge Scheindlin condemned the city for continuing these unlawful stops and frisks even after the Bronx prosecutor's office had become so concerned about their illegality that it stopped prosecuting cases based on them.[28]

On August 12, 2013, the judge, in a 195-page decision, ruled that the stop-and-frisk policy of the New York Police Department violated the constitutional rights of minorities in the city. She found that the department policy involved "indirect racial profiling" that led officers' to routinely stop and frisk "blacks and Hispanics who would not have been stopped if they were white."[29] She called for a federal monitor to oversee reforms, including the temporary use of body-worn cameras for some officers. Her remedy covered both lawsuits. She did not call for a ban on stop-and-frisk. Mayor Michael R. Bloomberg reacted angrily to her ruling and said the city would file an appeal.[30] The U.S. Court of Appeals for the Second Circuit stayed the remedies ordered by Judge Scheindlin and removed her from the case.[31]

The main victims of these street busts are African Americans who account for 13 percent of the United States population but constitute one-third of the national arrests for drug possession; while, for drug selling, blacks comprise almost half the national arrests.[32] In New York City, the NYPD, in their stop-and-frisk searches, arrested some 50,000 men in 2010, for low-level marijuana offenses, 86 percent of whom were blacks and Latinos.[33] The most common charge was criminal possession of marijuana in the fifth degree, a misdemeanor that can lead to a child-welfare inquiry, jeopardize occupational licenses, and turn up for years in background checks.[34] These misdemeanor arrests are very difficult to get expunged from a person's record, and even when they are expunged they can still show up.[35]

A high level of drug arrests in a neighborhood generates a high level of confidential informants. Those arrested for narcotics violations are frequently offered a chance to "work off" their sentence by becoming informants for the police.[36] Studies have shown that having a high concentration of the population incarcerated—especially for nonviolent drug offenses—has damaging consequences for residents and community relationships. According to an investigation of incarcerated drug law violators by the Sentencing Project,[37] 75 percent had never had a conviction for a violent offense, and 61 percent had been employed during the month before arrest.[38] Removing people like these from circulation, many for long periods of time, diminishes the work skills and income prospects of members of the community. In addition, removing fathers, mothers, and neighbors reduces the ability of an inner-city community to exercise informal social controls. Adding a large number of snitches to this mix erodes the ability of people in these neighborhoods to trust one another.[39]

Research by criminologists finds that when trust erodes, reliance on guns is likely to increase and violence to become more common.[40] Psychologist J. G. Miller argues: "No single tactic of law enforcement has contributed more to violence in the inner city than the practice of seeding the streets with informers . . . The practice undermines trust and breaks apart communities."[41] Snitches are always in danger of being injured or killed for collaborating with the police.[42]

Police contribute to the incendiary atmosphere by threatening to expose snitches as a way of pressuring them to continue providing information. As one street criminal expressed it, "You start informing then you got to keep informing cause if you stop they . . . gonna talk to the person that you told on and then they gonna wind up killing you." Another snitch explained, "They have you riding in the car . . . then let [others] know you're the snitch . . . The police gonna make it be known that you're the snitch . . . Get my head blown off!"[43]

Informants also claim the police engage in "freecasing"—i.e., planting illegal drugs—in order to boost their arrest record. They said the practice was "rampant."[44] As one interviewee put it, "Drop some boulders [crack] in your pocket. Send your ass in front of the judge. They gonna believe him before they believe you."[45] Another said, "They can't catch me with no drugs so . . . they freecase you . . . They put some heroin in my car [during a traffic stop] but I ain't have no heroin so they put it in my car . . . locked me up."[46]

These accusations of freecasing by police have been supported by evidence from an ex-NYPD narcotics detective: In 2011, Stephen Anderson testified in court that planting drugs on innocent people was done frequently; that it was a quick and easy way to increase arrest numbers.[47] Among NYPD officers the practice is known as "flaking." Detective Anderson had been caught flaking a woman and her boyfriend in 2008 and is now cooperating with the prosecutor. He plead guilty to "official misconduct" and faces two to four years in prison. The verdict came from Justice Gustin L. Reichbach in the State Supreme Court in Brooklyn. The justice referred to the "cowboy culture" of the police drug units and said, "Anything goes in the never-ending war on drugs."[48] Additional evidence comes from information acquired by the *New York Daily News* that the police in the Brooklyn and Queens narcotics squads were flaking often.[49]

The New York Court

While the federal courts are evaluating the constitutionality of NYPD's stops and frisks, the New York Court, the first-tier trial court, is "invisible and irrelevant," according to professor Steven Zeidman, of the City University School of Law.[50] He finds that the court is failing to perform the role the Supreme Court has "envisioned and mandated,"[51] namely, that it regulate the interactions between police and civilians. With 685,000 stops and frisks a year, the trial court should be calling police officers to testify about what they were doing and why. If the court determined that a stop was illegal, any evidence obtained would be excluded from a trial. The suppression of illegally obtained evidence is necessary in order to deter police from violating constitutional rights. Unfortunately, as Zeidman points out: "By abdicating its critical oversight role, the [New York] criminal court effectively shields police behavior from any meaningful external review or accountability and allows and encourages rampant stops and frisks to continue unabated."[52]

Francisco Zapata was stopped, frisked, and charged with misdemeanor marijuana possession. He knew his Constitution, having a copy of it in his cell phone, so he wanted a trial. But this was the Bronx, where there were 50,000 marijuana misdemeanor filings a year.[53] According to a study by Columbia University, 1 in 10 Bronx residents were stopped and frisked by police in 2010 and 2011. Court delays have been as long as five years.[54] But Zapata had legal representation by the Bronx Defenders, who provide legal help to poor residents charged with a crime. He was part of an effort by the Bronx Defenders, in cooperation with volunteers from the Cleary Gottlieb law firm, to challenge New York City's stop-and-frisk program by bringing 54 misdemeanor marijuana possession cases to trial. Eventually the effort had to be scrapped because not one of the 54 defendants succeeded in getting a trial. Instead, they wound up accepting pleas to avoid being required to reappear in court month after month, only to be told that the prosecutor "wasn't ready," or the arresting officer wasn't available that day. Lev L. Dassin, a former acting U.S. attorney in Manhattan, was in charge of the Wall Street firm's work on the project. He concluded, "The normal rules about being ready and having your day in court just don't apply. It's appalling."[55] Zapata came the closest of the 54 cases to getting a trial, but only after 11 court dates and 523 days. (When he missed one date because of work, he was threatened with arrest.) He finally saw his arresting officer take the stand as a witness, but while his lawyer was conducting a cross-examination the state dropped the case.[56]

The Bronx Defenders' attempts failed to stop the random NYPD stops and frisks, but their efforts highlighted how the inability to obtain a trial in the New York Trial Court has become a punishment in itself for huge numbers of people caught in the web of the criminal justice system. Here is a summary of what the Bronx Defenders learned:

> It [is] virtually impossible for clients to challenge unconstitutional stops and manufactured misdemeanors through the regular criminal legal process. Widespread police misconduct is systematically shielded from judicial scrutiny by court congestion and prosecutorial policies that create incentives for clients to plead guilty to lesser charges rather than see litigation through to the end. As a result, the staggering costs engendered by the current system—in the form of criminal records, fines, absences from school, missed days of work, evictions, deportations, and loss of parental rights—overwhelmingly fall on young men of color living in neighborhoods where these arrests are concentrated.[57]

It's impossible for a white middle-class adult like myself to know how it feels to fear that police will stop you and possibly abuse or even injure you almost every time you leave the house. One account by a young black man, Nicholas K. Peart, eloquently describes how he felt about being stopped and frisked by New York police officers at least five times.[58] Mr. Peart was a student at Borough of Manhattan Community College. He wrote, "When I was 14, my mother told me not to panic if a police officer stopped me. And she cautioned me to carry ID and never run away from the police or I could be shot. In the nine years since my mother gave me this advice, I had had numerous occasions to consider her wisdom." He recalls celebrating his eighteenth birthday with a cousin and a friend. They were sitting on benches in the median strip that runs down the middle of Broadway when suddenly "out of nowhere squad cars surrounded us. A policeman yelled from the window, 'Get on the ground!' I was stunned. And I was scared. Then I was on the ground with a gun pointed at me." Within the next few years he was stopped and frisked twice, for no apparent reason, while walking. In each case, police checked his ID and let him go. He knows that for young men in his neighborhood being stopped and frisked is a fact of daily life. He is afraid of the police: "I incorporated into my daily life the sense that I might find myself up against a wall or on the ground with an officer's gun at my head . . . And we all feel the same way—degraded, harassed, violated and criminalized because we're black or Latino."

In May 2011, he was stopped by two officers on his way to the store. They took his cell phone, wallet, and keys, handcuffed him, and put him in the back of the police car. One officer asked if he had marijuana and searched him. The other entered his apartment building, and, with his key, planned to get into his apartment. His 18-year-old sister was there with two younger siblings. She was terrified and tried to call him but the police had his cell phone. After the officer returned from the apartment building, they took off the handcuffs, told him to get out of the car, and drove off. (He didn't report whether the officer entered the apartment, nor did he say whether his possessions were returned.[59])

Stopping Stops and Frisks

In November 2013, Bill de Blasio was elected mayor of New York in a landslide, promising to rein in the use of stops and frisks by the NYPD. The number of stops of New Yorkers had been dropping dramatically even before de Blasio assumed office on January 1, 2014. The stops continued to plummet throughout 2014. In 2012, New Yorkers were stopped around 533,000 times; in 2013, 192,000 times; and, in 2014, 46,000 times. In each of these years around 55 percent of those stopped were African American, while around 30 percent were Latinos.[60]

In November 2014, Mayor de Blasio and the NYPD Chief Bill Bratton announced a major change in policy for officers approaching people with small amounts of marijuana. The new guidelines protect individuals who are caught with less than 25 grams of marijuana *even if* the drug is displayed openly from receiving a criminal record. New York's 1977 Marijuana Reform Act states that a person with less than 25 grams of marijuana should only receive a citation as long as the drug is concealed. But officers have frequently asked those they stop to empty their pockets or to permit a search of their vehicles, with the possible result of self-incrimination, because marijuana displayed openly is a violation of the law. With de Blasio's new policy, even if marijuana were openly displayed, the result would only be a citation, not an arrest. The individual would forfeit the marijuana and receive a summons to appear in court. The penalty would be a fine, but there would be no permanent record.[61]

In March 2015, conflicting attitudes emerged between Mayor de Blasio and Police Chief Bill Bratton toward the new guidelines for marijuana. The two men had stood side by side when the new marijuana policy was introduced in November 2014. But some four months later, Chief Bratton reported that homicides and shootings had increased over the past year and that the new marijuana policy was a factor. The police chief said, "People are killing each other over marijuana," and he compared the increase in crimes to the cocaine-related violence of the 1980s and 1990s. When the idea was first broached to relax the punishment for low-level possession of marijuana, Mr. Bratton declared, "I'm a strong believer that it should not be decriminalized."[62] Patrick Lynch, head of the Patrolmen's Benevolent Association, called the new marijuana policy "a dangerous half-measure that sends mixed signals and underscores the city's need to put more police officers on the streets." Lynch said, "From the point of view of us in law enforcement, any relaxation of enforcement against any kind of drug results in increased sales opportunities for dangerous drug dealers who freely use violence against their competitors."[63] Mayor de Blasio responded by reaffirming his support for the new guidelines arguing that arrests for low-level possession have disproportionately hurt blacks and Hispanics and damaged job prospects for otherwise law-abiding citizens. While stopping short of calling for the legalization of marijuana, de Blasio said that the experience of states that legalized the drug should be closely watched.[64]

It's not surprising that the mayor and the police do not see eye to eye on the issue of decriminalizing marijuana. The attitudes of Police Chief

Bratton and Patrick Lynch toward any policy threatening revenue that law enforcement can earn from the drug war reflects the consensus view of police and prosecutors. De Blasio's new policy is a financial threat to the NYPD. New York City receives millions of dollars every year from the Edward Byrne Memorial Grant Program, earning $4.4 million in 2014.[65] (Edward Byrne was a narcotics officer who was killed by a drug dealer.[66]) Recall that an investigation in 2001 by *Madison Capital Times* revealed that the size of the Byrne grants have been based almost entirely on the number of drug arrests.[67] De Blasio's new policy would cut down the number of drug arrests.

Part III

COVERT OPERATORS

CHAPTER 10

Criminal Informants

Police use informants in just about every type of case—white-collar crime, murder, burglary, and terrorism—but the most common use is in drug offenses.[1] The burgeoning war on drugs has triggered an explosion in criminal informants, and it's not hard to see why. Drug law violations involve willing buyers and sellers. Consequently, no one has a motive to complain or bring charges when the law is broken (except maybe angry neighbors). To arrest violators, police are often forced to operate undercover. As the U.S. Court of Appeals for the Seventh Circuit put it, referring especially to drug crimes, "Because [a] crime leaves no complaining witness, active participation by the [undercover] agents may be necessary to establish an effective case."[2]

Confidential informants (a.k.a. snitches) who navigate this underground economy are invaluable to law enforcement. They have usually been involved in drug crimes or other criminal activity themselves, and their motivation, as the late Representative Henry Hyde put it, is "to save their own skins."[3] Melvin Purvis, who tracked down John Dillinger and other notorious criminals, described informants this way in his book *American Agent*: "Those people of the underworld and the underworld's fringe who spy upon the activities of their fellow criminals and betray them to the law."[4]

To maintain a network of informants, law enforcement must pay them, either by reducing their charges and/or giving them money.[5] Snitches are so valuable that police try to keep their identities secret so they can continue to provide inside information. As a result, informants are usually not exposed by appearing in court. In a forfeiture hearing, property owners are often confronted with an officer who testifies what his informant told him; the owners cannot confront the snitch himself.[6]

Professor Alexandra Natapoff, a leading researcher of the informant industry, reports that "police, prosecutors, defense attorneys and judges all describe drug cases as relying on or creating informants . . . drug suspects routinely become informants themselves . . . [and] some police assert that they could not investigate drug cases without informants."[7] According to Dennis G. Fitzgerald, a former special agent of the DEA: "The DEA, the FBI and Customs are the largest federal consumers of informant services. Federal agents and local law enforcement are equally dependent on informants. It is an unusual organized crime and/or drug case that does not involve informants."[8]

One study of undercover police concluded that "one of the most critical requirements [for an officer] is the ability to cultivate informants for information on illegal activities and for contacts with active criminals. The relationship between an officer and an informant is . . . symbiotic, for they come to rely upon one another for services they can obtain only from each other." As one federal agent put it, "An informant is the easiest, quickest way to do police work . . . [He] can walk you in the front door and take you directly to the crook and introduce you face-to-face."[9]

A former detective superintendent of Scotland Yard explained the need for informants, especially in narcotics control: "I reckon that ten percent of the crimes committed in Great Britain would remain unsolved. That's the dilemma. That's why policemen are so vulnerable. We *must* use informers—You may have to let him go free after he's committed a crime because you can 'put the squeeze' on him afterwards"[10] (italics in the original).

Former Director of the FBI William Webster was passionate in extolling the importance of informants: "The informant is THE with a capital 'T' THE most effective tool in law enforcement today—state, local, or federal. We must accept that and deal with it."[11]

Informants are so crucial in helping solve drug crimes that officers are always on the lookout to expand their network. Dennis Fitzgerald tells us how the police do this.[12] Usually they offer a deal to an individual who has been arrested: Snitch for us and we'll get your charge reduced. Police may target a possible informant and wait until he is "suspected to be in possession of a controlled substance or other contraband. He is then 'arrested' following what is usually an illegal search and seizure. The subject, fearful of going to jail, may immediately agree to cooperate . . . He will work as an informant laboring under the impression that charges will be filed unless he cooperates."[13] Of course, cooperation means that the informant must continue to engage in illegal activities in order to acquire information about crimes for the police and the prosecutors.

Snitching has grown into an immensely profitable industry. Eric Schlosser reported that "in major drug cases an informer can earn a million dollars or more."[14] Forfeiture law awards snitches up to one-quarter of the assets that are confiscated on the basis of their testimony.[15] These payments are strongly defended by law enforcement. Gary H. Copeland, former director and chief counsel of the Department of Justice's Executive Office for Asset Forfeiture, revealed the government's motive in using snitches: "We're not paying it to them because we like them. We're paying it to them because they put money in the pot."[16] As Representative Henry Hyde put it: "One of the central pillars on which rests the dubious financial success of the federal forfeiture program is an army of well-paid secret informers."[17]

The large-scale use of criminal informants has caused many judges to complain that our criminal justice system is being corrupted.[18] There are many people in prison who are serving long mandatory minimum sentences who will do or say anything to shorten their sentence.
They have nothing to lose and everything to gain from their testimony, so they have an incentive to lie, and often do. Many have framed innocent people. According to Northwestern University Law School's Center on Wrongful Convictions, around 46 percent of capital convictions that have been overturned are a result of false informant testimony.[19] A 2005 study headed by law professor Samuel Gross found that almost 50 percent of wrongful convictions for murder in the United States from 1989 through 2003 were a result of lying by a "jailhouse snitch or another witness who stood to gain."[20]

A jailhouse snitch told a *60 Minutes* reporter how he was able, while in prison, to obtain confidential information about upcoming prosecutions. He fabricated incriminating information about the suspect and presented it to prosecutors in hopes of getting a reduction in his sentence.[21] Providing useful information to the DA is one of the few ways to get the harsh mandatory minimum sentences shortened. The U.S. Department of Justice reports that more than a quarter of federal drug defendants received lower sentences for providing "substantial assistance."[22] What determines whether the assistance is "substantial" depends entirely on the prosecutor.[23]

A major government investigation of jailhouse informants provided evidence on how inmates obtained information about upcoming cases and used it to provide assistance to prosecutors. The study was conducted by a Los Angeles County Grand Jury.[24] It lasted 10 years and included 120 witnesses, including 25 informants. The witnesses included people in all phases of law enforcement as well as scholars and private citizens. The testimony was shocking: Police used rewards and punishments to motivate inmates to provide false testimony for prosecutors in upcoming cases; there were numerous examples of lying and fabricating evidence by snitches; and, much of the phony evidence was supplied by officers.[25] The benefits inmates received for their testimony included such things as visits, food, movies, extra phone calls, as well as reduced sentences. They also received protection by being housed in a special place in the prison, called the "snitch tank."[26]

Prisoners claimed that law enforcement officials would supply them with information about crimes so that they would be able to secure incriminating statements from a defendant.[27] One inmate testified the police wanted him to provide evidence about a crime he knew nothing about. The officers fed him key information about the crime, taking him to the scene and "showing him pictures of the victim and the layout of the house." He subsequently testified in court that he had been the look-out during the crime.[28] Another informant claimed he was threatened unless he provided testimony; he said, "[I] was taken out of jail numerous times, shown the scenes of various crimes, and given police files."[29] Prisoners also stated that there were numerous other ways they were able to get information on upcoming trials: from arrest reports, photographs, and case files supplied by the DA; from information obtained from the coroner's office as well as the media; from friends and relatives attending court hearings; and from feedback on the accuracy of their upcoming testimony from detectives on the case.[30]

A recent case involving jailhouse snitches involves the Colombs, an African American family, who live in a two-bedroom bungalow in Church Point, Louisiana. Ann is a homemaker and her husband James is retired, having spent most of his career working in an oil field. He had been injured and their main income appears to be his disability check. There is nothing about the family that would suggest wealth. In 2006, federal charges were brought against Ann Colomb and her sons for running a cocaine ring in South Louisiana.[31] The U.S. attorney charged them with having sold some $15 million in illegal drugs over a 10-year period. The evidence came from more than 30 jailhouse snitches, who claimed to have repeatedly purchased cocaine from them.[32]

On the basis of this seemingly formidable testimony, the jury found Ann and her sons guilty. They faced a prison term that could have ranged from 10 years to life. But even as the trial was ongoing, the credibility of the jailhouse snitches' testimony started to collapse. Evidence from two different inmates revealed that groups of prisoners had been acquiring pictures of the Colombs, notes from prosecutors, and even grand jury testimony, so they could present incriminating evidence in hopes of getting a reduction in their sentences. The evidence against the snitches was precise and credible enough to destroy the government's case. U.S. District Judge Tucker Melancon set aside the jury's verdict, saying that "had the facts . . . been known to the jury when it began its deliberations . . . some, and possibly all of the defendants would have been acquitted." The government has declined to retry the case. Even though the case collapsed, the informants benefited from their false testimony. One got his life sentence reduced to 10 years; another had his life sentence cut to 15 years.[33]

In spite of overwhelming evidence than snitches are often liars, the escalation of the war on drugs has brought about a reversal in the law concerning their testimony. In 1962, a bootlegger was paid by Treasury agents for catching another bootlegger. The U.S. Court of Appeals for the Fifth Circuit threw the case out, saying that a conviction could not be based on evidence from an informant who stood to receive a contingent fee.[34] But, in 1987, this decision was overruled. Evidence from an informant now became acceptable, even if he stands to receive benefits for his testimony.[35] The decision of our courts to accept the self-serving testimony of snitches has clearly introduced corruption into our criminal justice system. As a consequence, many innocent people have lost their property or been sent to prison.

CHAPTER 11

Undercover Police

A uthorized criminality is an essential part of undercover policing.[1] The illegal activities—which almost always include an undercover officer paired up with one or more snitches—include supplying illegal drugs; working as a prostitute; forging documents; stealing IDs; getting drugs into prisons; laundering money from drug trafficking; counterfeiting bills; committing perjury; selling food stamps; and financing pornography.[2]

Undercover assignments are eagerly sought by police. The selection process is competitive and rigorous. Those chosen are typically young and usually do not receive formal academy training and socialization into the police culture until their undercover assignment is over. As criminologist George I. Miller explains, the job "is more civilian than police, and it would be counterproductive to socialize a person to be a police officer and then ask them to adopt a false identity."[3] Because only an elite few are selected, the assignment has high prestige.[4] Many of the recruits who have been offered the possibility of undercover work have made comments like, "Someone is offering me a chance to become a spy—really a neat thing."[5]

Some judges have ethical objections to undercover police breaking the law while enforcing it. As Justice Oliver Wendell Holmes expressed it: "I think it less evil that some criminals should escape than that the Government should play an ignoble part."[6] In spite of views like these, the courts have condoned illegal activity by undercover police as a way to acquire intelligence and gain the confidence of criminals. While there may be a limit in theory as to what an undercover officer can do when participating in an authorized crime, few if any cases have crossed that line. Judges are reluctant to impose restrictions on undercover police.[7] In fact, the following observation by the U.S. Court of Appeals for the Seventh Circuit is typical: "In the pursuit of crime, the Government is not confined to behavior suitable for the drawing room."[8]

The criminal activities of undercover police are subject to scant oversight and control by their bosses in law enforcement. One officer said: "They might tell me something to do, but the supervision was really minimal. They didn't have a real clear idea of what was going on—but that is what they had me out there for."[9] Another agent stated, "An undercover guy pretty much does what he wants; nobody bosses you around."[10] Yet, another undercover officer summed it up this way: "Vice is a strange part of the job. It's basically a lot of people doing what they want to do."[11]

According to a 1984 decision of the U.S. Court of Appeals, Tenth Circuit, the government doesn't even need probable cause to initiate an undercover investigation.[12] Gary Marx provides a frightening example of such an operation in the case of Arthur Baldwin who was the owner of a legal topless bar in Memphis.[13] The police wanted to close it down so they decided to investigate him to see if he was involved in any criminal activities. They lacked information to obtain a search warrant for electronic surveillance or search and seizure so instead, they set up a generalized undercover investigation. An agent "insinuated himself into Baldwin's life," working at the bar, chauffeuring him, caring for his child, and even living in his house for several months. Seeing some white powder on his dresser, the agent took it to be analyzed and it turned out to be cocaine. Baldwin was arrested and convicted. The police action in this case was perfectly legal.[14]

One authorized illegal role for undercover agents is to actively facilitate a crime. They often do this is by pretending to be accomplices—acting as thieves, hit men, corrupt cops, or drug suppliers.[15] For example, undercover agents have provided chemicals needed for manufacturing illegal drugs. One case, which involved supplying chemical materials for methamphetamine, was approved by the U.S. Supreme Court, which ruled that "the infiltration of drug rings and a limited participation in their unlawful . . . practices [is a] recognized and permissible means of investigation."[16]

Is there any limit on the extent to which police can act as an accomplice in the commission of a crime? There is: Undercover officers may facilitate a crime as long as the operation furthers the goals of law enforcement.[17] This standard may sound clear conceptually (to some), but in the trenches it becomes ambiguous. For one thing, goals may be in conflict: Should a crime be prevented or facilitated by undercover officers? Preventing a crime doesn't earn profits for law enforcement, but it's obviously a value for the public.[18]

Here is how an experienced cocaine smuggler presented this conflict between goals. He described the reaction of federal agents to a young and easily identifiable "amateur" smuggler about to fly to Latin America to bring cocaine back to the United States. "Rather than walk up to someone obviously headed for trouble—where they might flash a badge and say, 'Get smart kid, it's not going to work'—they will, as a matter of policy, allow him to risk his life with the local heavies, get a few snorts of pure [cocaine], and walk into jail at the airport back home."[19]

The federal agents will benefit; they will get welcomed publicity for preventing the illegal importation of cocaine into the United States; in addition, they will get credit for the bust. But, would the public have preferred instead that they simply warn the kid not to risk his life and ruin his future?

Do individuals who claim they are unjustly targeted by undercover police have any legal defense against authorized illegal activity? There are three possible types of protection for a person who believes their constitutional rights are being violated by an undercover officer who is involved in an authorized criminal activity: The officer could be prosecuted for personal criminal liability, or the targeted individual could mount a legal defense claiming entrapment, or the person could claim there was a violation of his due process rights.

Prosecuting the Officer

Undercover police are essentially immune from being sued for directly causing a crime. They are protected by the Public Authority Defense, namely, that the illegal conduct was for legitimate law enforcement purposes. This blanket immunity for undercover agents is routinely supported by prosecutors. In any event, this defense is so rare it's considered a "scholarly curiosity."[20]

Claiming Entrapment

The entrapment defense involves the claim that the target would never have committed the crime but was subjected to illegal inducements to do so (i.e., that he was bullied, threatened, or pressured). This defense is also rarely successful, because the courts' sole concern is whether the defendant was a willing and able participant in the crime. The entrapment defense is therefore also *not* an effective way to regulate the behavior of undercover police.[21]

Violating Due Process

Police conduct may, however, violate due process rights, which means violating standards of fairness and a sense of justice. But successful due process cases are also exceptional in undercover investigations; a claim of unjust behavior by the government usually fails, because, again, the usual focus of the courts is on whether the defendant had a predisposition to commit the crime.

Following are a couple of examples of successful due process defenses, which will give you an idea of how shocking undercover police behavior has to be to qualify for a violation of due process.

Two undercover officers repeatedly tried to get cocaine from their targets but kept getting sugar instead; they were so frustrated with the deception that they broke into one of the target's home in the middle of the night, drunk. Brandishing weapons, they confiscated two bags of cocaine. The resulting conviction was reversed, the state appeals court stating that this was "one of those rare cases" where police conduct constituted a denial of due process.[22]

In another extreme case, Los Angeles County Sheriff's deputies heard that a man named Rochin was selling narcotics. Going to his home, they found him in bed and saw two capsules on his nightstand. At that point Rochin swallowed the capsules. The police arrested him and took him to the hospital and had his stomach pumped. The capsules contained morphine. He was convicted by a California appellate court, but the U.S. Supreme Court overruled the conviction on due process grounds, stating that the deputies' conduct "shocked the conscience" and was therefore clearly unconstitutional.[23]

The following cases show where the court denied a defense based on the claim that due process had been violated.

The government initiated an undercover investigation of a man named Russell, suspecting that he and others were running an illegal laboratory supplying methamphetamine. An undercover narcotics agent went to Russell's home and offered to sell him a chemical (P2P) that is hard to obtain and is essential to the production of methamphetamine on condition that Russell show him the lab and give him a sample. Russell showed him the lab and said they had been making methamphetamine for some time. The agent returned with the chemical and watched while the suspects produced the drug. He did not actively participate but was courteous and helpful, picking up some aluminum foil that dropped onto the floor and putting it in the cooker. Russell then sold methamphetamine to the agent. He was then arrested and convicted on the charge of manufacturing and selling methamphetamine. His conviction was reversed on appeal to the Ninth Circuit on the grounds that his due process rights had been violated because there had been "an intolerable degree of governmental participation in the criminal enterprise."[24] The Supreme Court disagreed: A majority affirmed Russell's conviction, stating that he had not been entrapped because he had been producing the drug before the government became involved and that he was not an "unwary innocent" but an "unwary criminal."[25] The Court also stated that for undercover agents' to infiltrate and supply valuable ingredients in order to eradicate criminal organizations did not violate "fundamental fairness, [nor was it] shocking to the universal sense of justice [and therefore impermissible under] the Due Process Clause of the Fifth Amendment."[26]

In another case, a defendant named Hampton met a DEA informant in a pool hall.[27] Hampton mentioned he was short of cash and claimed that the informant suggested that they could earn some fast money by getting imitation heroin at the price of real heroin. The informant had a different story. He claimed that Hampton told him of a heroin source and that, at Hampton's suggestion, the informant had offered to contact buyers. They both told the same story as to what happened next. The informant arranged a meeting between Hampton and two buyers, who were also DEA agents. Prior to the meeting the informant supplied Hampton with a sample of real heroin, which Hampton sold to the agents. Before the second meeting with the agents, Hampton was arrested. At his trial, Hampton presented an entrapment defense because the government had supplied him with real heroin. He was convicted and the case went to the U.S. Supreme Court, which upheld the conviction. The Court, ignoring the entrapment argument, ruled that an accusation of outrageous conduct by undercover police could not be used as a due process defense because the defendant was predisposed to commit the crime. As Steven Meister concluded in his study of this Supreme Court case: "The Hampton majority seemed eager to devise arguments to prevent a defendant from challenging government investigative conduct on due process grounds."[28]

So, theoretically, there are three defenses for a person who is targeted by an undercover investigation. The Public Authority Defense could limit unacceptable police behavior by threatening to prosecute the police officer for illegal behavior. The other two, entrapment and due process, could immunize a defendant from criminal liability. In practice, however, successful use of any of these defenses is rare, and they are not likely to effectively regulate authorized criminality in undercover investigations. Furthermore, as Professor Elizabeth Joh concluded: "The trend of American criminal law has been one of removing barriers to conviction in the undercover context."[29]

Undercover assignments are highly coveted by young police recruits even though—or perhaps because—they involve serious risks, physical as well as psychological. The agents are posing as and associating with dangerous criminals, sometimes for months and even years, with very little supervision or support.

Agents are often challenged to ingest or inject illicit substances.[30] For example, as a result of the NYPD's 1997 antidrug initiative of deploying 3,000 undercover officers to buy illegal drugs and arrest the sellers, drug dealers started to get suspicious. They began testing their customers by pressuring them sometimes at gunpoint to sample drugs. Undercover police faced a dangerous dilemma: Take a drug like crack or methamphetamine or risk exposure with the possibility of injury or death. Coerced ingestion was common. One officer, who was ordered to take a hit from a crack pipe, said, "First I froze up. I told them I didn't do it, that I wouldn't do it. But, when they put the gun to me, I had to take the hit." He had headaches afterwards, but he said, "You've got to do whatever it takes to get these guys."[31] One supervisor said he would rather see the undercover police "shoot up" than risk getting hurt and that he would cover up the illegal act and make sure the agent didn't get addicted.[32]

Tests for undercover officers include more than just taking a hit from a crack pipe or participating in criminal assignments. Dealers scrutinize everything about their "customers." As the researcher Bruce Jacobs reports, "Curbside drug dealers are renowned for their alleged ability to read and interpret the 'vibes' that tell them whether a potential customer is 'OK.' Indeed, the prevailing sentiment among street sellers is that they can 'smell the poh-lice' a mile away."[33] Dealers scan a variety of personal clues. As one explained [a policeman's walk] "ain't like everyone else's walk. It's a certain kind of perfect walk, a cocky walk, like they know they gonna arrest your ass and take you to jail."[34] In another study, a dealer made a similar point, "You can just tell. It's the way they carry themselves. It's the way they act, the way they look, the way they dress—everything . . . They just don't know how to work the street."[35] Another suspicious clue is an unfamiliarity with the verbal subculture: "Do you know where I can get some drugs around here?" or "Whose got the dope around here?" are expressions that would ring alarm bells for drug sellers because, as one explained, "Why would he come on the set if he didn't know there was dope there in the first place?"[36]

Another danger for undercover police is that they may be seen as law violators by other officers or even by the public. When committing a crime, undercover agents are at risk of a lethal encounter because they are usually disguised as seedy characters. Gary Marx summarizes several tragic outcomes: In Houston, during a drug bust, a uniformed officer killed an undercover policewoman because she rushed to the scene with her gun drawn to help with the arrest. In Washington, D.C., a policeman in uniform who was responding to a robbery-in-progress killed an undercover officer who had his gun drawn.[37]

Some undercover programs have resulted in high injury and death rates for both police and citizens. In Detroit, for example, a program called STRESS ("Stop the Robberies—Enjoy Safe Streets") was ended after three years because 3 undercover agents were killed and 100 injured, while 16 alleged offenders were killed and 58 injured. The major problem was confusion over the identities of the officers who were disguised to blend in to the street environment.[38]

Psychological problems are a serious danger for undercover police, especially those in deep undercover. Immersed in a criminal culture, and presenting a false identity, they need to blend in and be accepted. They work in secret, are always in fear of being discovered, have almost no support, and are isolated from their colleagues and family. The only personal relationships they develop are with their snitches and the targets of their investigations. They frequently experience ambivalence and guilt over the continuous deception and eventual betrayal their role requires. Romantic involvements can become a problem. Undercover police may develop a closeness with members of the criminal subculture and a sympathetic understanding of how they became who they are.[39]

One officer reported that as a result of going undercover he became "a different kind of cop." He learned "what it's like to be on the other side of the fence," and he began "seeing the criminal element being just regular people, but caught up in their own thing."[40] Another said, "Boy, it can get gray out there . . . just because a guy's a criminal doesn't mean you can't like him, and that he doesn't have the same interest[s] as you do. They have company softball teams and wives and girlfriends. They drink beer and go fishing."[41] An agent who was in deep undercover said: "I started with drugs and [the roles were] clearly evident—white hats and black hats. Then . . . it was more like white hats and grey hats. But they were my only friends. [You] develop a closeness that is psychologically difficult to close off."[42]

Another officer explained the problems of deep undercover work this way: "I had an undercover apartment where I would stay a good amount of time. I soon met and started to run around with . . . a segment of society I didn't have a whole lot of experience with . . . They were my social life. They were my work life. They were everything."[43]

The intense stress of undercover work can be exacerbated by an agent's supervisor, who may be more concerned with making arrests than protecting the agent. One officer, Ben, who had spent two and a half years dealing with organized crime figures started having frightening symptoms:[44]

I'm wearing this recorder between my legs. I know they'd kill you in a minute . . . I'm there by myself. My nerves are really up. I'm starting to get to where I can't keep a meal down . . . I started to feel these chest pains . . . I would have diarrhea on a daily basis . . . I go to my sergeant . . . and say . . . I have a note from the doctor saying . . . too much stress. They'll have to let me out of this job. He laughs. I say, "What are you laughing about?" [He says] "We got a million dollars wrapped up in this. You're not physically hurt. You're going through stress. You'll be all right. You can handle it," . . . I was devastated.[45]

Finally, the day arrived when the criminals were arrested. Ben was present along with the troopers. One of the arrested men he had known well came up to him and said, "What did they pinch you for?" Ben answered, "I'm with them." "You cocksucker," he said and he spat at him. Another guy came up and said, "How could you do this Ben? You're my friend. How could you do this?" Ben reported feeling a heavy guilt. He referred to the man as "sixty some years old . . . like anybody's grandfather, a nice guy. I couldn't look at him. I had to put my head down . . . I felt like a piece of shit." This reminded Ben of another painful experience that was hard to shake off: "I knew this one guy whose kid was retarded. A lot of the money he was using for special schools for his kid. I know it was stolen money. But I also knew he wasn't going out whoring it. He was a family guy. How he put bread on the table was by stealing. He was paying a lot of money out for his retarded son to be educated [and] enough [left over] to just feed himself. I've thought of those people on Christmas morning when I wake up. I thought, 'Those kids' fathers aren't home because of me. I got that guy in trouble.'"[46]

Many undercover police express similar guilt feelings about turning in people they have been close to. One agent said: "I can remember . . . arresting these same people that had become my friends. I can't even talk about it now without getting emotional. They had trusted me . . . It took a long time to get over that."[47] Another said: "It's something . . . that just doesn't go away. It nags and eats at you. You feel really bad about it . . . their lives were ruined and their kids' lives . . . I don't think I could ever work narcotics again."[48]

At the end of a deep undercover operation with a motorcycle gang, an Alcohol, Tobacco, and Firearms (ATF) agent said, "Hard-core gangsters would be going to jail today, but for years I'd been calling these gangsters my brothers. I was both proud of my work as an undercover agent and sad about the ramifications my work would have for some of the men I'd grown close to . . . I knew their kids' names and they told me they loved me." He had no doubt that some of those he helped put in prison "would have died for me."[49]

As one vice-squad detective observed, "You're working with dope fiends and perverts all day, and a guy on the vice squad usually goes down; he deteriorates; he becomes like the people you work with . . . If I had stayed longer I would have deteriorated."[50] One officer who spent a year impersonating a street person as well as a member of a motorcycle gang reported: "I knew [it] was a role-playing thing, but I became total, 100 percent involved. I became what I was trying to tell people I was, and it confused me. Believe me, it confused me a lot."[51] In a *Penthouse* interview, Robert Leuci, who was the model for the book and movie *Prince of the City*, gradually saw a change in himself: "It seemed like I was becoming like the people I was after. I started looking like Mafia guys . . . They live a life of whispers. So then I found myself talking to my father in the same way."[52]

Deep undercover agents frequently report problems in their family relationships. The pressures on family life, as Gary Marx observed, are a result of "the odd hours, days, weeks away from home, unpredictability of work schedules, concern over safety, late night temptations and partying that the role may bring, and personality and life style changes that the agent may undergo."[53] The wife of one officer observed: "When you live undercover you live a lie. You can't confide in friends about the pressures on your husband; you can't even tell your children what their father really does. You live under constant strain."[54] One agent, who had been divorced during his three-year undercover operation, said: "Imagine having a relationship with someone where you can't talk about what you do and where you suddenly say 'I'll see you in a week' and just disappear. There is also stress on her because you may not come back."[55]

A study by psychologist Gary Farkas found that in his interviews with former and current undercover officers, 41 percent reported that adverse changes occurred in their relationships with family and friends; and 37 percent expressed anxiety when appearing in public with family and friends.[56] One officer explained: "[We] may have gone to a shopping mall . . . and see somebody who may be involved in a case or [who] may know who you are, so you wouldn't want your family to be part of it. So, I found myself . . . pretty much staying home with my family."[57]

Professor Michel Girodo conducted a study consisting of 271 federal undercover drug enforcement officers.[58] They were divided into two groups: one from men accepted as candidates for undercover work; the other, from officers who had operated as undercover agents. The study measured several psychiatric symptoms of both groups, such as depression, anxiety, phobias, paranoia, obsessive-compulsive, and imaginary complaints. The findings revealed that officers who had been undercover were more at risk than the normal population on every one of the psychological disturbances. By contrast, the psychiatric examination of men accepted as candidates for undercover work revealed they were less at risk than the normal population for the psychological disturbances that were measured.[59] In sum, Girodo's study found that undercover work turned healthy young men into those with serious psychiatric symptoms.

Girodo also found that the most common change in undercover drug enforcement police was the "tendency to use the language and social style of the sub-cultural group that has been infiltrated."[60] Among agents working in high-status operations, the most typical problem was exaggerated feelings of importance and sense of entitlement stemming from the luxurious, upper-class trappings of their role. (Girodo likens the high-level agents to Eliza Doolittle in Shaw's *Pygmalion*, who can never return to the streets after she's been a lady.) The most serious psychological problems occurred with agents who had long-term immersions in street subcultures and motorcycle gangs. Families of these agents reported an increase in aggression and emotional outbursts. The most common diagnosis was anxiety and depression. Girodo also found that the longer the time spent undercover, the greater the self-reported drug and alcohol use.[61]

There is physical danger for undercover agents even after their assignment is over. Drug dealers have a reputation for ruthless reprisals against those who have turned them in, and undercover assignments necessarily involve betrayal along with the hostility from those betrayed. As a result, former undercover police are warned to take extreme safety precautions such as changing their appearance (shaving beards, growing mustaches), checking to be sure they aren't being followed to and from work, and buying another car if they had used their own in their undercover work. One officer was assigned a bodyguard who stayed in his house during the evening hours. As one female agent said, "For almost a year after-wards, I drove to another officer's house in the morning and I rode in to work with him. Later they put a police radio in my personal car. They checked my gun and the battery in my radio every day. They were very protective. This is not because they felt I wasn't capable, they weren't sure what to do so they were careful."[62]

Judges, district attorneys, and police view the illegal activities of undercover agents as an unpleasant yet necessary fact. But an evalua-tion of undercover operations should include the inevitable social costs as well the benefits from the enhanced ability of law enforcement to catch criminals. Recall that one risk to society of undercover investi-gations is that they are often carried out by young and inexperienced officers. Operations are characterized by secrecy and a lack of account-ability. Anyone trying to obtain reliable, official information concerning the authorized criminal activities of undercover agents runs into a brick wall.[63] The Freedom of Information Act is supposed to guarantee access to the records of federal agencies, but the procedures and techniques of federal law enforcement are off limits, especially those concerning undercover policing. The courts have upheld these exemptions on the grounds that disclosure "would diminish the effectiveness of similar techniques in existing and future investigations."[64] Given this lack of information, how can we know whether the value of the arrests made through undercover means outweighs the harms of authorized criminal-ity by both police and informants?

Corruption in Undercover Policing

The stress, isolation, and unfettered nature of undercover work tempt agents to exceed the bounds of authorized criminality altogether. Given the astronomical profits in black market drugs, plus the fact that these illegal transactions take place between willing sellers and buyers, under-cover officers find themselves in possession of extremely valuable ser-vices, such as, looking the other way. Imagine that you're an undercover agent observing an illicit drug transaction. Who would know, who would complain, if you accepted a drug dealer's offer to augment your meager salary by just ignoring the whole thing? As a fellow officer told detec-tive Robert Sobel when he joined the Los Angeles narcotics division, "If you look the other way, I can make you a rich man." Sobel followed the advice, and made $140,000 over two years.[65]

Undercover police can sell other services to drug law violators as well: giving dealers information about drug stings or providing favorable testimony at a trial. Researchers report that undercover officers in almost every American city are on the payrolls of drug merchants.[66] Judge James Gray reports that "almost everyone in the legal profession knows someone who has succumbed to the temptation of large amounts of easy drug money."[67]

The corruption of undercover agents as a result of the drug war has been amply documented. Here are some examples.

- In the late 1960s, the Knapp Commission's investigation into the New York City police department found that about half of the narcotics agents had been indicted or discharged on grounds of corruption. In the New York office of the Federal Bureau of Narcotics and Dangerous Drugs, corruption was so rampant that almost every undercover agent was fired or transferred.[68]
- In the early 1980s, the entire homicide squad of nine detectives in the Metro Dade Police Department in Florida was indicted on federal charges of "racketeering, bribery, extortion and dealing in narcotics." Four of the detectives were convicted.[69]
- In 1994, New York City's Mollen Commission reported that corruption had become more vicious than the bribery scandals of earlier years with the police now "acting as criminals, especially in connection with the drug trade."[70]
- The number of federal, state, and local law enforcement officials in federal prisons for corruption, mostly in connection with illicit drugs, increased from 107 in 1994 to 668 in 2000.[71]
- In 1998, the General Accounting (now called the General Accountability) Office (GAO)—the investigative arm of Congress—reported that "several studies and investigations of drug-related police corruption found [that] on-duty police officers engaged in serious criminal activities, such as (1) conducting unconstitutional searches and seizures; (2) stealing money and/or drugs from drug dealers; (3) selling stolen drugs; (4) protecting drug operations; (5) providing false testimony; and (6) submitting false crime reports."[72]

This evidence raises the question of whether honest law enforcement can coexist with the drug war. A federal prosecutor who spent months investigating a Los Angeles sheriff had this to say on the question: "I realized how much of the story of police corruption revolved around drugs. The temptation to skim came from the constant contact with outlandish sums of untraceable drug proceeds . . . If you ask enough people—good, bad, or indifferent—to go into a room with a bag of apparently untraceable cash, sooner or later, someone will unzip the bag and take a bundle . . . And, regrettably, those are things we must ask some people to do every day."[73] A United Nations report on the drug war concluded, "In systems where a member of the legislature or judiciary, earning only a modest income, can easily gain the equivalent of some 20 months' salary from a [drug] trafficker by making one 'favorable' decision, the dangers of corruption are obvious."[74]

The pervasive corruption of public officials is not an aberration; it's intrinsic to the war on drugs, which operates undercover and free of public scrutiny. There is an unholy alliance between drug agents and drug traffickers, which is extremely valuable to both parties.[75] That's the reason that crackdowns on corruption connected with illicit drugs have been futile.

Part IV

CITIZENSHIP BARRIERS

CHAPTER 12

The Criminal Population

The United States has over 2.3 million people in prisons and jails; in addition, there are approximately 5 million on parole or probation.[1] Each year over 700,000 state and federal prisoners are released.[2] A majority are racial and ethnic minorities, many of whom have been taken out of impoverished communities, incarcerated for two or three years, and then released back into their neighborhoods.[3] Ex-inmates are often poorly educated, unskilled, physically disabled, lacking family support, dependent on drugs, and suffering from mental illnesses. They are a population with high levels of unemployment, little long-term work experience, and a great deal of involvement in the illegal labor market, where incomes are invariably higher than they can earn in legal jobs.[4]

Upon completion of their sentences they face major legal and social obstacles in finding stable and legitimate employment, locating decent housing, receiving public assistance, obtaining driver's licenses, salvaging endangered marriages, and retaining custody of their children. Based on current data, researchers estimate that more than two out of five ex-convicts will return to crime and lose their freedom within one year of release, and two-thirds will be back in prison within three years.[5] According to a sample from the Bureau of Justice Statistics, prisoners released in 1994 were arrested within three years for the following categories of crimes: violent offenses (21.6 percent), property offenses (31.9 percent), drug offenses (30.3 percent), and public order offences (28.3 percent), with many charged with more than one type of crime.[6]

Could treatment and rehabilitation programs improve these numbers? Until the mid-1970s the prevailing view was that the purpose of prison was to rehabilitate. As Judge Marvin Frankel expressed it in 1972: "[It is] fashionable nowadays to say that only rehabilitation can justify confinement."[7] But, by the end of the 1970s the American criminologist Michael R. Gottfredson declared that "the conventional wisdom in criminology is that rehabilitation has been found to be ineffective."[8]

In recent years, evidence has accumulated that properly designed and implemented treatment programs can reduce recidivism, provide job skills, and diminish substance abuse.[9] As professor Francis T. Cullen put it in 2002, in evaluating the studies on treatment and recidivism, "The empirical evidence is fairly convincing—and growing stronger as time passes—that treatment interventions are capable of decreasing recidivism."[10] Research has also shown that incarceration strengthens inmates' ties to antisocial and criminal networks, causing returning prisoners to be pulled away from legitimate work and toward crime.[11] Joan Petersilia has found that those who return home after incarceration have become "more desperate, more violence-prone, and more of a menace to society."[12]

Yet despite the documented dangers of incarceration and research showing that treatment can diminish criminal activity, prison programs designed to help inmates transition successfully back into society are scarce and have been cut in recent years. According to a 2010 report by the National Center on Addiction and Substance Abuse at Columbia University (CASA) almost 1.5 million prison and jail inmates (65 percent!) met the medical criteria for substance abuse and addiction, but only 11 percent had received any type of professional treatment. Of those who did, few had access to trained staff and pharmacological therapy such as methadone.[13] According to CASA, "An overwhelming body of evidence exists documenting that substance use disorders are preventable and treatable health conditions, and that cost effective screening, intervention and treatment options are available that can be administered effectively through the criminal justice system. Implementing these options can save taxpayers millions of dollars and reduce crime. Failure to do so makes no sense."[14]

Also critical to reducing recidivism are programs that encourage prisoners to participate in education and vocational training. Those services also declined from 1996 to 2006. The participation rate of state prisoners in 1996 was 57 percent, but by 2006 it had dropped to 45 percent. Similar cutbacks occurred for federal prisoners and inmates of jails.[15]

CASA's investigation also found that some 45 percent of federal inmates, 56 percent of state inmates, and 64 percent of jail inmates suffered from mental health problems. Relative to their peers, these prisoners after release experience more homelessness, more unemployment, more physical and sexual abuse, more alcohol and other drug problems, more criminal activity, and more involvement in the criminal justice system, "suggest[ing] that they are not being rehabilitated under the current system and instead are cycling in and out of incarceration."[16]

Prisoners coming home would have a difficult time adjusting even if our government were supportive, but that is emphatically not the case. Those leaving prison, along with those convicted of a crime not involving incarceration, will inevitably find themselves enmeshed in a maze of statutes that constitute barriers to their reintegration into society. Not only has Congress enacted federal legislation denying benefits to certain offenders, it has used the power of its purse motivating states to do so too. A guilty plea—even for a minor drug offense—automatically leads to possible penalties that continue long after a prison sentence has been served or parole, probation, or community service have ended.[17] These obstacles are referred to in the literature as "invisible punishments" or "collateral sanctions," and scholars describe them as "instruments of social exclusion."[18]

Consider the experience of Chris and Robin DiFranco, a white middle-class couple. Chris was one of thousands of felons in Florida who had completed his sentence but then had to endure a complex and expensive process simply to get a hearing before the clemency board, which had the power to decide whether or not to restore his basic civil rights.[19] His story gives a vivid idea of the bureaucratic gauntlet confronting a convicted felon attempting to become once again a full-fledged citizen.

In 1995, Mr. DiFranco pleaded guilty to conspiring with others to import marijuana. He was lucky to have been spared prison time because he had no prior convictions and had been only a minor player in transporting the drug. The judge sentenced Chris to five years of probation. He had a building contractor's license that he renewed every year. After completing probation, he thought his punishment was over. He filed an application to reinstate his contractor's license that included a question about whether he had ever been convicted of a felony. He answered honestly. Then the nightmare began. He was notified that he could not be eligible until he had completed the clemency process. He sent in the paperwork and despite repeated calls to the administrator in charge of the civil rights restoration files, his application sat unopened for over two years. Finally, they received a response: It was a 12-page questionnaire, asking detailed questions about the couples' parents, siblings, children born out of wedlock, complete marital history, and financial disclosures more detailed than those required for a mortgage. Further contacts with the Clemency Office led to a request for information on the whereabouts of all 42 coconspirators listed on Chris's indictment. Attorneys had told them that it usually cost more than $25,000 in such cases and more than two years just to get to a clemency hearing.

At last, with help from his parole office, Chris obtained a hearing with the clemency board chaired by then Governor Jeb Bush. He and Robin traveled from North Beach to Tallahassee and drove to the building that housed the Florida Clemency Board. After hearing a number of pleas, Chris said, "I had seen there was only one path to succeed before the commission . . . to show remorse, play the Christian Born Again Tune. So I did. I made a remorseful confession and I pleaded for mercy. Jeb Bush granted it . . . It took me more than three years and cost around $4,000. I was lucky. I know people that hired lawyers and spent $25,000 and after 5 years they are still in the process. How are people supposed to make an honest living out of prison if they cannot work?" Robin DiFranco said, "Most people wouldn't have kept as much documentation as we did. But I had everything." She also wondered how many "lower-income minorities" would have had the time and money to obtain certified copies of necessary documents, to travel, and to be able to talk "the right way" to bureaucrats. The answer appears to be, very few: Of the 600,000 ex-felons in Florida, only 1,067 had their civil rights restored in 2001. Not surprisingly, African Americans bear the brunt: According to the sociologist Christopher Uggen, Florida's 167,000 black ex-felons, representing 10.5 percent of the state's black adult population, have failed to obtain a restoration of their civil rights. By contrast, only 5.6 percent of the state's nonblack population have failed to restore their civil rights.[20]

CHAPTER 13

Invisible Punishments

Invisible punishments are legal obstacles that exist outside the traditional sentencing framework. They afflict people after they have completed the punishments meted out by a judge, be they incarceration, parole, or probation. Invisible punishments are a lifelong hazard for anyone with a criminal record on file with law enforcement agencies, a record that includes felony convictions, misdemeanors, and arrests—even arrests for first offenders who pleaded guilty to possessing marijuana. The formal sentence may be insignificant, but the real sentence comes down like a ton of bricks once the individual finds he is enmeshed in a complicated maze of statutes denying him a variety of rights. Judges and lawyers are not required to tell a defendant of these postsentence punishments.[1]

According to a task force of the American Bar Association, "Unbeknownst to this offender, and perhaps to any other actor in the sentencing process, as a result of his conviction he may be ineligible for many federally-funded health and welfare benefits, food stamps, public housing, and federal educational assistance. His drivers license may be automatically suspended, and he may no longer qualify for certain employment and professional licenses . . . He will not be permitted to enlist in the military, or possess a firearm, or obtain a federal security clearance. If a citizen, he may lose the right to vote; if not, he becomes immediately deportable."[2]

From the 1950s to the early 1980s, invisible punishments were widely criticized and restricted by state legislatures. After the mid-1980s, as a part of the escalating drug war, these sanctions proliferated.[3] While they have serious adverse consequences for ex-cons and others convicted of crimes, they require almost no expenditure of public funds, and are largely invisible to much of the public. Because they are not part of the sentence, they are usually not debated and are often tacked on to major pieces of legislation dealing with different topics.[4]

Between 65 and 71 million Americans are currently estimated to have some type of criminal record on file with state law enforcement agencies.[5] Many arrests on record never resulted in a conviction, and many convictions are old and minor. Criminal background checks are a standard part of the application procedure for employment, housing, welfare, and many other benefits. The growth of computerized record keeping allows this damaging and frequently erroneous information to be readily available. Some 33 states allow criminal histories to be accessed by the general public.[6]

In 2012, the *New York Times* criticized the federal government for paying too little attention to companies that collect and sell information to employers concerning the possible criminal backgrounds of prospective employees.[7] "Sloppy reporting was not a huge problem in the past when there were fewer companies gathering data and the only way to get information was to examine court records in person. But, in recent years, background checks have become a computer-driven industry, with companies buying often incomplete records in bulk from the courts or from other screening companies, and then not updating them."[8] Ninety percent of employers now use these data, which can circulated forever. One problem is that many reports show that an applicant was charged with a crime but do not record that he was exonerated. Another is that the background check may list the same offense several times, making it appear that the person has an extensive criminal record.

In certain states, people who have been convicted of a crime, no matter how minor or old, may find it impossible to have the record of their conviction erased. Twenty-seven states do not permit the expungement of any conviction records.[9] The laws in most states create roadblocks to employment for those who have been arrested but never convicted. Thirty-eight states currently permit all employers and occupational licensing agencies to ask about, and use in their hiring decisions, arrests that never led to a conviction. Ten states prohibit the use of that information, while three states allow only limited use.[10]

Let's look more closely at some of the invisible punishments.

Employment

A student in my drug war seminar at the University of North Carolina at Chapel Hill told the class how excited she was that her boyfriend was getting out of jail after serving three months for a drug law violation.

Some weeks later she was lamenting the fact that he was unable to get a job. "I guess he'll just have to go back to selling drugs," she said. Her boyfriend is likely to have two strikes against him in finding employment: He has a criminal record and he's African American.

It goes without saying that in some cases a firm's decision not to hire someone with a criminal record is reasonable and may even be necessary considering the possibility of an employer's being held liable for negligent hiring. Someone convicted of drunk driving should not be hired as a bus driver. A bank should not hire an applicant recently convicted of fraud.[11]

Numerous studies have addressed the question of how employers respond to a job seeker who has a criminal record.

One approach consists of surveys where employers are asked how willing they are to hire ex-cons. The economist Harry J. Holzer found that 60 to 70 percent of businesses would not hire someone with a criminal history, even in a tight labor market. His surveys found that employers would rather hire a welfare recipient, a high school dropout, or even a person with little experience, than an ex-con (1996).[12] A 2002 study by Holzer and colleagues concluded that "employers are, in general, quite averse to hiring ex-offenders . . . [they] fear the legal liabilities that could potentially be created . . . [and they] view their offender status as a signal of lack of reliability and trustworthiness."[13] This unwillingness to hire includes those with nonviolent drug law violations.[14]

Other researchers interviewed ex-prisoners about their labor market experiences. Mercer Sullivan interviewed 40 black, Hispanic, and white youths and found evidence suggesting the negative effects on employment of a criminal background.[15] For example, one Hispanic lost a job he had held for a year when his employer discovered he had been in prison. Another lost several jobs because he had to go to court every week and didn't want to tell his employers why he had to be absent. Alford Young interviewed 26 young African American men who had been in prison, several for nonviolent drug offenses. They all said that a prison record was a major obstacle to finding a job. Most wound up on the streets working in the underground economy.[16]

Some researchers attempt to isolate the direct effects of incarceration on employment, while statistically controlling for other relevant factors such as education, age, race, marital status, labor market conditions, and region.[17] These studies find that there is a significant negative relationship between a prison record and job prospects. Sociologist Bruce Western found detrimental effects on future labor income for those with criminal records, as well as harsher consequences for blacks than whites. He estimated that the percentage of lifetime income lost due to a prison record is 0.8 percent for whites, but 4.3 percent for blacks.[18] Western concluded that a prison record was more than a temporary setback that could be erased by time in the labor market: It diminished human capital and social networks and "hampered former inmates from entering that cadre of labor market insiders."[19]

Devah Pager employed a different type of study, one designed to measure the extent to which employment experience differs for blacks and whites, both with and without a criminal record.[20] She randomly assigned resumes to pairs of intensively trained black and white college students who were matched on the basis of physical appearance, interpersonal style, and any other characteristics that might influence an employer making hiring decisions.[21] The fictitious resumes showed equal levels of education and work experience. All applicants were given two types of resumes, one with and one without a criminal record, the latter consisting of a felony drug conviction and 18 months in prison, with reference to a supportive parole officer. The applicants applied for 350 jobs requiring no previous experience and only a high school education. They were given favorable work histories in entry-level jobs, with the applicants reporting that they had worked their way to a supervisory position prior to arrest and incarceration for a drug law violation. The study found:

- For whites, 34 percent with no criminal record were called back, while only 17 percent with a record were called back.
- For blacks, 14 percent of those with no criminal record were called back, while only 5 percent with a record were.[22]

So, in Pager's experiment, employers preferred whites with a criminal record over blacks with no record. While a criminal record reduced the likelihood of a call back for whites by 50 percent, it reduced it for blacks by about two-thirds. Pager concluded that "not only are blacks more likely to be incarcerated than whites; according to the findings presented here, they may also be more strongly affected by the stigma of a criminal record."[23]

Studies find that a major factor in reducing criminal activity by ex-offenders is stable employment.[24] For example, a 2005 study by Steven Raphael and David Weiman concluded, "For the lowest-risk parolees, our results suggest that having a job reduces the likelihood of being returned to custody [within three years] on a parole violation by 6 to 12 percentage points."[25] A long-term study of juvenile offenders by Robert Sampson and John Laub concluded that "job stability is central in explaining adult desistance from crime."[26] As New York City's probation commissioner describes the situation of former prisoners, "Either they work or they go back to jail."[27] According to criminologists Shawn Bushway and Peter Reuter, "Ample evidence suggests a link between individual employment and crime."[28]

Prior to the acceleration of the drug war, the primary institutions responsible for supporting prisoners during the reentry process were state departments of parole. They were part of the rehabilitation process and were charged with finding stable housing and employment, as well as providing guidance and supervision for released prisoners. As explained in 1973 by a National Advisory Commission on Criminal Justice Standards and Goals, "Parole staff must take the responsibility for finding needed resources for parolees in the community."[29] But in the past 30 years, there has been a radical transformation in the way parole operates. As criminologists James Austin and John Irwin describe it: "Instead of helping prisoners . . . the new parole system is bent on surveillance and detection. Parolees are routinely and randomly checked for illegal drug use, failure to locate or maintain a job, moving without permission, or any other number of petty and nuisance-type behaviors that don't conform to the rules of parole."[30] This failure by parole departments to provide support for ex-inmates has left the main burden for overseeing prisoner reentry to families and communities.[31] As Pager points out: "It is unlikely that these informal sources alone can effectively absorb the steady influx of [several hundred thousand] returning offenders [every year]." [32] In fact, many reentering offenders are on their own: The California Department of Corrections has estimated that, on any given day, between 30 and 50 percent of parolees were unemployed and homeless in Los Angeles and San Francisco.[33]

With public support shrinking and community support foundering under the growing strain of mass incarceration, occupations that were once *legally* available to released inmates and others with criminal records have become increasingly restricted as a result of the zero tolerance for drug law violators that developed in the 1980s and 1990s.[34] Occupational licensing agencies often fail to take into account how long ago an offense was committed or the offender's employment record after prison or conviction.[35] These agencies in most states can even deny jobs to people who have been arrested but never convicted of a crime.[36] Even those who have overcome substance abuse problems and have marketable job skills face these legal barriers to employment because of their convictions.[37] There are numerous cases where the nature of the crime is unrelated to the job at issue. Nearly 6,000 occupations in the United

States require licenses. Many of these would be appropriate for workers with even limited skills such as, "billiard room employees . . . barbers, embalmers, tank cleaners . . . and sellers of alcohol."[38]

Here are some examples:

- In New Jersey, any criminal history may disqualify a person from being a health care professional, including arrest without a conviction.[39]
- In California, parolees are prohibited from being lawyers, realtors, physicians, nurses, physical therapists, and educators.
- In Colorado, felons cannot be dentists, engineers, nurses, pharmacists, physicians, or realtors.
- In all states, the occupation of barbers is banned to ex-offenders.
- In many states, even arrest as a juvenile prevents employment in the criminal justice system.[40]
- In New York, ex-felons can be permanently denied licenses for jobs ranging from realtor to beer distributor.[41]
- In Illinois, of the 98 occupations requiring licenses, 57 place restrictions on applicants with a criminal record.[42]

Even for occupations that are legally accessible, ex-prisoners may not have the documents needed to apply for a license, such as a driver's license, usually required for obtaining a job. Putting one more obstacle in the way of anyone convicted of a drug law violation, Congress in 1992 passed a law requiring states to suspend for at least six months the driver's license of anyone convicted of a drug felony or lose 10 percent of the state's federal highway funds. As of 2009, 28 states including the District of Columbia automatically revoke or suspend licenses for some or all drug offenses.[43]

In 2010, Darrell Langdon was turned down for a position as a boiler-room engineer in the Chicago Public Schools because he had been convicted of possessing a half-gram of cocaine in 1985, a felony for which he received probation. The fact that he had been crime free for a quarter of a century didn't matter. Only after the Chicago Tribune publicized his case did the school system reverse its decision and agree to hire him.

In 2008, Lasheila Hawkins was released from a state jail in Texas after serving time for violating drug and prostitution laws. She met with counselors at the Department of Assistive and Rehabilitative Services, and together they worked out an "individualized plan for employment," which called for her to go to barber college. The department paid for her education at a private school, according to court documents. She passed all her tests and lined up a job after graduation. But, because of her criminal background, she was denied the license that was required for that occupation. When she appealed to an administrative law judge, he upheld the denial. When Glenn Neal, deputy director of the rehabilitation agency was questioned about this, he said he couldn't comment on specific cases but that vocational counselors were trained to take criminal history into account when planning postincarceration employment plans, so "I would be surprised if this happened very often." [44]

Housing

The most daunting challenge for a prisoner coming home is to find adequate, stable housing. Without this support ex-cons may be unable to make a successful reentry into society. Employment often hinges on a fixed living arrangement as does continuity in substance abuse and mental health treatment. If returning prisoners wind up homeless they are at an increased risk of being involved in criminal activities and being reincarcerated. So the safety of the public would require that the government concern itself with the housing needs of returning prisoners. Yet public policy does just the opposite. It places numerous obstacles in the way of ex-cons finding decent, stable housing, even for nonviolent drug offenders. [45]

Housing options are often limited by parole conditions that restrict ex-inmates from associating with anyone who has a criminal record, even family members. This prohibition presents a major obstacle for many parolees; for example, in a study of 309 returning prisoners in Baltimore, 60 percent had at least one family member who had been convicted of a crime. [46]

Private housing is usually prohibitively expensive, requiring first and last months' rent, plus a security deposit. To make matters worse, the supply of private rental units suitable for low income families has declined, while the demand has increased. [47] Even if an ex-inmate had the funds, landlords often conduct background checks and tend to reject anyone with a criminal record. [48] In a study of 306 ex-offenders in Seattle, "Virtually all of the interviewees said that housing was the most difficult need to meet, primarily because of lack of financial resources, limited credit and rental history, and discrimination as a result of ex-offender status." [49] A survey of the public found that a majority of respondents objected to having an ex-prisoner as a neighbor, even if the crime was a nonviolent drug offense. [50]

In an attempt to avoid homeless shelters or the streets, many ex-inmates try to find public housing. But the demand has soared mainly because of the increase in those returning from prison. At the same time, the supply has shrunk dramatically because federal spending on low-income housing has plummeted over the past 30 years.[51] Ex-prisoners attempting to enter public housing have not only run into the diminished availability, but have been prevented by laws that deny government subsidized housing to those convicted of certain crimes, including nonviolent drug offenses.[52] Studies find that 10 to 25 percent of returning prisoners are homeless within a year of their release. In major urban areas the number of ex-prisoners who are homeless has been estimated to be as high as 30 to 50 percent.[53]

In 1996, President Bill Clinton signed into law a policy called "One Strike and You're Out," designed to cleanse public housing of drug dealers and other criminals. The Department of Housing and Urban Development (HUD) launched the program. Under HUD's Public Housing Assessment System, local housing authorities were given concrete incentives to toughen admission and eviction standards: The more vigorously a public housing authority implemented one-strike evictions, the more bonus points they received from HUD in the competition for grant money and the more protection they received against oversight and monitoring.[54]

In 1997, HUD sent out a questionnaire to the 3,190 public housing managers asking how many were using the "one-strike" policy. Three-quarters said they were. Their response to the new policy was immediate and dramatic: In the six-month period after the program was adopted 19,405 people were denied admission because of drug-related or criminal activities, compared to 9,935 in the six months prior to program's inception. The number of tenants evicted jumped in similar fashion, increasing by 40 percent from one six-month period to the next.[55]

The eviction powers given to the public housing authorities are remarkably broad. No conviction is necessary. The incident could have been a trivial drug offense, could have occurred off the premises, and could have happened a long time ago. The housing authority simply has to persuade a judge by a preponderance of evidence (that is, more likely than not) that criminal activity occurred. The entire household could be evicted if any family member, or a guest, or anyone "under the control" of the tenant had been "proven" to have been involved in criminal activity.[56] The eviction process is stacked in favor of the housing authorities: Tenants have no right to a court-appointed lawyer, while the authorities employ experts.[57] One implication of the one-strike policy is that families living in public housing may be afraid to allow a family member or a friend released from prison to move in with them or even to visit.[58]

Here are a few personal stories of experiences with the public housing authorities under "One Strike and You're Out." (Names have been changed.)

- Shirly lived with her 16-year-old son and 14-year-old daughter. She obtained rental assistance from HUD. When her son started getting involved with drugs, she did everything she could to prevent it. She talked to his teachers and counselors. She even cut back on her minimum-wage work hours to spend more time with him. When she found illegal drugs in his room, she had him arrested. When he violated parole, she called the police. After being arrested again, he was placed in a juvenile institution. In spite of her efforts to control her son's behavior, HUD terminated her rental subsidy and she and her children lost their home.[59]
- In 1961, Frank was caught shoplifting, pleaded guilty, and served time in jail. In the years that followed he was a productive member of society and had no further brushes with the law. Forty years later, Frank, now a senior citizen, applied for admission to public housing. His application was rejected because of his old criminal record.[60]
- David and Ruth lived in a subsidized housing unit with their son, daughter, and granddaughter. Their son was on probation for a non-drug charge. In a routine police search of his belongings, pursuant to his probation, narcotics were found in a jacket pocket in his bedroom closet, and he was arrested. His parents told him he would have to move out. Based on the one-strike policy, the housing authority convinced the judge to evict the whole family.[61]

Many housing authorities objected to the "One Strike and You're Out" policy, reporting that law-abiding residents were being evicted because of the behavior of their children, relatives, or visitors. The law appeared to interpret "under the control of the tenant" to include anyone who visited the household; also, the term "on or off the premises" appeared to have no geographical limit.[62] The policy was subjected to numerous court challenges and the issue finally went to the U.S. Supreme Court in the case of *Department of HUD v. Pearlie Rucker et al.*, decided in 2002. It involved four tenants who were challenging their eviction notices by the housing authority in Oakland, California:[63]

- Pearlie Rucker, a 63-year-old woman, had been in public housing for 13 years. She lived with her mentally disabled daughter, two grandchildren, and a great grandchild. The housing authority attempted to evict the entire family because her daughter was caught possessing cocaine and a crack cocaine pipe three blocks from the apartment. Ms. Rucker claimed she regularly searched the residence for alcohol and illicit drugs and never found any, and she had no knowledge that her daughter ever used drugs.

- Willie Lee, 71, and Barbara Hill, 63, lived with their grandsons. Ms. Hill has been a public housing resident for more than 30 years, and Mr. Hill was a resident for over 25 years. The housing authority sought to evict the family because the grandsons were caught smoking marijuana in the parking lot of the apartment complex. Lee and Hill denied any knowledge of drug activity by their grandsons.
- Herman Walker, 75 and disabled, had lived in public housing for about 10 years. He was not capable of living independently and required the assistance of a caregiver. Three times within a two-month period, the caregiver and two guests were found with cocaine in Walker's apartment. Each time Walker was issued a notice of lease violation. With the third notice the housing authority moved to evict him. Only after that did Mr. Walker fire his caregiver.

The Supreme Court decided 8–0 (Justice Breyer abstaining) in favor of the housing authority. Justice Rehnquist delivered the opinion of the Court, stating that the relevant statute[64] "unambiguously requires lease terms that vest local public housing authorities with the discretion to evict tenants for drug-related activity of household members and guests whether or not the tenant knew, or should have known, about the activity. That this is so seems evident from the plain language of the statute."[65] Despite the Court's ruling in their favor, the housing authority of Oakland elected to permit three of the four Rucker plaintiffs to remain as tenants; only the disabled Herman Walker was evicted.[66]

Following the decision in Rucker, HUD sent a letter to the public housing directors encouraging them to show "compassion and common sense" in dealing with lease violations.[67] But—in what seems to be a clear contradiction of "compassion and common sense"—HUD also stated that housing authorities are not required to consider mitigating circumstances when they have determined that the terms of the lease have been violated by drug-related or other criminal activity.[68]

In the decade after Rucker, several state courts examined the role of the housing authorities' discretion in one-strike evictions. Nearly all the courts acknowledged that the Supreme Court has endorsed a strict liability standard, that is, that mitigating circumstances, such as the innocence of the tenant, need not be considered by a housing authority in deciding whether or not to evict.[69]

There are more than 2 million American families living in public housing. They are among the most impoverished in the country: 82 percent earn $20,000 a year or less, which is more than $3,000 below the official poverty line for a family of four. Forty percent are children under the age of 18, and 14 percent are 62 and older. Yet, Congress, the executive branch, and the Supreme Court have agreed that it's constitutional and acceptable policy that an entire family be evicted from public housing because one member, or even a guest, is involved in illegal drug or other criminal activity, even when the tenants are innocent of any wrongdoing. It's ironic that the U.S. Department of Housing and Urban Development (HUD), which profits from, and champions, the "One Strike and You're Out" policy, is the same federal agency responsible for providing the poor with safe and decent housing.[70]

One of the harshest consequences of this policy is the effect on children living in public housing who have committed—or are even suspected of having committed—a crime, even a minor drug offense.[71] The impact on them and their families can be disastrous. Public housing is for many families the only thing preventing them from homelessness. If they are evicted, they will be barred for three years from alternative public housing or government subsidies for renting private housing (called the Section 8 program).[72] Under state or local law, juvenile proceedings are confidential, even from public housing authorities (PHAs), but these authorities often succeed in getting information from the police and even from juvenile courts.[73] The most common reaction of a PHA to a juvenile delinquency case is to evict the entire family, often acting even before the case has been resolved. Other PHAs put the family in a catch-22, ruling that they can stay in public housing only if they dispossess their offending child.[74]

The one-strike policy conflicts with the goal of the juvenile justice system, which is the rehabilitation of juvenile offenders. A juvenile court may determine that the needs of a child are best met by remaining with the family and receiving counseling or therapy. But if the court learns that the family is being evicted from public housing or that the child will be barred from home, it may decide that the juvenile will have to be placed in a correctional facility. The question then is, what happens when the youth is released from the facility, as is currently the case for about 100,000 juveniles a year?[75] Homelessness is one outcome. A 2006 study in Minnesota found that 46 percent of homeless youngsters between the ages of 10 and 17 had been in correctional institutions.[76] Many of these youths were banned by "No Trespass" orders issued by PHAs from reunifying with their families who were still living in public housing.[77]

Over the past 30 years there has been explosion in the homeless population in the United States.[78] It has grown from a small group of people "stereotyped as bums and winos" to a more diverse mix of individuals.[79] The number of Americans who had experienced periods of homelessness each year was estimated in 2004 to be as high as 3.5 million.[80] The simultaneous escalation in both the prison and homeless populations over the past 30 years is hardly surprising when you compare their profiles. Both groups are disproportionately male, young, African American, impoverished, unemployed, limited in educational attainment and literacy skills and have high rates of substance abuse and mental illness.[81] As we've seen, ex-prisoners face a high risk of winding up in a homeless shelter or on the streets. Studies also find that people who are homeless are overrepresented in prison.[82] One 2005 investigation found that of the 1,426 homeless people interviewed, some 23 percent had a history of imprisonment.[83] Researchers cite many reasons why the homeless have a high risk of winding up in prison:

- A homeless existence is public, with street people often seen as offensive and threatening. They may be imprisoned as a result of arrests for even minor offenses.[84]
- The system often fails to provide the homeless access to services, such as health care, mental health care, and substance abuse treatment.[85]
- Many spaces in urban areas have been placed off limits to homeless people, who often refuse to abide by these restrictions because these locales may offer jobs, health services or social connections.[86]

Professors Katherine Beckett and Steve Herbert interviewed 41 homeless people in Seattle who had been legally banished from certain areas of the city; they found that only one-third "mostly complied" with the ban.[87] Here is an example of the difficulties faced by homeless people who have been excluded from certain areas. One woman was banished from both the public parks and the SODA zones (Stay Out of Drug Areas), areas which provided important services for her and also included the residence of her mother. So she ignored the ban at the risk of going to jail. Here is what she said: "I stay here at the shelter. I've got to use all, all of DESC (Shelter, Housing and Services for Homeless Adults[88]) . . . and you tell me I can't be here? They got the clothing, they got the food, they got the medical attention . . . Where am I gonna move? . . . [Complying with a SODA order] is kind of difficult for me because I use the public health

area down there, I have a case worker down there. I go through there . . .
The DSHS office (Department of Social and Health Services) [is there]. I
have to go to the DSHS office . . . to get my benefits and stuff . . . I can't
stay out of these areas."[89]

Professor Steven VanderStaay traveled around the United States col-
lecting testimonies from homeless people. Here is part of his interview
with a 28-year-old Puerto Rican woman, named Hell, who is homeless
in Philadelphia, Pennsylvania. "I was in a couple of shelters and any
shelter I was in, it was dirty. We had cockroaches the size of mice. I'm
not crazy, I'm serious. And the food . . . and violence. There's a whole lot
of violence . . . It's like you're here under martial law . . . If you choose
not to go to a shelter, and [choose to live] . . . on the street, than you have
to worry about being raped and beat up . . . [and you] have the problem of showering, trying to keep clean, and sleeping. Because downtown
you're not allowed to sleep. The cops chase you all over the city . . . You
have to be strong if you're going to be homeless."[90]

Abundant research has documented that homeless people are at high
risk of suffering from serious health problems, such as, substance abuse,
depression, suicide, and contracting infectious diseases like TB and AIDS.[91]

Welfare

Many returning from prison have relied on public assistance to pay for
housing, job training, and substance abuse treatment. These benefits
have helped ex-convicts overcome addiction, find a job, and avoid criminal activity. But a welfare law passed in 1996 increased the difficulty of
obtaining these benefits. It was enacted by Congress with bipartisan support (allowing, literally, two minutes for debate!) and signed by President Bill Clinton. The law dramatically changed the American welfare
system. It ended a 60-year commitment to the poor by eliminating the
individual entitlement to welfare, replacing it with a block grant to the
states called Temporary Assistance to Needy Families (TANF).[92] Benefits
are limited to five years, and require recipients to work to receive benefits. A little-known provision of the law states that there is "a lifetime
ban on eligibility for TANF assistance and food stamps for individuals
with drug felony convictions."[93] *A drug law violation is the only offense
singled out for this lifetime federal sanction.* A person who has completed a prison sentence for rape or armed robbery can qualify for TANF
and food stamps, but not someone convicted of selling or possessing
even a small quantity of illicit drugs, regardless of whether that person is
a first-time offender or a minor. No one convicted of a drug law offense

is exempt from the ban, not even pregnant women, those in treatment for drug addiction, people with AIDS, or people who have been crime free for decades.[94]

States can opt out or modify the ban, but otherwise it's permanent. As of 2009, only 11 states (ME, MI, NH, NJ, NM, NY, OH, OK, RI, VT, WA), in addition to Washington, D.C., have eliminated the ban entirely; 9 have kept the ban with no modification (AL, AK, GA, MS, MO, NE, ND, WV, WY); and 30 have limited the ban in some way, allowing those with drug felony convictions to get some or all welfare benefits if they satisfy certain conditions, such as participating in a drug treatment program or meeting a required waiting period or having a conviction that involved only "possession" but not "trafficking."[95] Concerning trafficking, Professor Gabriel J. Chin points out that "the definition of dealing is so broad that virtually all users are dealers."[96] According to federal law, sharing a single marijuana cigarette with a friend constitutes trafficking.[97] Federal courts of appeal have ruled that "sharing drugs with another constitutes 'distribution,'" even if "no commercial scheme is involved."[98] In addition, possession of a controlled substance, even marijuana, if defined as a felony under state law, can constitute trafficking.[99]

Welfare reform has presented many recipients with a catch-22: They use welfare benefits to help pay for substance abuse treatment but lose their benefits *because* they have substance abuse problems.[100] Studies have found that between 10 and 20 percent of the adults receiving TANF have alcohol and drug problems and that welfare payments frequently help them pay for room and board during substance abuse treatment. Many states are screening TANF recipients for drug problems, and terminating the benefits of those found to be dependent.[101]

Education

Congress has also passed legislation punishing anyone convicted of a drug offense by suspending their education benefits. The 1998 Higher Education Act specified that beginning in 2001 any student convicted of a drug law violation would be ineligible for federal financial aid for one to two years after conviction, depending on whether it was a person's first conviction.[102] No such disqualification applied to convictions for burglary, rape, or manslaughter. This legislation is still a part of our nation's drug policy. As of 2011–2012, 72.8 percent of full-time undergraduates receive federal aid.[103]

In 2012, Cornell University economists Michael Lovenheim and Emily Owens investigated the effects of this legislation. They found that "the temporary prohibition of Federal aid caused a large decline in the fraction of drug offenders who enrolled in college within two years of graduating from high school."[104] Many of these students simply waited to enroll until they were eligible for federal benefits, while some were less likely ever to attend college. In addition, Lovenheim and Owens found "no evidence that the law had a deterrent effect on drug offenses." In fact, among their sample of students with drug convictions, those who had been subjected to the restrictions on financial aid were 60 percent more likely to be convicted of another drug crime within three years of graduating high school than those who were not subjected to the restrictions.[105]

Voting

It was election day, 2000, in Florida. Neither presidential candidate, George W. Bush or Al Gore, could claim victory; the race was too close to call. Whoever won the state's electoral votes would become the next president. Thomas Johnson wanted to cast his ballot for Bush,[106] but Johnson had to stay home that day. He was denied the right to vote by Florida law because he was an ex-offender. In 1992, he had been convicted in New York of selling cocaine and carrying a weapon without a license. After serving his sentence, he moved to Florida in 1996. Today, Thomas Johnson is the director of a Christian residential program for ex-offenders.

He was not the only Florida ex-felon who was barred from the voting booth that day; there were 613,513 others.[107] In this case, the disenfranchisement of ex-felons likely altered the outcome of the presidential election. Researchers Uggen and Manza estimate that if as few as 13.6 percent of the ex-felons had voted, with 69 percent voting Democratic, Gore would have won Florida by 31,000 votes.[108]

As the U.S. population under criminal justice supervision has soared in recent decades, so have the millions of people disenfranchised because of felony convictions—from 1.17 million in 1976 to over 5.85 million in 2010.[109] About a quarter are incarcerated, but the rest have finished their prison sentences and are on probation or parole, which means that over 4 million people who work and pay taxes in their communities are banned from the voting booth. This total includes about a million African American ex-felons.[110]

Felons who have completed their sentences and are theoretically no longer under the control of the criminal justice system are barred from voting in 11 states. Felons from these states make up about 45 percent

(2.6 million) of the disenfranchised population.[111] Nationally, almost 7.7 percent of African Americans are disenfranchised, as compared to 1.8 percent of non–African Americans. In Florida, Kentucky, and Virginia, at least 20 percent of blacks can't vote. Two states, Maine and Vermont, permit all felons to vote, including those in prison.[112]

In recent years a few states have overturned some of the voting restrictions for ex-felons, while other states have adopted more restrictive regulations.[113] As to the constitutionality of barring felons from voting, the Supreme Court ruled in *Richardson v. Ramirez* (1974) that felon disenfranchisement did not violate the equal protection clause of the Fourteenth Amendment because the amendment permits states to impose voting restrictions for "participation in rebellion, or other crime."[114]

The voting ban in the United States contrasts dramatically with practices in many other countries. Sixteen European countries allow all prisoners to vote in elections.[115] Prisoners can also vote in Canada, Israel, South Africa, Hong Kong, and other countries.[116]

Families

The most obvious and perhaps most tragic invisible punishment associated with incarceration is the separation of families and the resultant detrimental effects on children. With few exceptions, criminal statutes pay no attention to the impact of a criminal conviction on family relationships and children.[117] Studies find that when parents are incarcerated children as young as two to six "suffer a variety of adverse outcomes," such as, "anxiety, withdrawal, hyper-vigilance, depression, shame . . . guilt . . . anger, aggression, and hostility toward caregivers and siblings."[118]

One out of three women, and one out of four men, are in prison because they violated drug laws, a nonviolent offense.[119] Currently, 98,200 inmates in federal prison—51 percent of the federal prison population—were incarcerated for possession, trafficking, or other drug-related offenses. Drug offenders comprise 16 percent (210,200 inmates) of the total state prison population.[120] About half of the children left behind are under the age of 10. Over 60 percent of imprisoned women, and the majority of men, report being a parent.[121]

It's not surprising that abundant research has documented that "imprisonment of a parent disrupts intact, viable families."[122] It's difficult for incarcerated parents to maintain contact with their children. A key factor is the harshness of our sentencing laws, which ensures that imprisoned parents will be separated from their minor children for a significant portion of the child's life. The average time served in prison for drug offenses in 2012 was 68 months (down from 82 months in 2008).[123]

Another barrier between incarcerated parents and their children is the physical distance between prisons and home. More than 60 percent of parents are in state prisons that are typically in remote, rural areas, located more than 100 miles from the prisoners' homes. Incarcerated mothers are on average 160 miles away from their children; they are typically farther away than fathers because prisons for women are scarce.[124] In New York State, the main prison for women is about 400 miles from New York City. In California, two-thirds of the state's incarcerated mothers are held in two institutions that are in the remote town of Chowchilla, eight hours away from the urban centers where the great majority of their children live.[125]

In August 2013, the Federal Bureau of Prisons, U.S. Department of Justice, decided to transfer over 1,100 women out of Danbury prison in Connecticut to a prison in Alliceville, Alabama, and other prisons possibly even farther away.[126] Danbury is 60 miles from Hartford, 70 miles from New York City, and 150 miles from Boston. It is accessible by car, train, and public transportation. By contrast, Alliceville is over 1,000 miles from these cities and has no airport, train, or other long-distance public transportation. Eleven U.S. senators have questioned the need to close the Danbury women's prison and have complained about the damage this will do to the children and to the mothers who will wind up isolated from their families. As Senator Chris Murphy (D-CT) put it, "I think you are effectively cutting off communication between the women and their families by moving them to rural Alabama. Certainly, these women did something wrong, but their children didn't. It shouldn't be the policy of the Board of Prisons to cut off communication between a 7-year-old and her mother, regardless of what her mother did wrong."[127]

Abundant research documents how critical it is to a child's well-being to stay in regular communication with an incarcerated parent.[128] Unfortunately, contact with children is rare in prisons. A survey found that almost 60 percent of both mothers and fathers had never received a personal visit from their minor or adult children and over 40 percent had never even talked to their children on the phone.[129] The reasons most often cited for the rarity of visits are the geographical distance, the expense, the lack of transportation, and the unwillingness or inability of caregivers to bring children.[130]

Prison policies contribute to the difficulty of maintaining contact with families, often making visiting difficult and humiliating. Approval for a visitation can take several weeks; an original copy of the child's birth certificate and a document establishing a guardian's authority may be required; visitors frequently have to wait in line for hours, sometimes without access to bathrooms; children may undergo a pat search, even a "diaper peek"; visiting hours are usually scheduled during daytime hours when caregivers are working; and, those who violate the prison's dress code may be turned away.[131] As one inmate told Joan Petersilia: "In my own experience, I have noticed that prison officials often disrespect visitors . . . They are patronized, made to wait exorbitant amounts of time, told what types of clothing is permitted . . . My own mother's experience at one California facility was so bad I told her to never come see me there again."[132]

Prisons pay little attention to how a child may be affected by visiting their parent. Donna Wilmott was serving two years in prison on a conspiracy charge. (She is currently the family advocacy coordinator at Legal Services for Prisoners with Children in San Francisco.) She spent the first few weeks in solitary confinement and was allowed only window visits. She told her husband not to bring her four-year-old daughter to visit her: "I was desperate to see her, but I didn't want to put her through that. If you put a glass barrier between a child and a parent it's crazy-making for the child . . . It's almost like putting the parent in a box. The message the children gets is, 'Your mother is so bad you can't touch her. She's dangerous.'"[133]

The expense of visiting a prison can be prohibitive for many families. The anthropologist Donald Braman investigated the case of Lilly whose son Anthony had been in prison for 10 years since he was 18 for involvement in a fight.[134] Lilly, in her early 50s, is a single parent with three children. She has never been to high school and is functionally illiterate. Lilly supplements her fixed income of $530 a month by working at odd jobs such as day care provider, cook, and beautician. She worries constantly about Anthony, who has been seriously beaten in prison and has skin and breathing problems. Her efforts to visit have been frustrating, something she attributes to the abusive way prison officials treat visitors. Most families can readily list a number of "needless indignities suffered during visitation, the most common of which is flat refusal of entry on any of a number of grounds, but which often extend to cavity searches and the offhand insult."[135] Lilly recalled that Anthony's 63-year-old grandmother tried to visit but was turned away because she was wearing a "sweatshirt that was the wrong color."[136] Lilly visits monthly, which involves a two-day trip in a rental car, food, and a motel. The cost is between $150 and $200, a cost shared by her extended family.

She accepts the collect phone calls from her son, even though they are exorbitantly expensive. Her average phone bill is over $100 a month. As she put it, "Lord, just look at my phone bill. You know the only people this helps is the corporations."[137]

Lilly is right. Corporations have profited from phone calls at the expense of poor families like hers. There have been sweetheart deals between corrections departments and phone companies, where the prisons get a kickback from every call. Collect calls often cost $1 to $3 a minute; in addition, phone companies have charged an upfront fee as high as $4.99 for just making a call. Outside of prison, Americans, even without Skype, can easily get unlimited domestic calls for $9.99 a month.[138]

In his book *Going Up the River*, the Pulitzer Prize–winning journalist Joseph T. Hallinan explored the revenue prisons take in from phone calls by inmates: "When I began my travels, I had no idea . . . that a single pay phone inside a prison could earn its owner $12,000 a year . . . But, corporate America did. Giant firms like AT&T lined up at prison gates. The inmates on the other side of the fence, AT&T estimated, place $1 *billion* a year in long-distance phone calls. But unlike you or me, the inmates don't get to pick their long-distance carrier—the prison does. And so AT&T and its competitors learned that the way to get inmates as customers was to give the prison a legal kickback: on a $1 call the prison might make $0.40 or $0.50. In no time, correction departments became phone-call millionaires" (italics in the original).[139]

Prison officials defend the kickback by arguing that phones in prisons require special security features, such as recording, monitoring, and blocking calls. This defense was unconvincing to New York State, which eliminated the kickback and required prisons to provide service at the lowest possible cost. The federal government has also surmounted this alleged difficulty by using a computerized system that allows inmates to place monitored calls to a limited group of phone numbers.[140] As *The New York Times* reported in September 2012: "Members of Congress and civil rights groups are pushing the Federal Communications Commission (F.C.C.) to rein in telephone companies that, in many states, charge inmates spectacularly high rates that can force their families to choose between keeping in touch with a relative behind bars and, in some cases, putting food on the table . . . The F.C.C. . . . has been weighing this issue for nearly a decade."[141] Finally, in the fall of 2013, the Commission attempted to end this injustice when it "prohibited price-gouging by the private companies that provide interstate telephone service for prison and jail inmates."[142]

Parents who have been incarcerated, even for a minor drug offense, run the serious risk of losing their children permanently.[143] These ex-inmates face an uphill battle in maintaining their parental rights because their criminal record impedes their ability to find stable work and shelter. The largest number of child welfare interventions that remove children from their families are not for abuse, they are for neglect.[144] As Professor Naomi Cahn points out, "neglect" is usually a manifestation of poverty. Consequently, "children may be removed for poverty alone."[145] An Illinois study found that almost 10 percent of children were taken from their families because of a lack of adequate food or shelter, rather than any act on the part of the parents; while another 12 percent were removed because of a lack of supervision.[146] While neglect can be lethal, Cahn interprets these cases as "resource problems, not the problems of abusive or neglectful parents, [and that] removing children from their families of origin may disrupt the otherwise strong emotional bonds between family members and have a particularly severe impact on the child."[147] After reviewing the various studies, Duncan Lindsey concluded that "inadequacy of income, more than any other factor, constitutes the reason that children are removed [from their parents]."[148] Research by Professor Dorothy Roberts also concluded that "the huge role of neglect—has much more to do with poverty than the public is willing to acknowledge."[149] Peter Digre, the head of the Los Angeles Child Welfare Department testified before a congressional sub-committee that poverty was the reason that about half the children in his system were removed from their homes.[150]

Our public officials extol and glorify "The Family" as much as they do the American flag. Here are the words of our Supreme Court:[151] "The Court has frequently emphasized the importance of the family. The rights to conceive and to raise one's children have been deemed—in various Supreme Court rulings—as: 'essential,'[152] 'basic civil rights of man,'[153] and '[r]ights far more precious . . . than property rights.'"[154] Politicians of all stripes also employ this glorification of the family as one of their mantras.

Yet, Congress passed legislation in 1997 that damaged the families of parents with prison records resulting from even minor drug offenses. The law was the Adoption and Safe Families Act (ASFA).[155] It accelerated the movement of children who were languishing for years in foster care into more permanent situations, such as adoption or reunification with their family. Clearly, the law has had some beneficial effects. But ASFA stacked the cards against imprisoned parents by setting an impossibly short time period for many to meet the goals necessary to reunify with their children who were in foster care. Subject to certain exceptions (discussed below), the law requires states to terminate parental rights when children have been in foster care for as long as 15 of the past 22 months.[156] ASFA's speeded-up time clock has resulted in a growing number of incarcerated parents losing their children, because the average time served by prisoners was 25 months. Even for drug possession, the average prison time exceeded 15 months (it was 17 months).[157] Several states have even begun the termination of parental rights for children who have been in foster care for as little as 12 months.[158] ASFA tilts the playing field toward adoption by providing a subsidy to the states of several thousand dollars per child adopted. The law provides no corresponding incentive for returning a child to its family. States could be motivated by this bonus to move children into adoption without adequate consideration.[159]

The law requires that "reasonable efforts" be made not to remove children from their family unnecessarily. But research by Professor Peter Schneider finds that children, especially those with an incarcerated parent, are often rushed into adoption regardless of whether it's in the child's best interest.[160] Not only do many parents lose their children while they are in prison, but even after release they may not have sufficient time to do what is required to restore parental rights. ASFA requires parents to convince their state court that the problems that led to the child's removal have been corrected. But lack of services in prison may result in parents' continuing to have the same problems that led to their child's removal. As we've seen, substance abuse treatment and counseling programs are rarely available in prison. In addition, ex-offenders confront multiple obstacles to finding a stable job, locating decent housing, accessing drug treatment, and obtaining public benefits. Failure in these areas could result in losing their children to adoption when that is not in the best interests of the child.[161]

Understandably, ASFA eliminates the requirement of making a reasonable effort to preserve parental rights where parents have been convicted of murder, voluntary manslaughter, or acts of serious violence against their children.[162] But, as professor Elise Zeeland points out, the fact that a parent was incarcerated often provides sufficient grounds for removal, even if the criminal offense was not serious and has no bearing on the parent's ability to care for the child.[163] At least half the states now consider incarceration per se as a reason to move a foster child to adoption. Professor Philip Genty found that in the five years following the 1997 enactment of ASFA, the average number of reported annual terminations of parental rights due to parental incarceration was 562, as compared to an average of 182 in the five years preceding ASFA.[164]

Foster care policy targets children who are at higher risk than the national average for committing crimes, dropping out of school, becoming addicted to drugs, having mental health problems, carrying a sexually transmitted disease, or winding up on the streets. Around 800,000 children spend time in foster care each year, and the average stay is two years.[165] Despite the risk of poor life chances for these children, it may not be clear that removing them from their parents and placing them in foster care will be beneficial. While a substance abusing family is harmful for children, removal could also be harmful. As one example, a serious problem with foster care is its instability: The average child is moved from one family to another at least once, and a quarter are moved three or more times.[166]

Rigorous recent studies have attempted to measure the effects on children of foster care versus home care. The research focused on a sample of children who had been evaluated by investigators to be marginal as to whether they should be moved into foster care or left with their parents. Part of the sample wound up in foster care and part remained with their family. Prior to placement, these two groups did not differ in the seriousness of their behavior problems. The future behavior of the two groups was then compared, providing a measure of the impact of foster care relative to home care for a sample of children who were initially considered marginal for placement. Research by economist Joseph J. Doyle Jr. found that "children on the margin of placement tend to have better outcomes when they remain at home."[167] Specifically, he found that foster care resulted in higher arrests, convictions, and incarcerations, along with higher teen birth rates and lower earnings as adults. Research by Catherine Lawrence et al. obtained similar results.[168]

Financial Penalties

Almost every encounter with the criminal justice system results in some type of financial penalty. The New York State Bar Association concluded in 2006 that "the financial penalties imposed, directly or indirectly, as a result of a criminal conviction, are among the least recognized of the invisible punishments."[169] These court-ordered payments benefit numerous government agencies and private businesses, including, probation departments, child-support enforcement offices, drug testers, and substance abuse treatment centers. States have authorized these fees and fines to recoup the administrative costs resulting from those arrested, prosecuted, imprisoned, and supervised within the criminal justice system. These financial penalties have proliferated over the past quarter century. They are so hidden and scattered throughout state codes and are so dependent on the type of crime and locale that attorneys and policy makers are rarely able to comprehend the full punishments attached to a particular conviction or sentence. Twenty-seven percent of the fees and fines imposed on felony convictions are for drug offenses.[170]

Here are some of the financial penalties.[171] Most convicted persons are required to pay fees to cover a variety of court expenses, such as maintaining facilities, servicing of warrants, and even contributions to police retirement funds. Offenders also pay a book-in fee at the time of arrest; a per diem for stays in jail pending trial; payments for reports on the defendant relevant to sentencing; fees defraying the costs of a public defender; payments toward the costs of residential or work release centers; fees covering costs of parole and supervision; and restitutions to victims. As Adam Liptak reported in *The New York Times* in 2006, "Private probation companies charge $30 to $40 a month for supervision. Halfway houses charge for staying in them. People sentenced to community service are required to buy $15 insurance policies for every week they work. Criminals on probation and parole wear global positioning devices that monitor their whereabouts—for a charge of as much as $16 a day.

"The sums raised by these ever-mounting fees are intended to help offset some of the enormous costs of operating the criminal justice system. But even relatively small fees—$40 per session, say, for a court-ordered anger management class or $15 for a drug test—can have devastating consequences for people who emerge from prison with no money, credit or prospects, and who live in fear of being sent back for failing to pay."[172]

These penalties can bury an ex-offender in a debt of $10,000 or more.[173] In addition, people often enter prison owing child support payments that build up while they are in prison. A 2007 study commissioned by the Justice Department's Bureau of Justice Assistance describes cases of newly released inmates who find they have a debt of as much as $25,000 the minute they step outside the prison gate. For example, a study in one state found that people released on parole owed an average of $16,600 for child support. In another state the debt for those released from prison averaged more than $20,000.[174]

Ex-inmates who default on repaying these debts can suffer devastating consequences to their finances and even to their freedom. Lagging in debt payments, they may have their wages deducted or their assets seized; they may have the costs associated with debt collection added to the balance they owe; they may face penalties such as community service, curfew, or electronic monitoring; or, they may even wind up back in prison for "contempt of court or willful nonpayment."[175]

Consider the case of DeMarcus Sanders, 26, an African American from Waterloo, Iowa. A police officer pulled him over for playing his music too loud. The officer claimed he smelled marijuana so he searched the car and found a single marijuana seed on the floor. Mr. Sanders pleaded guilty and was sentenced to 30 days in jail. He lost his janitorial job and credits for college courses he was taking. Even though it's been a few years since his arrest, he still owes the state $2,346 for fines, fees, court costs, and room and board at the jail. His arrest for possessing marijuana in Iowa led to a six-month suspension of his driver's license. In order to reinstate his license, Mr. Sanders would have to pay off a certain percentage of his debt to the state. Waterloo has little public transportation, so it's difficult to hold down a job and care for his eight-year-old son. He has had to turn down a job in a nearby city because it's 45 minutes away and he doesn't have a license to drive. Most recently, he was working small jobs and living with his parents.[176]

Beverly Dubois is a former park ranger in Washington State. She was convicted of growing and selling marijuana and served nine months in jail. She left jail with a debt of $1,610—$1,000 for a county "drug enforcement fund," a $500 "victim assessment fee," and $100 in court costs. (She said, "I still don't know who the victim was.") Ms. Dubois, disabled as a result of a car accident, lived on disability payments of $600 a month. She was required to pay $10 a month toward her debt. But, in spite of her payments, her debt continued to grow because of the 12 percent interest rate assessed annually by the State of Washington. "I will never have it paid off in my lifetime," she said. Unless the current system changes, Ms. Dubois is right.

While the Supreme Court has ruled that defendants cannot be imprisoned for failure to pay off their debts, they can be jailed for failing to report to their probation officer. Many people who fall behind on debt payment fail to appreciate this distinction and give up attending parole sessions.[177] An example is Sabrina Byrd, a single mother of three, who was charged with a misdemeanor fine of $852 in College Park, Georgia. Because she couldn't pay her fine, the court put her on probation and set up a payment plan requiring that she pay down the fine; in addition, she was required to pay a service fee of $39 a month to a private company authorized to supervise misdemeanor probationers. The $124 monthly payment schedule was more than Byrd could afford, so she stopped attending probation meetings. In 2003, she was arrested and sentenced to 25 days in jail for violating probation.[178]

Byrd's experience in the criminal justice system has become common, as predicted in 1986 by the National Institute of Corrections: "The added stress caused by inability to pay [probation supervision fees] may cause probationers to miss appointments . . . sometimes resulting in revocation [of parole] for failure to comply with the conditions of probation."[179] Kirsten D. Levingston, of the New York University School of Law, interprets cases like these as examples of powerful interests profiting "from keeping prisons and jails full—private prison investors, powerful correctional officers' unions, telephone companies, and various service industries (such as medical, transportation, and food service industries)—all gain directly from keeping prisons in business."[180] Here is a statement in the 2010 annual report of the Corrections Corporation of America—the largest private prison company—pointing out that any relaxation of the drug war could hurt their bottom line: "The demand for our facilities and services could be adversely affected by the relaxation of enforcement efforts, leniency in conviction or parole standards and sentencing practices, or through the decriminalization of certain activities that are currently proscribed by our criminal laws. For instance, any changes with respect to drugs and controlled substances or illegal immigration could affect the number of persons arrested, convicted, and sentenced, thereby potentially reducing demand for correctional facilities to house them."[181]

Border Searches

The Fourth Amendment requires that all searches be based on probable cause, but routine searches at the border are a special case. A "routine search" includes "investigating a person's luggage, personal belongings, outer clothing, wallet, purse, and even a person's shoes." It may also involve the use of a drug-detection dog and include photocopying material as well as installing electronic devices in the articles searched.[182] The Supreme Court has given the Customs Service and other agencies with authority over the national border complete discretion to engage in routine stops and searches at any point of entry to the United States. This "border exception" to the Fourth Amendment is based on the authority granted by the Constitution to Congress "[t]o regulate Commerce with foreign Nations."[183] The Customs Service is free to choose its suspects as well as its methods in preventing illegal objects from entering the country. Next to terrorism, the highest priority for the agencies that patrol our borders is not untaxed items like jewelry or whiskey. It's illicit drugs.[184]

There are so many millions of travelers entering the United States every year that Customs cannot scrutinize people individually. So the agency has relied on a drug-courier profile consisting of 43 factors to determine who merits a "non-routine search."[185] These are more intrusive than routine searches and may include prolonged detention, a strip search, a body cavity search, an x-ray search, and the destruction of property.[186] Nonroutine searches are often conducted on people who are suspected of having swallowed balloons filled with illegal drugs.[187] Narcotics and other contraband are frequently smuggled into the country in the body cavities of travelers. According to a 2009 Congressional Research Service Report to Congress, cavity searches "have become more commonplace . . . [and] may include inspections of the vagina or rectum, or the use of emetics."[188] The Supreme Court has stated that a nonroutine search could include "strip, body cavity, or involuntary x-ray searches."[189] However, the Court has not expressed any view on what level of suspicion is required to establish a nonroutine search.[190] That task has been left to the lower courts, which require that agents simply have a "reasonable suspicion of illegal activity to conduct a non-routine border search."[191]

But reasonable suspicion in this context means that Customs agents employ their drug-courier profile, which (as we've seen) could target anyone. The courts are substantially in agreement that factors that can be taken into account to determine reasonable suspicion include: nervousness, unusual conduct, an informant's tip, bulky or loose-fitting clothing, unemployment, inadequate luggage, evasive answers, or traveling to or from a city known for illegal drugs.[192] For example, in one case, a federal court found reasonable suspicion when the person was traveling alone, had one unchecked suitcase, was young and attractive, came from Bogotá, Colombia, and was wearing a loose-fitting dress. These factors matched the drug-courier profile for carriers of narcotics in that region.[193]

In *U.S. v. Montoya de Hernandez* (1985), the Supreme Court was confronted with a woman suspected of balloon swallowing who refused to allow an x-ray search.[194] Customs detained Ms. De Hernandez for more than 16 hours and would not let her leave until she had carried out a monitored bowel movement into a waste basket. The Supreme Court ruled that it was reasonable to detain her for that period of time in order to verify or dispel the agents' suspicion that she was smuggling drugs in her alimentary canal. Chief Justice William Rehnquist defended this decision as being responsive to "the veritable national crises in law enforcement caused by [the] smuggling of illegal narcotics."[195]

David A. Harris states that Customs has the "most sweeping set of police powers that exists under our laws."[196] Given this power, it would not be surprising to find that blacks and Hispanics are disproportionately subjected to nonroutine searches at the border. By the late 1990s, allegations of racial profiling at Customs had become widespread. Black women in particular were being singled out for nonroutine searches. One study of these searches described them as "more harrowing and degrading" than the term "intrusive" would suggest.[197]

One of the people informed about the strip searches of black women by Customs is Edward Fox, a civil rights lawyer. As of 2002 he had represented some 90 African American women who complained of intrusive searches at O'Hare Airport in Chicago. He estimated that his class-action lawsuit will eventually include some 1,300 women. Fox heard over and over again that intimate searches were approved by low-ranking customs agents without even the approval of a supervisor. Publicity about these intimate searches led to new leadership at the Customs Service, which promised to eliminate racial profiling.[198]

But we are now living in the "age of terrorism" and our government has pledged to tighten security at our borders. Pursuant to recommendations by the 911 Commission, several bills have come before Congress to tighten border security. For example, in 2005 the House of Representatives passed a bill that called for increasing border inspectors by at least 250 each of year from 2007 through 2010. A similar measure was passed by the Senate.[199] How will security measures like these affect nonroutine searches for drugs in the future?

Summary

Federal drug laws enacted in the 1980s created policing for profit, causing arrests and incarcerations to skyrocket. Millions of nonviolent and otherwise law-abiding Americans have become marked as criminals. After completing the sentences meted out by judges, drug law offenders find themselves enmeshed in a complicated maze of penalties—called invisible punishments—which are likely to last a lifetime. For even the most minor drug law violators, thousands of occupational licenses are not available; public housing is often off limits; parole officers focus on harassment, not help; federal welfare benefits are permanently cut off; federal education benefits are suspended; driver's licenses may be suspended or revoked; voting rights are often denied; and, a huge debt typically burdens returning prisoners. Perhaps the most tragic victims are the children of incarcerated parents; in spite of the paeans to "The Family" that traditionally flow from our government officials, Congress has so shortened the period during which these parents can rehabilitate themselves and reclaim their children from foster care, that many lose their parental rights permanently.

Drug law violators not only suffer these and other invisible punishments, they are the sole victims of some of them: The permanent deprivation of federal welfare benefits applies only to drug offenses. No other crime, be it murder or rape, earns this lifetime punishment. The same is true for the suspension of federal education benefits for college students convicted of a drug offense. The suspension applies to no other crime.

The effects of invisible punishments are clear: They impede drug law violators from reestablishing the rights of first-class citizenship, possibly for life.

Part V

DRUG TESTING

CHAPTER 14

Drug Testing Students

Drug testing has become so widespread an invasion of our privacy that it might surprise you to know that U.S. courts once routinely struck down random drug testing as an unreasonable search and seizure. Except for police, prison inmates, and athletes, citizens were rarely tested, and then usually only when there were grounds for suspicion. This tradition was maintained until the late 1980s, when it gave way to the antidrug rhetoric of the war on drugs. The result has been a nationwide proliferation of suspicionless drug testing.[1] Businesses began randomly testing employees. Parents became so frightened by government propaganda that they became willing to sacrifice privacy rights to protect their children's health. So, schools also joined the war on drugs by implementing a "zero tolerance" policy, involving drug testing and drug-detection dogs.[2]

In the late 1980s, in the small community of Vernonia, Oregon, school officials perceived an increase in illegal drug use. They panicked, declaring the student body to be in "a state of rebellion."[3] When drug sweeps with dogs and antidrug classes failed to stem the "rebellion," the officials instituted a policy of mandatory drug testing for athletes in the fall of 1989. Parents of athletes were required to submit a form consenting to the drug testing. Eligibility for athletics was made contingent on the results of the test. Once a week, 10 percent of all student athletes had to submit a urine sample to be analyzed for illegal drug use.

The policy was challenged in court when a student was denied the opportunity to play football because his parents refused to consent to the test. The lawsuit claimed a violation of the student's Fourth Amendment right to be free of unreasonable searches and seizures. The school district appealed all the way to the U.S. Supreme Court, which ruled in support of the school.[4] The Court, in a previous decision, had already downgraded the Fourth Amendment protection for public school students based on the rationale that school authorities have a compelling interest in maintaining order.[5] In the Vernonia ruling, the Court pointed out that athletes have an even lower expectation of privacy than non-athletes because they undress in locker rooms; as Justice Scalia put it, "School sports are not for the bashful." The Court went on to make the following arguments:

- Participation in sports is voluntary;
- No one is arbitrarily singled out, because all athletes are subject to testing;
- The tests themselves are performed under minimally intrusive conditions; and, finally,
- There is a serious drug abuse problem that justifies drug testing.

The effect of this 1995 Supreme Court decision was to open the way for drug testing athletes in schools throughout the country.[6]

But, schools began pushing the envelope beyond athletics.[7] They started requiring suspicionless drug tests as a condition for eligibility to a range of extracurricular student activities such as marching band, choir, or debate club. There was also random testing of students who drove back and forth to school. In the extreme case of Lockney, Texas, the entire junior high school student body was drug tested.

These policies were challenged on constitutional grounds. The question was whether they were covered by the Vernonia ruling, which only applied to athletes. This led to conflicting rulings by the federal circuit courts. In 2002, a case involving Tecumseh High School in Oklahoma was accepted for review by the Supreme Court.[8] The school had been conducting random and suspicionless drug testing of students in a wide range of extracurricular activities, including cheerleading, pompon squad, band, choir, color guard, Future Farmers of America, and Future Homemakers of America.[9] In a 5–4 decision, the Court ruled that public schools have the authority to perform random drug tests on all middle and high school students participating in extracurricular activities.[10]

In a law review article, Christopher A. Gorman criticized the Supreme Court's ruling, arguing that the Court failed to take into account the embarrassment and humiliation expressed by many of the students as well as the failure of the test procedures to satisfy professional medical standards.[11] As Gorman put it,

> The Tecumseh District utilizes teachers and coaches to administer drug screenings, whereas in other contexts, medical personnel, anonymous to the test subject and trained to preserve patients' privacy expectations, often conduct drug screenings. Evidence presented to the district court indicated that Tecumseh school personnel had fallen far short of meeting the professional norms that trained medical personnel would certainly uphold in conducting a drug screening. Moreover, the teachers and coaches conducting the drug screening in the Tecumseh District may often have a personal relationship with the students being tested. This relationship is likely to cause great discomfort to students and intensify the invasiveness of the procedures by forcing students to examine a urine sample with a teacher or other school personnel in an authoritative position.[12]

As a practical matter, policy concerning drug testing public school students is determined by school districts. Policies vary widely across the nation, even among districts within a state. But as a result of the Supreme Court's 2002 Tecumseh decision, random drug testing of students in athletics as well in other extracurricular activities has become common in schools across the country.[13]

This brings us to the obvious next question: Does random drug testing diminish students' use of illicit drugs? The Supreme Court dealt with the question this way in its Tecumseh ruling: "Testing students who participate in extracurricular activities is a reasonably effective means of addressing the School District's legitimate concerns in preventing, deterring, and detecting drug use."[14]

John Walters, the drug czar in 2002, also endorsed drug testing students as a way to diminish illegal drug use. He was then the director of the Office of National Drug Control Policy (ONDCP), which is responsible for crafting our nation's policy toward illegal drugs. Here is the view of the ONDCP expressed in a 2002 booklet entitled *What You Need to Know about Drug Testing in Schools*: "There are those, of course, who will represent the Court's [2002] decision as a blow against privacy and a victory for 'Big Brother.' These concerns are largely unfounded, however, and to focus on them is to ignore the enormous potential benefits of drug testing. Already, testing has been shown to be extremely effective at reducing drug use in schools . . . As a deterrent, few methods work better."[15]

The American public also apparently believes that testing reduces drug use. A 2002 Gallup poll found that 70 percent approved drug testing of students, while 29 percent disapproved.[16] A CBS/New York Times poll in 1989 showed that a majority of Americans believed that drug testing would reduce use by a "great deal," and was more effective than stiffer penalties, education programs, treatment programs, or eradicating drugs in foreign countries.[17]

These views conflict with the findings of two major empirical investigations of this issue. *These studies found no evidence that drug testing affected students' consumption of, or attitudes toward, illicit substances.*

In 2006, the U.S. Department of Education evaluated the effects of drug testing using a sample of 36 high schools with 4,723 students in grades 9 through 12.[18] About half the schools were randomly assigned to drug testing, while the remaining schools were not permitted to implement testing until after the student survey was concluded. The study failed to find a significant difference between the two groups of schools in their use of the drugs tested whether the drugs included alcohol and tobacco along with the illicit drugs, or not.[19] In addition, the percentage of students who reported that they "definitely will" or "probably will" use illicit substances in the next 12 months showed no difference between the groups of schools with or without drug testing.[20]

Researchers from the University of Michigan also conducted a study of the impact of drug testing in high schools.[21] The data covered the period 1998 through 2002 and was supported by the National Institute on Drug Abuse. Two subsets of data that included 10th and 12th graders were analyzed: one group consisted of approximately 4,000 male athletes from 297 high schools; the other sample consisted of 10,400 "heavy" drug-using students in 557 high schools—specifically, students who had reported using marijuana 20 or more times in their lifetime.[22] Over the five years of the study, about 19,000 students were drug tested. The study found that random drug testing of athletes was not a "significant predictor" of their illicit drug use, including the consumption of marijuana. There was also no evidence that "the heavy drug-using segment of the student population, specifically, is deterred from using marijuana or other illicit drugs by random or for-cause testing."[23]

In evaluating these studies, the RAND Drug Policy Research Center concluded that drug testing has not been shown to curtail the use of illicit drugs by students. In testimony before a House Committee, a RAND Corporation spokesman approved the priorities of the Fiscal Year 2011 budget request of the Obama administration because it eliminated "spending on some programs for which there was little or no scientific support, in particular student drug testing."[24]

The American Academy of Pediatrics, after reviewing the studies on drug testing students, also concluded: "Currently, [2007] there is little evidence of the effectiveness of school-based drug testing in the scientific literature."[25] The review warned that "drug testing poses substantial risks—in particular, the risk of harming the parent-child and school-child relationships by creating an environment of resentment, distrust, and suspicion."[26] In addition, the Academy noted that "it is fairly easy to defeat drug tests, and most drug-involved youths are all too familiar with ways to do so"; moreover, "Standard drug tests do not detect many of the drugs most frequently abused by adolescents, such as alcohol, ecstasy (MDMA), and inhalants."[27]

Few physicians support school-based drug testing. A 2006 national poll found that 83 percent of physicians disapproved of drug testing in public schools. The doctors surveyed were in pediatrics, family medicine, and adolescent medicine.[28]

In sum: The scientific evidence finds that drug testing fails to diminish the use of illicit drugs by adolescents, nor does it alter their attitudes toward the risks of these substances. Moreover, pediatricians warn that drug testing risks harming the parent–child and school–child relationships.

CHAPTER 15

Employee Drug Testing

In 1988, Congress passed a law requiring companies with federal contracts to drug test employees.[1] In 1989, the U.S. Supreme Court gave the green light to mandatory, suspicionless testing of workers in positions that involve safety and national security hazards. The Court ruled that these concerns overrode the Fourth Amendment rights of employees.[2] The federal government does not regulate drug testing in the private sector; rather, it delegates that authority to the states and to certain government agencies.[3]

In the years following this legislation and Court ruling, workplace drug testing by both private and government employers became widespread as well as controversial. Critics, like the ACLU, condemn random testing, arguing that it is often "unrelated to the tasks required to do the job, produces inaccurate results, and remains unproven as a means of stopping drug use."[4]

As companies ramp up drug testing, there are growing complaints from workers, who cite invasions of privacy and the unfairness of losing their jobs for taking legal medications. For example, in October 2010, Velma Sue Bates received a devastating phone call. She was fired from her job of 22 years with Dura Automotive Systems.[5] Why? Had she done anything wrong? No. The company had decided to add hydrocodone and oxycodone to their drug screening. Ms. Bates, whose job was trimming car window moldings on an assembly line, had been prescribed hydrocodone for back pain by her doctor. Along with the shock, she was humiliated, saying that people would never believe she was fired for using a legal drug: "You tell somebody you lost your job because you're on prescription medication and they're like, 'Yeah, right.'" She understood the safety concerns of the company, but added, "If the medicine they're taking is not good for them or the workplace, then there should be some sort of program where they can teach us how that affects you or see if something else can be worked out. But that was not an option for us."[6]

According to Dr. Seddon R. Savage, a pain specialist at Dartmouth College and president of the American Pain Society, "In general, well-prescribed opioids at a stable dose that are well supervised in most healthy people won't cause sedation or other cognitive problems."[7] Dr. Robert T. Cochran Jr., a Nashville pain specialist who is treating three of Dura's former employees, agreed with Dr. Savage and added, "I think they [Dura] terminated some people who were not in any way compromised."[8] Christopher J. Kuczynski, assistant legal counsel in the Equal Employment Opportunity Commission's policy division for the Americans with Disabilities Act, points out that "the employer must have a reasonable belief the person is unable to do the job or poses a threat based on a medical condition."[9]

Ms. Bates and five others sued Dura. In 2014, the U.S. Court of Appeals ruled in their favor. The court referred the issue to a jury, which awarded compensatory and punitive damages of more than $870,000 to Ms. Bates and each of four others.[10]

Injuries in the workplace are a serious public health issue in the United States. According to a news release by the Bureau of Labor Statistics, there were 3 million injuries and illnesses reported in the private industrial sector in 2011.[11] The Centers for Disease Control and Prevention reported that there were 2.6 million admissions to emergency rooms for job-related injuries and illnesses in 2010.[12] Does drug testing reduce these numbers?

The RAND Corporation reviewed 33 selected empirical studies that analyzed the relationship between drug testing, substance use, and workplace injuries. While there were many conflicting findings, most studies found that companies that tested tended to have both lower substance use and less occupational injuries. RAND pointed out, however, that the limitations of these studies made it impossible to say that either of these outcomes were a result of drug testing.[13] There were several relevant factors not adequately accounted for in the studies. For example:[14]

• Drug testing often occurs along with other workplace policies to diminish drug use, such as, employee assistance programs, education programs, and peer interventions. In these cases, researchers may have failed to isolate the independent effects of testing.

- Punishments imposed for a positive drug test vary across employers, and these diverse sanctions are not accounted for in many studies of workplace drug testing.
- When a company institutes drug testing, individuals who use drugs may avoid that company. RAND found no studies that incorporated this possible self-selection effect.

Several studies also found that the positive association between substance use and workplace injuries may be due to factors that independently cause both outcomes, that is, a person who is more likely to abuse substances, including alcohol, is also more likely to incur the risk of injury on the job even without drugs.[15] Some of these studies found that when these high risk factors for individuals were controlled for, the positive relationship between substance use and workplace injuries disappeared.[16]

Professor Robert J. MacCoun came to the same conclusions as RAND: "Support for a general deterrent effect of drug testing is mixed. The available studies are correlational and hence subject to a variety of inferential problems."[17] MacCoun also criticized testing because it is vulnerable to false positives (incorrectly assigning guilt) as well as false negatives (incorrectly finding lack of guilt). For example, false positives for marijuana can be triggered by contaminants as well as prescription and over-the-counter medications. False negatives could result from temporary abstention or loading up on water, not to mention the detailed advice on Web sites on how to defeat a drug test.[18]

In the U.K., an investigation of drug testing on the job was initiated in 2002 and lasted for 18 months. Evidence was obtained from "employers and employees, providers of drug testing services, trade unions and business organizations, insurers and police officers, occupational health physicians and health and safety specialists, natural and social scientists, lawyers, philosophers and other experts in drug testing policy."[19] Here are the major findings:

- Any link between drug use and accidents or low performance is "inconclusive."[20]
- There was no evidence for a clear link between drug use and accidents in safety-critical industries, although drug- and alcohol-induced intoxication is obviously a source of risk in such environments.[21]
- There was no evidence that drug testing at work has a significant deterrent effect on drug use.[22]
- Evidence suggests that alcohol is a greater cause for concern in the workplace than illicit drugs.[23]

- Those interviewed emphasized the potentially divisive nature of drug testing and the costs of excluding responsible and capable people from employment.[24]
- Authorizing employers to investigate private behavior conflicts with liberal-democratic values.[25]
- Drug testing does not measure current intoxication and reveals information about drug use that has no relevance for performance.[26]

A 2006 Canadian investigation of workplace safety[27] also concluded that there is a "lack of credible scientific evidence that urine tests improve workplace safety."[28] The study also pointed out that "the motives for drug testing in Canada are mostly linked to safety concerns, rather than part of a more general 'war on drugs' that is prevalent in the United States."[29]

The contrast between U.S. and Canadian attitudes toward workplace drug testing is stark. According to the Canadian Human Rights Commission Policy on Alcohol and Drug Testing, the following types of testing are "*not acceptable* . . . because they cannot be established as bona fide occupational requirements" (italics in the original):[30]

- preemployment drug testing,
- preemployment alcohol testing,
- random drug testing, and
- random alcohol testing of employees in non-safety-sensitive positions.[31]

For safety-sensitive positions, random alcohol testing is considered reasonable, but random drug testing is prohibited except where there is "reasonable cause" or after an accident.[32]

While acknowledging that the abuse of drugs can have adverse effects on health and safety, the Canadian Human Rights Commission believes that drug testing is generally unacceptable because it's a violation of human rights and is not a reliable measure of whether a person is—or is not—capable of performing their job.[33]

Summary

The proliferation of drug testing of students and workers over the past 30 years has infringed on privacy rights with no health or safety benefits to show for it. Major empirical studies find *no evidence that drug testing diminishes the use of, or attitudes toward, illicit drugs.* There are, however, negative effects in addition to the assault on privacy rights. The

American Academy of Pediatrics warns about harm to children because of the environment of distrust and suspicion caused by drug testing. Results from drug tests are vulnerable to errors, but flawed or not they can damage reputations, result in job losses, and cause a suspension of education benefits.

In spite of the damages of drug testing and the consensus of the scientific evidence that it doesn't work, a majority of Americans support it.[34] Moreover, people appear to perceive drug testing as normal. Expressions of anger or indignation at this invasion of privacy are rare. On the contrary, government agencies and corporations proudly announce that they conduct drug tests. In his first week on the job as secretary of defense, Robert Gates reported in his memoir that the Department of Defense required that he take a drug test. He wrote, "Even the Secretary of Defense was not exempt from that."[35] Shopping at Lowes recently my wife and I were struck by a sign at the entrance assuring us that "all our employees are drug tested."

Part VI

Is the War Ending?

CHAPTER 16

Good News!

My students knew before I did! On April 4, 2013, the moment we began our seminar on the drug war, they excitedly informed me that more than half the American people now favored legalizing marijuana. A national survey had found that 52 percent favored legalization, while 45 percent did not.[1] The rapid increase in support for legalizing marijuana over the past two decades has been astonishing: In 1991, only 17 percent of Americans said yes and 78 percent said no; but, by October 2013, Gallup reported that 58 percent approved while 39 percent disapproved; among Millennials the increase went from 21 to 67 percent over this period.[2] My students—all in their first year at the University of North Carolina—were optimistic that the war against drugs was coming to an end.

On August 12, 2013, Ethan Nadelmann, executive director of Drug Policy Alliance, a nonprofit organization whose principal goal is to end the war on drugs, sent out an e-mail with the following first sentence: "What a day! If only every Monday morning was like this." He related three pieces of "good news" that happened within hours of each other:

1. On a CNN special on marijuana the previous night, Dr. Sanjay Gupta, President Obama's first pick for surgeon general of the United States, issued a public apology, saying, "We have been terribly and systematically misled [about marijuana] for nearly 70 years, and I apologize for my own role in that."

2. U.S. District Court Judge Shira Scheindlin ruled that the New York Police Department's stop-and-frisk practices are unconstitutional, that the city had "adopted a policy of indirect racial profiling . . . [and] the city's highest officials have turned a blind eye to the evidence that officers are conducting stops in a racially discriminatory manner."[3]

3. Attorney General Eric Holder announced changes in federal sentencing practices that could result in fewer people getting locked up in federal prison for low-level drug law violations. Holder stated that "in some cases, mandatory minimums . . . have resulted in unduly harsh sentences . . . that do not reflect our Principles of Federal Prosecution. Long sentences for low-level, non-violent drug offenses do not promote public safety, deterrence, and rehabilitation."[4] Holder said that the Justice Department would direct federal prosecutors to charge defendants in certain low-level, nonviolent drug offenses in such a way that they would not be eligible for mandatory minimum sentences. Lawyers with expertise in criminal law said that prosecutors could do this by omitting from the official charging documents the amount of drugs involved in the arrest.[5]

It is unclear how many drug offenders would see shorter prison terms under Holder's proposal.[6] According to Scott Burns, executive director of the National District Attorney's Association, "United States Attorneys . . . no longer prosecute or send to prison those who are first time offenders or those who have committed low level drug offenses . . . unless it is a serious case and often must involve a firearm."[7] The attorney general also instructed attorneys to inform the judge as to the quantity of drugs involved, but judicial discretion is limited by the mandatory minimum sentencing laws.[8] Moreover, Holder's reform applies only to federal not state crimes. It's uncertain how state and local law enforcement will respond to Holder's reform if at all, and they are the ones arresting and incarcerating low-level, nonviolent drug law violators.

There was still more good news: In November 2012, Colorado and Washington legalized marijuana for recreational use for those over 21.[9] These state laws violate federal law, which classifies marijuana as a dangerous drug and its distribution "a serious crime."[10] The federal government remained silent about these state laws until August 29, 2013, when Attorney General Holder informed the governors of Colorado and Washington that the Department of Justice will not block their experiment as long as they set up effective regulations to protect public health and safety.[11] Here are some of the circumstances under which federal marijuana law would be enforced:

- distributing it to those under 21,
- allocating revenue to criminal enterprises,
- diverting it to other states,
- driving drugged,
- growing it on public lands, and/or
- using it on federal property.

In the midterm elections on November 4, 2014, Alaska and Oregon joined the list of states that allow the drug to be sold and used for those over 21.[12] While the federal government could find many reasons to override these state laws, the prospect is highly unpopular with the public. In a USA Today/Gallup poll, 63 percent of Americans disapproved of the federal government overruling states that legalize marijuana. Pew's polling found similar results: disapproval by 64 percent of independents, 59 percent of Democrats, and 57 percent of Republicans.[13]

By contrast with the public, the reactions of many public officials to Holder's policy were skeptical and contentious. In a hearing on these state marijuana laws before the Senate Judiciary Committee on September 10, 2013, Senator Patrick Leahy (D-VT), the committee's chairman, argued that there was a "persistent uncertainty" about how the Justice Department could resolve conflicts between federal and state laws. He pointed out that financial institutions and landlords could be prosecuted for racketeering, money laundering, and trafficking under current federal laws. Senator Charles E. Grassley (R-IA), the ranking Republican, was angry that the Justice Department was willing to accept the states' marijuana laws under any circumstances. He argued that the new federal policy was a step toward broad legalization of the drug, which would be disastrous for public safety and might violate international treaties. He said that marijuana's status as an illegal drug "isn't based on a whim. It's based on what science tells us about this dangerous and addictive drug."[14] John Urquhart, Sheriff of King County, Washington, testified that the state was "handcuffed" by not knowing how financial institutions could conduct marijuana-related business. Kevin A. Sabet, a former drug policy adviser in the Obama administration, who opposed legalization, said that some marijuana operations were not being adequately regulated by Colorado and Washington and were violating the Justice Department's regulations designed to protect public health and safety.[15]

Questions about the state marijuana laws remain:

- Congress did not change the drug laws, so what if a future president were a drug warrior?
- The circumstances under which federal law would override state laws are vague; how will they be interpreted?
- Will the U.S. attorneys heed the attorney general? Several have already said they will continue to crack down on marijuana dispensaries, and they have.[16]

Perhaps the most remarkable piece of good news occurred on January 16, 2015: U.S. Attorney General Eric Holder—as he was preparing to leave the office he had held since February 3, 2009—made the surprise announcement that state and local police would henceforth be barred from using federal law to seize cash, cars, and other property without warrants or criminal charges. This practice had been in effect since 1984.[17] If Holder's action were sustained it would result in a loss of millions of dollars to law enforcement across the country including the office of the U.S. attorney general! The future impact of Holder's controversial action is uncertain: It could be modified or revoked by a future attorney general or, of course, Congress. Law enforcement will fight Holder's decision tooth and nail; they attacked it the moment it was announced.[18] Even if his ruling is sustained, it contains significant loopholes that were discussed in Chapter 3.

CHAPTER 17

The War's Beneficiaries

These dramatic policy reversals are welcome news to many. Are they a harbinger of a fading drug war or merely momentary blips? I believe it's too early to celebrate. Based on the evidence documented in this book, the forces energizing the war are powerful and will not easily be dislodged. Consider the following groups that benefit.

Police officials, both federal and state, have become addicted to profits from drug arrests and property confiscations. As a result, a powerful national law enforcement lobby has sprung up to protect the revenue they take in from the war. The U.S. attorney general has also profited. It's ironic that a war to eliminate illicit drug transactions furnishes police and prosecutors with a financial incentive to perpetuate those transactions.

The war provides financial benefits for many other groups as well:

- Government agencies that receive money to fight the war, such as, the National Guard, the Coast Guard, Customs and Border Protection, Department of Justice, and the Department of Defense.[1]
- Prison employees whose jobs and salaries are supported by those incarcerated as a result of drug convictions.
- Rural communities whose income, employment, and political clout, benefit from local prisons that house convicted drug law violators.
- Private corporations that provide services to prisons, such as, phone service, food preparation, vocational training, and inmate transportation.
- Private, for-profit prisons that have sprouted up and proliferated to take advantage of mass incarceration.[2]
- Private firms that perform the drug testing of students and employees.

In addition, many are motivated to support the war because of racist attitudes. There is overwhelming psychological evidence that stereotyping drug law violators as men of color infects most of us. Unconscious racial bias is ubiquitous, and conscious racism clearly still flourishes.[3] So, for example, when the reputation of the Los Angeles Police Chief Daryl Gates remained unscathed after asserting before the Senate Judiciary Committee that casual drug users "ought to be taken out and shot," it seems obvious to me that Gates employed the term "casual drug users" as a widely accepted code phrase for African Americans and Hispanics.[4]

Finally, many Americans back the war because they believe—mistakenly, as shown in Part V—that drug testing students protects them from getting hooked on drugs. A 2010 Roper poll found that 76 percent of respondents said that drug abuse was a "very" or "somewhat" serious problem in the local schools[5]; and surveys in 2013 reported that around 40 percent oppose even legalizing marijuana and favor increased government spending to fight the war.[6]

As a reflection of how politically powerful the groups are that are promoting the war, consider how dramatically Barack Obama's views of illicit drugs changed once he assumed the presidency—from casual and lighthearted to punitive and aggressive. What happened? I suggest that, as president, Obama was forced to recant his previous public statements and promises because of pressures from influential interests that benefit from the war.

In his book, *Dreams from My Father*, Obama recounts that as a young man, when he was upset and confused, he found that "pot had helped, and booze, maybe a little blow [i.e., cocaine] when you could afford it ... [and though] the high didn't solve whatever it was getting you down, it could at least help you laugh at the world's ongoing folly and see through all the hypocrisy and bullshit and cheap moralism."[7] In 2006, in a meeting with magazine editors, Senator Obama joked that, unlike Bill Clinton who famously "didn't inhale," he, as a kid, "inhaled frequently. That was the point."[8] These jovial comments hardly sound like he considered the use of marijuana, or even cocaine, to be a criminal act.

In 2004, as a candidate for the U.S. Senate, Obama advocated decriminalizing marijuana and declared the drug war "an utter failure."[9] Yet, as president, he has opposed legalizing marijuana. In addition, his administration still classifies it—contrary to the scientific evidence—as a Schedule I drug, namely, one that's dangerous and has no medical value.[10] Obama could order marijuana removed as a Schedule I drug with a stroke of his pen.

During his campaign for president, he stated that medical marijuana was an issue best left to the states: "I'm not going to be using Justice Department resources to try to circumvent state laws on this issue."[11] In an interview in March 2008, with the *Mail Tribune* newspaper in Oregon, Obama said, "My attitude is that if it's an issue of doctors prescribing medical marijuana as a treatment for glaucoma or as a cancer treatment, I think that should be appropriate because there really is no difference between that and a doctor prescribing morphine or anything else."[12] He publicly vowed to end the Bush administration's crackdowns on providers of medical marijuana in states where it was legal. But, as president, Obama broke this promise: His SWAT team raids on medical-marijuana dispensaries exceeded those of George W. Bush, even though legalizing marijuana for medical purposes has long been overwhelmingly supported by the public.[13] As Rob Kampia, executive director of the Marijuana Policy Project, put it, "There's no question that Obama's the worst president on medical marijuana."[14] Ethan Nadelmann, director of Drug Policy Alliance, said, "The [Obama] administration is going after legal dispensaries and state and local authorities in ways that are going to push this stuff back underground again."[15] The governor of Rhode Island, Lincoln Chafee, a former Republican senator, described Obama's circumvention's of state [medical marijuana] laws as "utter chaos."[16]

As a presidential candidate, Obama also promised to "review drug sentences to see where we can . . . reduce the blind and counterproductive sentencing of nonviolent offenders."[17] The president has the power to free people who do not belong in jail; yet, after 55 months in office, he had granted only one commutation out of 8,126 applications—that is, 0.01 percent—the stingiest record of any president in recent years; even President Nixon granted 7 percent.[18] As recently as February 28, 2013, President Obama denied 1,500 commutation petitions; and, in late 2013, he commuted the sentences of eight drug offenders, out of more than 8,000 federal prisoners serving time under outdated crack cocaine laws.[19]

As an incoming president, Obama authorized a dramatic break from the drug war rhetoric and policy of previous administrations: His drug czar, Gil Kerlikowske, in his first press conference, assured the American people that the administration would eliminate the bellicose analogy with war that had been an obstacle to dealing with drug issues. He told *The Wall Street Journal* in May 2009 that "we're not at war with people in this country."[20] He said the administration would deal with drugs as a public health issue, rather than as a criminal justice issue alone.

But that turned out to be only rhetoric; the Obama administration did just the opposite: It beefed up the federal grants that rewarded police for arresting drug law violators, while criticizing President George W. Bush for cutting back on them.[21] In addition, the Pentagon under Obama increased the military equipment donated to police and multijurisdictional drug task forces, equipment used in SWAT raids.[22] In 2011, Craig Barrett, the program manager for the agency that oversees the Pentagon giveaways reported: "[This] has been a historic year for the program. We reutilized more than $500 million [in military hardware] . . . This passes the previous mark by several hundred million dollars."[23] As Radley Balko observed: "Millions of pieces of equipment designed for use on a battlefield—such as tanks, bayonets, M-16s, and armored personnel carriers—have been given to domestic police agencies for use on American streets, against American citizens."[24] By boosting antidrug grants, and the militarization of the police, Obama has bolstered the drug war.[25]

My purpose in focusing on Obama's about-face on U.S. drug policy is to neither criticize him nor excuse him, but to provide what seems to me to be a dramatic example of how powerful the forces are that support the war on drugs.

Part VII

Summary and Conclusions

CHAPTER 18

Inevitable Damages

Ramping up the drug war in the 1980s damaged our country in ways that were inevitable and should have been foreseeable. Laws made it profitable for state, local, and federal police to arrest nonviolent drug offenders and to confiscate their property without requiring clear and convincing evidence of a criminal charge. In addition, the Supreme Court, along with the rest of the country, had moved sharply to the right, diminishing the likelihood of constitutional protections against harsh and racially discriminatory drug laws.[1] Given these conditions, it was inevitable that many of our human and property rights would be eroded:

- Arrests and incarcerations for nonviolent drug offenses would soar, ruining the lives of thousands of individuals and their families, especially of racial minorities.
- Police would take advantage of the profits obtainable from the civil asset forfeiture laws, eroding Americans' property rights.
- SWAT teams would be motivated to raid homes in search of illicit drugs, resulting in injuries and fatalities to residents as well as officers.
- Law enforcement would devote fewer resources to profitless, nondrug crimes, such as assault, and manslaughter.
- The zero tolerance for drug law violators would result in police being unleashed to engage in random "consent" searches for illicit drugs on buses, trains, and highways, searches that would inevitably be racially biased.

A drug war would cause damages to society even if police did not directly profit from it. Drug law violations are victimless crimes, because buyers and sellers are willing transactors. Consequently, officers must go undercover to apprehend offenders. Corruption becomes unavoidable, because the war operates underground largely free of regulation and public scrutiny, and where police are subjected to bribes from profitable cartels. Some will succumb. There's an "unholy alliance" between undercover officers and drug lords, which is valuable to both parties.[2] That's the reason government crackdowns on corruption connected with drugs have been futile, which raises the question of whether honest law enforcement and a drug war can ever coexist. As Joseph D. McNamara, a former chief of police, put it: "As someone who spent 35 years wearing a police uniform, I've come to believe that hundreds of thousands of law-enforcement officers commit felony perjury every year testifying about drug arrests."[3]

Undercover police need informants to help them navigate the criminal underground in just about every type of crime, but the majority are used in drug crimes. Informants, a.k.a. snitches, are usually criminals. Their sole concern is getting their charges reduced or getting money by convincing prosecutors they have provided significant information. False informant testimony is common, and many defendants have been sent to prison as a result.[4]

Another characteristic of the drug war is that the percentage of violators who can feasibly be arrested is very small; for example, there are some 39 million illicit drug users, but there are only around 1.5 million people arrested a year for drug law offenses.[5] Police couldn't possibly arrest 39 million Americans a year. (The *total* number of annual arrests for *all* crimes is about 13 million.)[6] But the flip side of this impossibility is that police have enormous discretion as to where they send their troops to fight the war. How do they decide? If police stereotype blacks and Hispanics as drug felons—which overwhelming evidence finds that almost all of us do—they will target these groups. If, in addition, our laws fail to penalize law enforcement for racial discrimination—which is unfortunately the case—then we should not be surprised to find that people of color are disproportionately punished for drug offenses—which they are. *A war on drugs opens the door to inevitable racial injustices by law enforcement.*

Any war demonizes the enemy. In the drug war, that enemy includes some 125 million Americans over the age of 12 who have violated the drug laws at some time in their lives.[7] Over 500,000 are currently in U.S. prisons or jails because of drug offenses (a nonviolent crime); in addition, some 1.3 million are on parole or probation for drug law violations.[8] And these punishments are only the tip of the iceberg: Anyone convicted of even the most minor drug offense *will* face a maze of penalties that continue long after a prison sentence has been served, or parole and probation have ended. These offenders will have to struggle to regain full rights of citizenship. They will confront obstacles in obtaining health and welfare benefits, such as food stamps, public housing, and federal education assistance. They may have their driver's license suspended and lose their right to vote. They will be handicapped in finding a job and will find themselves blocked from many occupations because they have lost the eligibility for the required licenses.[9] Some of these punishments are meted out only to drug law violators, not to murderers or rapists.

Wars involve bloodshed, and the drug war is no exception: Drug cartels have no access to the legal system to settle disputes. They need weapons to protect themselves against police and each other, so they're well primed for battle; in addition, the turf is profitable and worth fighting for. The main cause of homicides linked to drug markets are turf battles between illicit drug cartels. The victims of this gang warfare are not only drug traffickers, they include police and innocent bystanders caught in the crossfire.[10]

Law enforcement profits from drug offenses, but earns zero profits from nondrug crimes. This differential creates an incentive for police to reallocate their efforts from nondrug to drug crimes. Rigorous empirical studies have shown that this relative profitability of drug arrests has been responsible for increases in other types of crime, including robbery, burglary, property crimes, violence, and even homicides.

Finally, when the government criminalizes the production and distribution of a drug, it surrenders the right to regulate its quality. Black market drugs are at risk of contamination, sometimes with toxic substances; they are also frequently of unknown potency, a major cause of overdoses. A public health hazard caused by the war has been well documented: Addicts who inject illicit drugs often wind up on the streets where they share needles. According to the Centers for Disease Control and Prevention, contaminated needles resulting from sharing are responsible for a quarter of the AIDS cases in the United States, including some 9,000 cases of AIDS among American children under the age of 13.[11]

CHAPTER 19

Drug War Benefits?

In this book we have focused on the harms caused by the war on drugs. But no public policy can be all bad. Can it?

According to the DEA, the goal of the drug war is to "dismantle major drug trafficking organizations and . . . remove drugs . . . from our neighborhoods."[1] Has this been accomplished? Consider the evidence:

If punitive prohibition had been successful and the drugs had been removed from our neighborhoods, the price of illicit drugs should have increased. In fact, the opposite happened. The price per pure gram of heroin, cocaine, crack, and methamphetamine have all dramatically declined. For example, in 1981, the price of cocaine was $669, while in 2011 it was $177, with similar price movements in the other hard drugs.[2] The average price of marijuana has revealed no trend.[3]

Even though the war failed to drive up drug prices, it might have succeeded in making drugs harder to obtain. Data pertinent to this question come from the University of Michigan Survey of high school seniors, which failed to reveal any pattern: The percentage of students who reported that marijuana, cocaine, crack, and heroin were "fairly easy or very easy to get" fluctuated from the 1980s to the present without any discernible trend.[4]

There have been several empirical studies of efforts by police to suppress drug trafficking and consumption. They invariably illustrate the futility of these attempts. For example:

- Mark Kleiman, in a classic study of a four-year police crackdown in Lawrence, Massachusetts, found an upsurge in violent crime but no evidence of a reduction in drug consumption.[5]

- The RAND Corporation analyzed an intensification of the drug war in 1986 in Washington, D.C. Law enforcement arrested 30,000 people in the first 17 months, but as soon as police operations returned to normal, so did the drug markets.[6]
- A police crackdown displaced a major drug gang in East Harlem, New York City, in 1992. Captain Ronald Welsh, the head of the narcotics unit said it was a "big case" and the most successful operation ever carried out. But he soon realized the benefits were short lived. "There's still heroin on that corner, other guys moved right in to pick up the slack."[7]
- ODALE[8] was the name of a temporary federal strike force created by President Nixon to curtail illicit drug transactions in Phoenix and San Diego. With the help of state and local police, ODALE arrested every drug dealer in those cities. The director of ODALE, retired judge Volney V. Brown, summed up the results this way: "We had spent tens of thousands of federal dollars, and sent scores of pushers to prison, but there was no lasting effect on the availability or price of illicit drugs."[9]

Because police crackdowns have failed to diminish illegal drug use, you might expect that the removal or relaxation of criminal sanctions would likewise have negligible effects on drug consumption; and, indeed, that's what the empirical studies have found. For example:

- In the 1970s, 11 states in the United States decriminalized possession of small amounts of marijuana. Studies found no difference in consumption in these states compared to those that did not. There are similar findings for Australia, Italy, and Spain.[10]
- In 1976, the Netherlands removed criminal penalties for using marijuana. A study by Peter Reuter and Robert J. MacCoun of the RAND Drug Policy Research Center found that "the change had little if any effect on levels of use during the first 7 years of the new regime."[11]
- In 2001, Portugal removed criminal penalties for possession of all street drugs including heroin and cocaine.[12] Drug usage rates have remained about the same, while deaths and sexually transmitted diseases have declined.[13]
- A 2008 Survey by the World Health Organization of 85,052 households in 11 countries, including the United States, found that the rates of marijuana and cocaine use were *not* related to the harshness of a country's drug policy.[14]

Further evidence of the ineffectiveness of criminal sanctions for illicit drug transactions comes from officers who have served on the front lines.

As Edward Ellison, former head of Scotland Yard's Anti-Drug Squad, summed it up: "We have attempted prohibition. All that happened was that courts became clogged with thousands of cases of small, individual users, and a generation of young people came to think of the police as their enemies. There were no resources left to fight other crime. I say legalize drugs because I want to see less drug abuse, not more."[15]

According to Raymond Kendall, former head of the international police force, Interpol: "Making drug abuse a crime is useless and even dangerous . . . Every year we seize more and more drugs and arrest more and more dealers but at the same time the quantity available in our countries still increases . . . Police are losing the drug battle worldwide."[16]

Former police chief Joseph D. McNamara points out the basic economic rationale as to why a war on drugs cannot succeed: "About $500 worth of heroin or cocaine in a source country brings as much a $100,000 on the streets of an American city. All the cops, armies, prisons, and executions in the world cannot impede a market with that kind of tax free markup. It is the illegality that permits the obscene markup."[17]

Former Seattle police chief Norm Stamper explains his opposition to drug prohibition: "We've arrested tens of millions of Americans for non-violent drug offenses, most for simple possession of marijuana. We've damaged or ruined the lives of countless citizens who've lost school loans, publicly subsidized housing, and jobs. And yet, drugs are more readily available—especially to our kids—at lower prices and higher levels of potency than in the history of the drug war . . . Even the staunchest drug warriors are in agreement: This is one war whose mission remains unaccomplished, a costly battle with no victory in sight."[18]

In a 2005 National Survey of 22,587 police chiefs and sheriffs, 82 percent answered "no" when asked: "Has the national war on drugs . . . been successful in reducing the use of illegal drugs?" (The percentage who answered "yes" as opposed to "no opinion" was not recorded.) In addition, over two-thirds said "yes" when asked if there had been an increase in "OxyContin and other Schedule II Narcotics" in their community.[19] Interestingly, in spite of the fact that more than four out of five officers believe the drug war is a failure, 61.2 percent of them oppose legalizing marijuana, even "for those who have a legitimate medical need for the drug."[20] By contrast, a national poll by AARP at about the same time as the police poll (November 2004), found that 72 percent agreed that "adults [should] be allowed to legally use marijuana for medical purposes if a physician recommends it."[21]

Scholars who study the drug war routinely condemn it, as do judges who are often forced to impose harsh sentences they see as outrageous. Here are a few examples:

"America's highly punitive policy of prohibition is intrusive, divisive, and expensive and leaves the United States with a drug problem that is worse than that of any other wealthy nation" (Robert J. MacCoun and Peter Reuter, RAND Drug Policy Research Center).[22]

"Deterrent strategies have not been successful in reducing drug use. Enforcement strategies have consumed resources, aggravated health risks associated with drugs, and increased levels of violence surrounding drug markets. Drug policy has also increased profits for drug dealers and attracted other young people into selling . . . Severe sentencing laws applied broadly and indiscriminately have undermined, rather than reinforced, the moral authority of the law" (*American Society of Criminology*).[23]

"[M]any of our drug laws are scandalously draconian and the sentences are often savage . . . The war on drugs has done considerable damage to the fourth amendment and . . . something is very wrong indeed when a person gets a longer sentence for marijuana than from espionage" (Judge Morris S. Arnold, U.S. Court of Appeals, Little Rock, Arkansas).[24]

"The day in the fall of 1988 that I was mandated to sentence Luis Quinones, an eighteen-year-old with no prior record, to ten years of real time because he was a bouncer in an apartment where drugs were being sold, I faced our national drug policy and . . . concluded that our present policy of criminal prohibition was a monumental error" (Robert W. Sweet, District Judge in New York City).[25]

Finally, even the former U.S. drug czar Gil Kerlikowske believes the drug war has failed! In May 2010 he told the *Associated Press*: "In the grand scheme, it has not been successful. Forty years later, the concern about drugs and drug problems is, if anything, magnified, intensified."[26]

Final Comment

Ending America's war on drugs would free enormous resources that could then be used for the benefit of our society. According to budgetary estimates by Jeffrey A. Miron and Katherine Waldock, our federal and state governments would gain around $88 billion a year (in 2008 dollars) by legalizing all street drugs—some $41 billion through eliminating the government spending needed to enforce the war, plus about $47 billion from additional tax revenues derivable from the currently illicit drugs. The total financial benefit to our governments from legalizing only marijuana would be around $17 billion.[27]

Regulated legalization would also bring health benefits: Illicit drugs would be safer because they would no longer be supplied by gangsters. Drugs from the black market are dangerous, because they are often contaminated and of unknown potency. Legalization would free consumers to access drugs of known quality and strength, and if they had problems they could seek medical help without fear of arrest.

This book has documented how the war against drugs has introduced corruption into our criminal justice system by allowing law enforcement to profit from drug arrests and property forfeitures. The consequent damages have been numerous and are deeply embedded in the social and legal fabric of our country. These include an erosion of our property rights, violent SWAT raids on our homes, and harsh punishments of millions of nonviolent Americans, especially men of color. The only way to deal a mortal blow to this corruption is to turn the control of *all* illicit drugs over to our governments, as we did with alcohol, rather than continuing to leave it in the hands of the underworld.

Notes

Introduction

1. See "A Living Death: Life without Parole for Nonviolent Offenses," by the ACLU Foundation, November 2013, pp. 156–157.

2. Haldeman's diary.

3. Ehrlichman interview with Dan Baum, and reported by him on radio in Boulder, CO, on February 24, 1998, available at http://you-tube.club/watch/?v=O-X7bAW43-c.

4. Reported in *The New York Times*, February 29, 1988.

5. "Casual Drug Users Should Be Shot, Gates Says," by Ronald J. Ostrow, *Los Angeles Times*, September 6, 1990.

6. The Comprehensive Crime Control Act of 1984; and "Edward Byrne Memorial Justice Assistance Grant Program; Legislative and Funding History," by Nathan James, *CRS Report for Congress*, January 12, 2007.

7. http://www.lpboulder.org/quotes/.

8. See *Drugs: America's Holy War*, by Arthur Benavie, pp. 90–92.

9. http://www.mapinc.org/drugnews/v03/n640/a07.html.

10. See, for example, "Breaking Down Holder's Move to Limit Civil Asset Forfeiture Abuse," by Radley Balko, *Washington Post*, January 16, 2015.

11. http://www.medscape.com/viewarticle/837011.

Chapter 1

1. The U.S. Supreme Court's ruling in *Webb v. United States* (1919) upheld the constitutionality of the Harrison Narcotic Act of 1914, which held that it was illegal for physicians to maintain addicts, who

were consequently forced to turn to the criminal black market to get their illicit drugs. The *Webb* decision inaugurated the drug prohibition era, which is still with us. See, for example, *Drugs: America's Holy War*, by Arthur Benavie, ch. 3, especially pp. 24–27.

2. See Ronald Reagan's remarks on signing Executive Order 12368, concerning federal drug abuse policy functions, June 24, 1982.

3. See the president's message announcing federal initiatives against drug trafficking and organized crime, in *Weekly Comp. Pres. Doc.*, vol. 18, October 14, 1982, pp. 1311, 1313–1314; See, for example, "Policing for Profit: The Drug War's Hidden Economic Agenda," by Eric Blumenson and Eva Nilsen, *University of Chicago Law Review*, vol. 65, no. 1, winter 1998, p. 45.

4. Ibid.

5. www.csmonitor.com/1986/0609/afill09a.html.

6. See "Policing for Profit," by Marian R. Williams, Jefferson E. Holcomb, Tomislav V. Kovandzic, and Scott Bullock, *Institute for Justice*, March 2010, p. 11.

7. See *Why Our Drug Laws Have Failed and What We Can Do about It*, 2nd ed., by Judge James P. Gray, 2012, p. 127; "Overview of Asset Forfeiture Law in the United States," by Stefan D. Cassella, *United States Attorneys' Bulletin*, 2007, p. 12; "Reforming the Civil Asset Reform Act," by Eric Moores, *Arizona Law Review*, vol. 51, no. 777, 2010, p. 787; and "The Forfeiture Racket," by Radley Balko, *Reason*, January 27, 2010.

8. "Policing for Profit," by Marian R. Williams, Jefferson E. Holcomb, Tomislav V. Kovandzic, and Scott Bullock, *Institute for Justice*, March 2010, p. 15.

9. Ibid., pp. 104, 161; *Forfeiting Our Property Rights*, by Rep. Henry Hyde, p. 7; "Civil Forfeiture: A Fiction That Offends Due Process," by David Benjamin Ross, *Regent University Law Review*, 2000, p. 268; and "Restoring Civility—The Civil Asset Reform Act of 2000: Baby Steps towards a More Civilized Civil Forfeiture System," by Barclay Thomas Johnson, *Indiana Law Review*, vol. 35, 2002, p. 1058.

10. *Drug Agent's Guide, Drug Enforcement Administration*, rev. ed. (1981; repr. 1987) by Harry L. Myers and Joseph Brzostowski, pp. 15–19.

11. "Overview of Asset Forfeiture Law in the United States," by Stefan D. Cassella, *United States Attorneys' Bulletin*, 2012, p. 12; "Reforming the Civil Asset Reform Act," by Eric Moores, *Arizona Law Review*, vol. 51, no. 777, 2010, p. 787; and, "The Forfeiture Racket," by Radley Balko, *Reason*, January 27, 2010, ascribing the 20 percent estimate

to attorney David Smith, author of the legal treatise *Prosecution and Defense of Forfeiture Cases.*

12. The authorized federal agencies are the FBI, DEA, Bureau of Alcohol, Tobacco, Firearms and Explosives (ATF), and the U.S. Postal Inspection Service (USPIS). Under limited circumstances, the U.S. Attorney's Office (USAO) may also directly adopt seizures. Department of Justice, *Guide to Equitable Sharing for State and Local Law Enforcement Agencies*, April 2009, pp. 2–3.

13. There was no defense for an innocent owner until the Civil Asset Forfeiture Reform Act of 2000 (CAFRA), which did not apply to the states. See Chapter 3.

14. See section IV, part A, General Authorization of Attorney General's Guidelines on Seized and Forfeited Property (July 1990), as specified in 28 U.S.C. § 524 (c).

15. In 1992, Congress extended the Equitable Sharing Program to include the U.S. Treasury by creating the Treasury Assets Forfeiture Fund. All Treasury agencies now make deposits into this fund, which is much smaller that the Justice Department's Fund; See "Policy Briefing," by Scott Ehlers, *The Drug Policy Foundation*, 1999, p. 6.

16. *A License to Steal*, by Leonard W. Levy, p. 23.

17. Prior to the Civil Asset Forfeiture Reform Act of 2000 (CAFRA), the standard to establish guilt was probable cause, a lower standard than preponderance of evidence. Probable cause is still the standard of proof for federal seizures by customs agents and other Treasury agencies, as opposed to the higher standard required of the DEA or FBI, agencies of the Department of Justice. The majority of federal forfeitures are made by the Justice Department. See, for example, "Restoring Civility—The Civil Asset Reform Act of 2000: Baby Steps towards a More Civilized Civil Forfeiture System," by Barclay Thomas Johnson, *Indiana Law Review*, vol. 35, 2002.

18. See "Policing for Profit," by Marian R. Williams, Jefferson E. Holcomb, Tomislav V. Kovandzic, and Scott Bullock, *Institute for Justice*, March 2010, p. 47.

19. Ibid., pp. 12–13.

20. Ibid., p. 7.

21. Ibid., p. 15.

22. Ibid., p. 80, and interviews by the author with a former member of the narcotics squad in Chapel Hill, NC.

23. "Escalating the War on Drugs: Causes and Unintended Consequences" by Bruce Benson, *Stanford Law & Policy Review*, March 22, 2009, p. 9.

24. See "Policing for Profit," by Marian R. Williams, Jefferson E. Holcomb, Tomislav V. Kovandzic, and Scott Bullock, *Institute for Justice*, March 2010, p. 8.

25. "Civil Asset Forfeiture and Federal Equitable Sharing," by Marian R. Williams, Jefferson E. Holcomb, and Tomislav V. Kovandzic, posted November 6, 2012, by *ASU News* filed under General, Government and Justice Studies, Research, Today.

26. *A License to Steal*, by Leonard L. Levy, p. 144; and "Are Seizures Legalized Theft?" by David Cauchon, *USA Today*, May 18, 1992.

27. Quoted in *Forfeiting Our Property Rights*, by Rep. Henry Hyde, p. 29.

28. See "The Forfeiture Racket," by Radley Balko, *Reason*, January 27, 2010.

29. http://www.washingtonpost.com/sf/investigative/2014/09/06/stop-and-seize.

30. "Addicted to the Drug War: The Role of Civil Asset Forfeiture as Budgetary Necessity in Contemporary Law Enforcement," by John L. Worrall, *Journal of Criminal Justice*, vol. 29, 2001, pp. 171–187.

31. "Drug Enforcement's Double-Edged Sword. An Assessment of Asset Forfeiture Programs," by M. Miller and L. Selva, *Justice Quarterly*, vol. 11, 1994, p. 325.

32. Student interview of an officer in North Carolina who had worked in the narcotics squad, March 2010.

33. See, for example, http://www.wral.com/news/local/story/6833320.

34. Ibid.

35. "A Fine Too Far: State Stamp Laws for Drugs Make a Mockery of the Tax Code," *The Economist*, February 18, 2010.

36. Executive Office for U.S. Attorneys, Department of Justice, *U.S. Attorneys Bulletin*, vol. 38, no. 180, 1990, quoted in *Forfeiting Our Property Rights*, by Rep. Henry Hyde, p. 35. The attorney general in 1990 was Richard Lewis "Dick" Thornburgh.

37. "The Forfeiture Racket," by Radley Balko, *Reason*, January 27, 2010.

38. *The New York Times*, September 3, 1993, p. A17.

39. "Presumed Guilty: The Laws Victims in the War on Drugs," by Andrew Schneider and Mary Pat Flaherty, *Pittsburgh Press*, August 11–September 16, 1991, cited in *Forfeiting Our Property Rights*, by Rep. Henry Hyde, p. 6.

40. http://www.justice.gov/opa/pr/attorney-general-prohibits-federal-agency-adoptions-assets-seized-state-and-local-law. Accessed January 16, 2015.

41. See "Holder Limits Seized-Asset Sharing Process That Split Billions with Local, State Police," by Robert O'Harrow Jr., Sari Horwitz, and Steven Rich, *The Washington Post*, January 16, 2015.

42. http://www.justice.gov/opa/pr/attorney-general-prohibits-federal-agency-adoptions-assets-seized-state-and-local-law; and, for example, "Eric Holder's Asset Forfeiture Decision Won't Stop the Widespread Abuse of Police Power," by Jonathan Banks, *New Republic*, January 15, 2015.

43. See, for example, "Despite Holder's Forfeiture Reform, Cops Still Have a License to Steal," by Jacob Sullum, *Forbes*, January 22, 2015.

44. http://www.justice.gov/opa/pr/attorney-general-prohibits-federal-agency-adoptions-assets-seized-state-and-local-law.

45. See, for example, "How Much Civil Asset Forfeiture Will Holder's New Policy Actually Prevent?" by Radley Balko, *The Washington Post*, January 20, 2015.

46. Ibid. Smith's statement is in response to questions from Radley Balko.

47. "Holder Limits Seized-Asset Sharing Process That Split Billions with Local, State Police," by Robert O'Harrow Jr., Sari Horwitz, and Steven Rich, *The Washington Post*, January 16, 2015.

48. Ibid.

49. Ibid.

50. "Policing for Profit," by Marian R. Williams, Jefferson E. Holcomb, Tomislav V. Kovandzic, and Scott Bullock, *Institute for Justice*, March 2010, p. 80. The only state that does not have a civil asset forfeiture program is North Carolina, where only criminal asset forfeiture is allowed.

51. As shown in ibid., part II: States are legally entitled to receive 100 percent of the value of forfeitures in 26 states, while 17 states are certified to receive less than 100 percent, but often wind up getting all or most of it. It's only in 8 states that police and prosecutors are barred from getting any profits from forfeitures. There are also other differences between the state forfeiture laws and the federal law; for example, the required burden of proof necessary to convict property is higher than that of the Department of Justice in 15 states, but lower in 9, with the same in the rest. In addition, in 6 states the property owner is assumed innocent, while, in the rest of the states as well as under federal law, the property owner is assumed guilty until proven innocent.

52. *Rise of the Warrior Cop*, by Radley Balko, pp. 221–222.

53. See "Edward Byrne Memorial Justice Assistance Grant Program: Legislative and Funding History," by Nathan James, *CRS Report to*

Congress, January 12, 2007, pp. 2–3. Additional grants were established by Congress during the 1990s. Whatever their stated purpose—whether it was community policing or programs to fight local crime—researchers found that there's no way to control how grant money was spent once police departments receive it.

54. "A Special Report: Hooked on SWAT," by Steven Elbow, *Capital Times,* August 18, 2001.

55. *Rise of the Warrior Cop,* by Radley Balko, p. 243.

56. Uniform Crime Reports, Crime in the United States, FBI, annual.

57. "How the Government Bribes Police to Arrest People for Smoking Pot," by Aaron Cantu, *Alternet,* June 5, 2014.

58. See, for example, *Drugs: America's Holy War,* by Arthur Benavie, pp. 68–69.

59. "7 Ways the Obama Administration Has Accelerated Police Militarization," by Radley Balko, The Huffington Post, July 10, 2013.

60. "Overview of the American Recovery and Reinvestment Act of 2009," U.S. Department of Justice, available at www.ojp.usdoj.gov /recovery.

61. See "Escalating the War on Drugs: Causes and Unintended Consequences," by Bruce Benson, *Stanford Law & Policy Review,* March 22, 2009, pp. 10–11. The provision was section 6077.

62. Ibid., p. 10.

63. Ibid.

64. Ibid.

65. See "Holder Limits Seized-Asset Sharing Process That Split Billions with Local, State Police," by Robert O'Harrow Jr., Sari Horwitz, and Steven Rich, *The Washington Post,* January 16, 2015.

66. "The Next Stage of Forfeiture Reform," by Eric D. Blumenson and Eva Nilsen, *Federal Sentencing Reporter,* vol. 14, no. 2, September/ October 2000, pp. 14–15.

67. *Forfeiting Our Property Rights,* by Rep. Henry Hyde, pp. 50–51.

68. Ibid., p. 50.

69. "Crime in the United States 2013—Arrests," *FBI Uniform Crime Report* (Washington, D.C.: U.S. Dept. of Justice, November 2014), p. 2.

70. See "Prisoners in 2011," *Bureau of Justice Statistics,* by E. A. Carson and W. J. Sabol, U.S Department of Justice (Washington, D.C., 2012); "A 25-Year Quagmire: The War on Drugs and Its Impact on American Society," *The Sentencing Project,* by M. Mauer and R. King (Washington, D.C., 2007).

71. See *War Comes Home,* by the ACLU, June 2014, pp. 37–38.

Chapter 2

1. See "Policing for Profit," by Marian R. Williams, Jefferson E. Holcomb, Tomislav V. Kovandzic, and Scott Bullock, *Institute for Justice*, March 2010, p. 28.

2. *United States v. $124,700*, 458 F.3d 822 (8th Cir. 2006).

3. See, for example, "Cocaine Contaminates Majority of U.S. Currency," *Scientific American*, by David Biello, August 16, 2009.

4. "Policing for Profit," by Marian R. Williams, Jefferson E. Holcomb, Tomislav V. Kovandzic, and Scott Bullock, *Institute for Justice*, March 2010, p. 16.

5. Ibid.

6. Ibid.

7. See http://www.cnn.com/2009/CRIME/05/05/texas.police.seizures/.

8. Ibid.

9. "Reforming the Civil Asset Reform Act," by Eric Moores, *Arizona Law Review*, vol. 51, no. 777, 2010, p. 787; and "The Forfeiture Racket," by Radley Balko, *Reason,* January 27, 2010, ascribing the 20 percent estimate to attorney David Smith, author of the legal treatise *Prosecution and Defense of Forfeiture Cases.*

10. See, for example, "The Forfeiture Racket: Police and Prosecutors Won't Give Up Their License to Steal," by Radley Balko, *Reason,* January 27, 2010; and "Anthony Smelley Will Get His Money Back," by Radley Balko, *The Agitator*, February 26, 2010.

11. Ibid.

12. See, for example, "The Drug War's Hidden Economic Agenda," by Eric D. Blumenson and Eva Nilsen, *The Nation*, March 9, 1998.

13. "Reforming the Civil Asset Reform Act," by Eric Moores, *Arizona Law Review*, vol. 51, no. 777, 2010, p. 788.

14. "Drug Enforcement's Double-Edged Sword: An Assessment of Asset Forfeiture Programs," by J. Mitchell Miller and Lance H. Selva, *Justice Quarterly*, vol. 11, no. 2, June 1994, p. 319.

15. "The Next Stage of Forfeiture Reform," by Eric D. Blumenson and Eva Nilsen, *Federal Sentencing Reporter,* vol. 14, no. 2, September/October 2001, p. 8.

Chapter 3

1. See "Police Seize 'Drug House'" by Kari Pugh, *Fredericksburg News*, March 23, 2004; and "Dealer Sent to Prison," by Keith Epps, *Fredericksburg News,* January 6, 2005.

2. Ibid.

3. See "Police Seize 'Drug House'" by Kari Pugh, *Fredericksburg News*, March 23, 2004; and "Dealer Sent to Prison," by Keith Epps, *Fredericksburg News,* January 6, 2005.

4. Ibid.

5. *Calero-Toledo v. Pearson Yacht Leasing Co.* 416 U.S. 663 668 (1974); and, for example, "Restoring Civility—The Civil Asset Forfeiture Reform Act of 2000: Baby Steps towards a More Civilized Civil Forfeiture System," by Barclay Thomas Johnson, *Indiana Law Review*, vol. 35, 2002, pp. 1054–1055.

6. *Bennis v. Michigan* (94–8729), 517 U.S. 1163 (1996); and "Restoring Civility—The Civil Asset Forfeiture Reform Act of 2000: Baby Steps towards a More Civilized Civil Forfeiture System," by Barclay Thomas Johnson, *Indiana Law Review*, vol. 35, 2002, pp. 1054–1055.
7516. U.S. 442 (1996), p. 456.

8. "Almost Blind Justice: Sometimes, Even the Innocent Are Guilty," by Stephen Chapman, *Chicago Tribune*, March 7, 1996.

9. "Legal Fiction and Forfeiture: An Historical Analysis of the Civil Asset Forfeiture Reform Act," by Todd Barnet, *Duquesne University Law Review*, fall 2001, p. 17.

10. The source for this data is "Policing for Profit," by Marian R. Williams, Jefferson E. Holcomb, Tomislav V. Kovandzic, and Scott Bullock, *Institute for Justice*, March 2010, part II.

11. See, for example, "Hold on to Your Assets: The Supreme Court Reviews Illinois' Awful Asset Forfeiture Law," by Radley Balko, *Reason*, September 8, 2009; "Justices Hear Arguments on Property Seized by Police," by Adam Liptak, *The New York Times*, October 14, 2009; and "Justices Hint Seizure Case May Be Moot," by DMC-ADMIN, *Wisconsin Law Journal*, October 19, 2009.

12. "Justices Hear Arguments on Property Seized by Police," by Adam Liptak, *The New York Times*, October 14, 2009.

13. See http://www.law.cornell.edu/supct/html/08-351.ZO.html.

14. "Hold on to Your Assets: The Supreme Court Reviews Illinois' Awful Asset Forfeiture Law," by Radley Balko, *Reason*, September 8, 2009.

15. "The Forfeiture Racket: Police and Prosecutors Won't Give Up Their License to Steal," by Radley Balko, *Reason*, January 27, 2010; and "Reforming the Civil Asset Forfeiture Reform Act," by Eric Moores, *Arizona Law Review*, pp. 797–799.

16. http://www.justice.gov/jmd/afp/02fundreport/2014affr/report2b.htm.

17. "The Forfeiture Racket: Police and Prosecutors Won't Give Up Their License to Steal," by Radley Balko, *Reason*, January 27, 2010.

18. See *Department of Justice Forfeiture Assets Fund*, January 2014, p. 7. Available at http://www.justice.gov/afp/annual-financial-statements.

19. http://www.justice.gov/jmd/afp/01programaudit/index.htm.

20. See, for example, "Policing for Profit: The Drug War's Hidden Economic Agenda," by Eric Blumenson and Eva Nilsen, *The University of Chicago Law Review*, vol. 65, no. 1, winter 1998, p. 42.

21. See "Drug Agents' Guide to Forfeiture of Assets," *Drug Enforcement Administration*, U.S. Department of Justice, 1987.

22. "Reforming the Civil Drug Forfeiture Statutes: Analysis and Recommendations," by William Carpenter, *Temple Law Review*, 1994, p. 1104.

23. "Civil Forfeiture: A Fiction That Offends Due Process," by David Benjamin Ross, *Regent University Law Review*, 2000, p. 261.

24. "Reforming the Civil Drug Forfeiture Statutes: Analysis and Recommendations," by William Carpenter, *Temple Law Review*, 1994, pp. 1105–1107.

25. "Civil Forfeiture: A Fiction That Offends Due Process," by David Benjamin Ross, *Regent University Law Review*, 2000, pp. 261–262.

26. *A License to Steal*, by Leonard W. Levy, p. 88.

27. *Caplin & Crysdale, Chartered v. United States*, 491 U.S. 617,629 (1989); See, for example, "Restored Civility—The Civil Asset Forfeiture Reform Act of 2000: Baby Steps towards A More Civilized Civil Forfeiture System," by Barclay Thomas Johnson, *Indiana Law Review*, vol. 35, 2001, p. 29, 1045.

28. For example, see "Widowed Cancer Survivor Fights Federal Land Seizure," by Scott Johnson, *Montgomery Advertiser*, September 27, 2009.

29. Ibid.

30. Ibid.

31. http://docs.justia.com/cases/federal/district-courts/alabama/almd ce/2:2007cv00694/36133/107/.

32. See, for example, "Crime Pays for Police," by Larry Salzman, *Boston Herald*, October 10, 2011.

33. http://ij.org/massachusetts-civil-forfeiture-release-1-24-2013.

Chapter 4

1. See "Militarizing American Police: The Rise and Normalization of Paramilitary Units," by Peter B. Kraska and Victor E. Kappeler, *Social*

Problems, vol. 44, no. 1, February 1997, p. 4; See, also, "Overkill: The Rise of Paramilitary Police Raids in America," by Radley Balko, *CATO Institute*, 2006.

2. "Militarizing American Police: The Rise and Normalization of Paramilitary Units," by Peter B. Kraska and Victor E. Kappeler, *Social Problems*, vol. 44, no. 1, February 1997, p. 1.

3. *Rise of the Warrior Cop*, by Radley Balko, p. 308.

4. "Soldiers of the Drug War Remain on Duty," by Timothy Egan, *The New York Times*, March 1, 1999.

5. "Militarizing American Police: The Rise and Normalization of Paramilitary Units," by Peter B. Kraska and Victor E. Kappeler, *Social Problems*, vol. 44, no. 1, February 1997, p. 3.

6. Ibid., p. 4.

7. "A Special Report: Hooked on SWAT," by Steven Elbow, *Capital Times*, August 18, 2001.

8. See "SWAT Teams," by Radley Balko in The Huffington Post, November 12, 2011.

9. "A Special Report: Hooked on SWAT," by Steven Elbow, *Capital Times*, August 18, 2001.

10. Ibid.

11. Ibid.

12. "SWAT Teams," by Radley Balko in The Huffington Post, November 12, 2011; and *Rise of the Warrior Cop*, by Radley Balko, pp. 206–210.

13. "War Comes Home," by the ACLU, June 2014, pp. 2, 37.

14. Ibid., p. 38, and figure 7.

15. "Drug Raids Usually Hit Mark, Occasionally Bomb," by Craig Jarvis, *Raleigh News and Observer*, July 7, 1998.

16. "Suburban Family Terrorized as Cops Raid Wrong House," by Jon Sall, *Chicago Sun-Times*, March 28, 1998.

17. "Kelly Sticks Up for Cop Searches," by Frankie Edozien, *New York Post*, June 5, 2003; and "More NYPD No-Knocks: New Yorkers Tell Their Tales of Botched Raids," by Rivka Gewirtz, *Village Voice*, June 18–24, 2003.

18. "Researching the Police Military Blur: Lessons Learned," by Peter Kraska, *Police Forum*, vol. 14, no. 3, 2005, p. 43.

19. *America's Longest War*, by Steven B. Duke and Albert C. Gross, p. 123; and *Why Our Drug Laws Have Failed and What We Can Do about It*, 2nd ed., by Judge James P. Gray, p. 96. See the Supreme Court ruling in *Illinois v. Gates*, 462 U.S. 313 (1983).

20. *Wilson v. Arkansas* (1995).

21. *Hudson v. Michigan* (2006).

22. See "Overkill: The Rise of Paramilitary Police Raids in America," by Radley Balko, *CATO Institute*, 2006, p. 5.

23. Ibid., p. 1.

24. Ibid.

25. "SWAT Raid Roughs Up Wrong Guys," by Jesse Bogan, *San Antonio News-Express*, November 21, 2002.

26. "Warrant Targets Wrong Home, Wrong Man," by Adam Wright, *The Chronicle-Telegram*, June 28, 2006.

27. See "Overkill: The Rise of Paramilitary Police Raids in America," by Radley Balko, *CATO Institute*, 2006, p. 32.

28. "Jury Finds Winnabow Man Guilty in Assault on Officer," by Millard K. Ives, *Wilmington Morning Star*, October 30, 2002; See *State of North Carolina v. Pellham*, no. COA03-636, filed: May 4, 2004.

29. "'It Just Went Wrong,' Sheriff Says of Slaying," by Phillip Ramati and Joe Kovac Jr., *Macon Telegraph*, April 5, 2006.

30. "Georgia Supreme Court Says Accused Cop Killers Eligible for Death Penalty," by Celeste Smith, NewsCentralGA.com, November 22, 2010; see http://caselaw.findlaw.com/ga-supreme-court/1010031 .html.

31. "Fair Pleads Guilty, Sentenced to Life in Whitehead Slaying," by Amy Leigh Womack, *The Telegraph*, June 15, 2012.

32. http://www.13wmaz.com/news/story.aspx?storyid=204074.

33. See http://www.youtube.com/watch?v=6b-67q0vlCw for a list of YouTube videos of SWAT raids.

Chapter 5

1. *California v. Acevedo*, 111 S. Ct. 1982, 2002 (1991); and *Smoke and Mirrors*, by Dan Baum, pp. 177–179.

2. *The New Jim Crow*, by Michelle Alexander, pp. 134–136.

3. *Harmelin v. Michigan*, 111 S. Ct. 2680, 2706 (1991).

4. www.justice.gov/dea/agency/penalties.htm.

5. *Sourcebook of Criminal Justice Statistics*, Bureau of Justice Statistics, U.S, Department of Justice, 2008, table 5.31.

6. *Hutto v. Davis*, 454 U.S. 370 (1982).

7. Ibid.; see, also, "Supreme Court Roundup; 40-Year Drug Term Held 'Legislative Prerogative,'" Special to *The New York Times*, January 12, 1982; and *The New Jim Crow*, by Michelle Alexander, p. 89.

8. *Harmelin v. Michigan*, 111 S. Ct. 2680, 2706 (1991).

9. *The New Jim Crow*, by Michelle Alexander, p. 89.

10. "The Hidden Problem of Time Served in Prison," by Marc Mauer, *Social Research*, summer 2007, pp. 701–703.

11. *Why Our Drug Laws Have Failed and What We Can Do about It*, 2nd ed., by Judge James P. Gray, pp. 105–106.

12. *Alabama v. White*, 496 U.S. 325 (1990), pp. 328–332; and *Illinois v. Gates*, 462 U.S. 213 (1983).

13. *Rise of the Warrior Cop*, by Radley Balko, pp. 150–151; and *Smoke and Mirrors*, by Dan Baum, pp. 177–179.

14. *US v. Leon*, 468 U.S. 897 (1984).

15. *Why Our Drug Laws Have Failed and What We Can Do about It*, 2nd ed., by Judge James P. Gray, p. 107.

16. *Rise of the Warrior Cop*, by Radley Balko, p. 151.

17. See *No Equal Justice*, by David Cole, pp. 16–22; and http://supreme.justia.com/cases/federal/us/501/429/case.html. See, also, *The New Jim Crow*, by Michelle Alexander, pp. 63–65.

18. "The Right to Be Secure," by Joseph P. Kahn, *Boston Globe Magazine*, April 7, 1991; also, *No Equal Justice*, by David Cole, p. 16.

19. *No Equal Justice*, by David Cole, pp. 17–19; and *Bostick v. State*, 554 So. 2d, pp. 1153, 1158, Florida, 1989.

20. Ibid.

21. 501 U.S. 429 111 S.Ct. 2382 115 L.Ed.2d 389 Florida, Petitioner, Terrance Bostick, available at https://bulk.resource.org/courts.gov/c/US/501/501.US.429.89-1717.html.

22. Ibid.

23. *No Equal Justice*, by David Cole, p. 18.

24. Ibid., p. 19; see 501 U.S. 429 111 S.Ct. 2382 115 L.Ed.2d 389 Florida, Petitioner, Terrance Bostick, available at https://bulk.resource.org/courts.gov/c/US/501/501.US.429.89-1717.html.

25. "Black and Blue Encounters' Some Preliminary Thoughts about Fourth Amendment Seizures: Should Race Matter?" by Tracey Maclin, *Valparaiso University Law Review*, vol. 26, no. 243, 1991, p. 248. Available at: http://scholar.valpo.edu/vulr/vol26/iss1/19.

26. Ibid., p. 262.

27. Ibid., pp. 249–250.

28. *No Equal Justice,* by David Cole, pp. 39–40; and, *The New Jim Crow*, by Michelle Alexander, pp. 56–57, 105–106.

29. *Whren v. United States*, 517 U.S. 806 (1996).

30. *Ohio v. Robinette* (95–891), 519 U.S. 33 (1996); *No Equal Justice,* by David Cole, pp. 30–31; and *The New Jim Crow*, by Michelle Alexander, p. 67.

31. 73 Ohio St. 3d, at 650, 653 N. E. 2d, at 696.

32. *Ohio v. Robinette* (95–891), 519 U.S. 33 (1996).

33. See *Schneckloth v. Bustamonte*, 412 U.S. 231 (1973).

34. Ibid.; See "Fourth Amendment Lessons from the Highway and the Subway: A Principled Approach to Suspicionless Searches," by Ricardo J. Bascuas, *Rutgers Law Journal,* vol. 38, 2007, pp. 763–764.

35. See, for example, "Fourth Amendment Lessons from the Highway and the Subway: A Principled Approach to Suspicionless Searches," by Ricardo J. Bascuas, *Rutgers Law Journal*, vol. 38, 2007, pp. 761–769; *Profiles in Injustice*, by David A. Harris, ch. 3; and *The New Jim Crow*, by Michelle Alexander, pp. 69–71.

36. "Driving While Black," by Gary Webb, *Esquire*, April 1, 1999; and, *Profiles in Injustice*, by David A. Harris, pp. 22–23.

37. Ibid.

38. "Fourth Amendment Lessons from the Highway and the Subway: A Principled Approach to Suspicionless Searches," by Ricardo J. Bascuas, *Rutgers Law Journal*, vol. 38, 2007, p. 763; and *The New Jim Crow*, by Michelle Alexander, p. 70.

39. Ibid.

40. "Flawed Enforcement: Why Drug Task Force Highway Interdiction Violates Rights, Wastes Tax Dollars, and Fails to Limit the Availability of Drugs in Texas," by Scott Henson, *American Civil Liberties Union—Texas Chapter*, p. 11.

41. See "Fourth Amendment Lessons from the Highway and the Subway: A Principled Approach to Suspicionless Searches," by Ricardo J. Bascuas, *Rutgers Law Journal*, vol. 38, 2007, p. 762.

42. Ibid., p. 763.

43. Ibid., p. 766.

44. *United States. v. Place*, 462 U.S. 696 (1983).

45. "Sniffing Out the Fourth Amendment: Ten Years Later," by Hope Walker Hall, *Maine Law Review*, vol. 46, 1994, pp. 151–152.

46. See *Illinois v. Caballes*, 543 U.S. 405 (2005); "Fourth Amendment Lessons from the Highway and the Subway: A Principled Approach to Suspicionless Searches," by Ricardo J. Bascuas, *Rutgers Law Journal*, vol. 38, 2007, p. 762; *The New Jim Crow*, by Michelle Alexander, pp. 69–70; and *Profiles in Injustice*, by David A. Harris, pp. 48–52.

47. *Illinois v. Caballes*, 543 U.S. 405 (2005).

48. http://www.oyez.org/cases/2010-2019/2012/2012_11_817. One restriction on the use of drug-sniffing dogs is at the front door of a house, which was ruled by the Court to be a search for purposes of the Fourth Amendment in *Florida v. Jardines* (2013).

49. *Rodriguez v. United States*, April 21, 2015.

50. Two Chapel Hill, NC, police officers that I interviewed told me that the Supreme Court ruling in Rodriguez would have no effect on their use of dog sniffs in traffic stops.

51. For the evidence and citations referred to in this paragraph, see "Policing for Profit," by Marian R. Williams, Jefferson E. Holcomb, Tomislav V. Kovandzic, and Scott Bullock, *Institute for Justice*, March 2010, p. 24. (The 2009 study can be found in an article in *Scientific American*, August 16, 2009, by D. Biello.)

52. Ibid.

53. *Why Our Drug Laws Have Failed and What We Can Do about It*, 2nd ed., by James P. Gray, p. 73.

54. "An Assault, a SWAT Team, a Drug Raid, and Some Sex Toys," by Radley Balko, The Huffington Post, November 26, 2011.

55. *Why Our Drug Laws Have Failed and What We Can Do about It*, 2nd ed., by James P. Gray, p. 70; and "1 in 3 Killers in LA County Are Punished," *Los Angeles Times*, December 1, 1996, Orange County ed., p. A1.

56. "An Assault, a SWAT Team, a Drug Raid, and Some Sex Toys," by Radley Balko, The Huffington Post, November 26, 2011.

57. For a discussion of the statistical studies touched on here, see "The War on Drugs: A Public Bad," by Bruce L. Benson, a paper prepared for a *Research Symposium on Bad Public Goods*, Northwestern University School of Law, September 2008, pp. 13–36.

58. See "The Impact of Marijuana Law Enforcement in an Economic Model of Crime," by Edward M. Shepard and Paul R. Blackley, *Journal of Drug Issues*, vol. 37, spring 2007, pp. 407–408; and the discussion in *Drug War Harms*, by Jeffrey A. Miron, ch. 4.

59. See, for example, *Drugs: America's Holy War*, by Arthur Benavie, pp. 35–42; and Chapter 18.

60. "An Empirical Analysis of Imprisoning Drug Offenders," by Ilyana Kuziemko and Steve D. Levitt, *Journal of Public Economics*, 88 (2004) 2043–2066.

Chapter 6

1. Ibid.; and http://www.law.cornell.edu/supct/html/95-5841.ZO.html.

2. See, for example, "Fourth Amendment Lessons from the Highway and the Subway: A Principled Approach to Suspicionless Searches," by Ricardo J. Bascuas, *Rutgers Law Journal*, vol. 38, 2007, p. 760.

3. See *McCleskey v. Kemp* 481 U.S. 279, 327 (1989) Brennan, J. dissenting, available at http://www.law.cornell.edu/supct/html/historics

/USSC_CR_0481_0279_ZO.html, Justice J. Powell delivered the decision of the Court. See also *No Equal Justice*, by David Cole, pp. 132–141; *The New Jim Crow*, by Michelle Alexander, pp. 106–109; and, *Unequal under Law*, by Doris Marie Provine, pp. 146–148, 156.

4. Ibid.

5. *McCleskey v. Kemp*, 481 U.S. 279 (1987); see, for example, http://www.law.cornell.edu/supct/html/historics/USSC_CR_0481_0279_ZD2 .html.

6. Ibid.; see, for example, *The New Jim Crow*, by Michelle Alexander, pp. 108–109.

7. Ibid.

8. See, for example, *Mobile v. Bolden* (1980), which upheld the principal for an election system; also, see *The Case against the Supreme Court*, ch. 1, by Erwin Chemerinsky.

9. See "Incarceration and the Imbalance of Power," by Angela J. Davis in *Invisible Punishment*, edited by Marc Mauer and Meda Chesney-Lind, pp. 63–65; and *The New Jim Crow*, by Michelle Alexander, p. 112.

10. "Incarceration and the Imbalance of Power," by Angela J. Davis in *Invisible Punishment*, edited by Marc Mauer and Meda Chesney-Lind, p. 63.

11. *Yick Wo v. Hopkins* (1886).

12. See *No Equal Justice*, by David Cole, pp. 157–161; *Unequal under Law*, by Doris Marie Provine, pp. 147–148; "Incarceration and the Imbalance of Power," by Angela J. Davis in *Invisible Punishment*, edited by Marc Mauer and Meda Chesney-Lind, pp. 63–65; and *The New Jim Crow*, by Michelle Alexander, pp. 113–116.

13. *No Equal Justice*, by David Cole, p. 160.

14. Ibid.; and *United States v. Armstrong*, 517 U.S. 456 (1996), opinion of the Court.

15. Ibid.

16. *No Equal Justice*, by David Cole, p. 159; and *The New Jim Crow*, by Michelle Alexander, pp. 114–115.

17. *The New Jim Crow*, by Michelle Alexander, p. 115.

18. Ibid., pp. 134–135; and *Unequal under Law*, by Doris Marie Provine, pp. 154–156.

19. *Whitewashing Race*, a collaborative effort by Michael K. Brown, Martin Carnoy, Elliott Currie, Troy Duster, David B. Oppenheimer, Marjorie M. Shultz, and David Wellman, 2003, p. 38.

20. "Content of Our Categories," by Linda Hamilon Krieger, *Stanford Law Review*, 1995, p. 1171.

21. *The New Jim Crow*, by Michelle Alexander, p. 134; *Whitewashing Race* a collaborative effort by Michael K. Brown, Martin Carnoy, Elliott Currie, Troy Duster, David B. Oppenheimer, Marjorie M. Shultz, and David Wellman, 2003, pp. 38–39; *Unequal under Law*, by Doris Marie Provine, pp. 154–156; and "Behind the Court's Civil Rights Ruling," by David Dante Troutt, *The New York Times*, April 29, 2001.

Chapter 7

1. *The New Jim Crow*, by Michelle Alexander, pp. 98–99.

2. "The Automaticity of Race and Afrocentric Facial Features in Social Judgments," by Irene V. Blair, Charles M. Judd, and Jennifer L. Fallman, *Journal of Personality and Social Psychology*, vol. 87, no. 6, 2004, p. 764.

3. "The Associated Press Racial Attitudes Survey," October 29, 2012, p. 29.

4. "The Police Officer's Dilemma: Using Ethnicity to Disambiguate Potentially Threatening Individuals," by Joshua Correll, Bernadette Park, Charles M. Judd, and Bernd Wittenbrink., *Journal of Personality and Social Psychology*, vol. 83, no. 6, 2002, pp. 1314–1329. See, also, "Seeing Black: Race, Crime, and Visual Processing," by Jennifer Eberhardt, Valerie J. Purdie, Phillip Atiba Goff, and Paul G. Davies, *Journal of Personality and Social Psychology*, vol. 87, no. 6, 2004, pp. 876–893; and "Prejudice and Perception: The Role of Automatic and Controlled Processes in Misperceiving a Weapon," by B. Keith Payne, *Journal of Personality and Social Psychology*, vol. 81, no. 2, 2001, pp. 181–192. For a summary, see *The New Jim Crow*, by Michelle Alexander, pp. 103–105.

5. See, for example, "Race and Criminal Justice," by Alfred Blumstein, in *America Becoming: Racial Trends and Their Consequences*, vol. 11, edited by Neil Smelser, William Julius Wilson, and Faith Mitchell, 2001, pp. 23–24; and *When Prisoners Come Home*, by Joan Petersilia, p. 28.

6. See also *Malign Neglect*, by Michael Tonry, pp. 65–66, table 2–3. These data on the differential rates of violent crimes by whites versus blacks do not control for other relevant factors that could account for these crime rates, such as, poverty, discrimination, or incarceration history.

7. "Elements of Well-Being Affected by Criminalizing the Drug User: An Overview," by Martin Y. Iguchi, Jennifer A. London, Nell Griffith Forge, *Public Health Reports, National Institute of Drug Abuse*, vol. 117,

supplement 1, 2002, p. S147, available at http://www.ncbi.nlm.nih
.gov/pmc/articles/PMC1913697/pdf/pubhealthrep00207-0151.pdf.

8. Ibid.

9. "Racial Disparities in the Criminal Justice System," by Marc
Mauer, *The Sentencing Project*, October 29, 2009, pp. 3–4; and *Race to
Incarcerate*, by Marc Mauer, p. 30. For additional research, see *Whitewashing Race*, a collaborative effort by Michael K. Brown, Martin
Carnoy, Elliott Currie, Troy Duster, David B. Oppenheimer, Marjorie M.
Shultz, and David Wellman, 2003, p. 139; "Racial Disproportionality
of U.S. Prison Populations Revisited," by Alfred Blumstein, *University
of Colorado Law Review*, vol. 64, pp. 743–760; and "Racial Dispro-
portionality in the American Prison Population: Using the Blumstein
Method to Address the Critical Race and Justice Issue of the 21st Century," by Brett E. Garland, Cassia Spohn, and Eric J. Wodahl, *Justice
Policy Journal*, vol. 5, no. 2, fall 2008, pp. 14–19.

10. Available at: http://www.ussc.gov/ANNRPT/2003/table34.pdf;
http://www.oas.samhsa.gov/Nhsda/2k3tabs/Sect1peTabs1to66
.htm#tab1.43a; and reported in "Cracks in the System," ACLU, p. 8.

11. "Racial Disparities in the Criminal Justice System," by Marc
Mauer, *The Sentencing Project*, October 29, 2009, p. 3; and *Whitewashing
Race*, by Michael K. Brown et al., p. 139.

12. See, for example, "Drug Use, Drug Possession Arrests, and the
Question of Race: Lessons from Seattle," by Katherine Beckett, Kris
Nyrop, Lori Pfingst, and Melissa Bowen, *Social Problems*, vol. 52, no. 3,
2005, p. 421.

13. "Crime in the United States, 2013," U.S. Department of Justice—
Federal Bureau of Investigation; and, *SAMHSA*, Center for Behavioral
Health Statistics and Quality, National Survey on Drug Use and Health,
2013, p. 15 and figure 2.1.

14. The arrests data can be found in "Crime in the United States,
2013," U.S. Department of Justice—Federal Bureau of Investigation,
while the number of illicit drug users is available in *SAMHSA*, Center
for Behavioral Health Statistics and Quality, National Survey on Drug
Use and Health, 2013, p. 15 and figure 2.1.

15. "Blacks Feel Brunt of Drug War," by Ron Harris, *Los Angeles
Times*, April 22, 1990.

16. "A Window of Opportunity: Addressing the Complexities of the
Relationship between Drug Enforcement and Racial Disparity in Seattle," by Tal Klement and Elizbeth Wiggins, *The Defender Association*,
2001, p. 202.

17. "Prosecutorial Discretion and Racial Disparities in Sentencing: Some Views of Former U.S. Attorneys," by Lynn Lu, *Federal Sentencing Reporter*, February 17, 2007, p. 92.

Chapter 8

1. See, for example, "Drug Arrests at the Millennium," *Society*, vol. 39, no. 5, by Erich Goode, p. 43.

2. "Race, Drugs, and Policing: Understanding Disparities in Drug Delivery Arrests," by Katherine Beckett, Kris Nyrop, and Lori Pfingst, *Criminology*, vol. 44, no. 1, 2006, p. 119, table 3.

3. "A Window of Opportunity: Addressing the Complexities of the Relationship between Drug Enforcement and Racial Disparity in Seattle," by Tal Klement and Elizabeth Siggins, *The Defender Association*, 2001, p. 201.

4. Ibid., pp. 202, 206.

5. Ibid., pp. 199–200.

6. Ibid., p. 207.

7. Ibid., p. 208.

8. Ibid.

9. "Race, Drugs, and Policing: Understanding Disparities in Drug Delivery Arrests," by Katherine Beckett, Kris Nyrop, and Lori Pfingst, *Criminology*, vol. 44, no. 1, 2006; "Drug Use, Drug Possession Arrests, and the Question of Race: Lessons from Seattle," by Katherine Beckett, Kris Nyrop, Lori Pfingst, and Melissa Bowen, *Social Problems*, vol. 52, no. 3, 2005; and "A Window of Opportunity: Addressing the Complexities of the Relationship between Drug Enforcement and Racial Disparity in Seattle," by Tal Klement and Elizabeth Siggins, *The Defender Association*, 2001. For a summary, see *The New Jim Crow*, by Michelle Alexander, pp. 124–125.

10. "Race, Drugs, and Policing: Understanding Disparities in Drug Delivery Arrests," by Katherine Beckett, Kris Nyrop, and Lori Pfingst, *Criminology*, vol. 44, no. 1, 2006, pp. 126–127, figure 2.

11. "A Window of Opportunity: Addressing the Complexities of the Relationship between Drug Enforcement and Racial Disparity in Seattle," by Tal Klement and Elizabeth Siggins, *The Defender Association*, 2001, p. 211. The statement is by Steve Freng of HIDTA (High Intensity Drug Trafficking Area), a federal agency that coordinates regional drug enforcement activity.

12. "Race, Drugs, and Policing: Understanding Disparities in Drug Delivery Arrests," by Katherine Beckett, Kris Nyrop, and Lori Pfingst, *Criminology*, vol. 44, no. 1, 2006, pp. 127–128, figure 3.

13. "Drug Use, Drug Possession Arrests, and the Question of Race: Lessons from Seattle," by Katherine Beckett, Kris Nyrop, Lori Pfingst, and Melissa Bowen, *Social Problems*, vol. 52, no. 3, 2005, p. 434.

14. "A Window of Opportunity: Addressing the Complexities of the Relationship between Drug Enforcement and Racial Disparity in Seattle," by Tal Klement and Elizabeth Siggins, *The Defender Association*, 2001, p. 186.

15. "Drug Use, Drug Possession Arrests, and the Question of Race: Lessons from Seattle," by Katherine Beckett, Kris Nyrop, Lori Pfingst, and Melissa Bowen, *Social Problems*, vol. 52, no. 3, 2005, p. 434.

16. Ibid., pp. 428–429. See, also, p. 432, where the study estimated that crack plus heroin constituted only about one-third of the total outdoor drug transactions, while crack arrests were 75 percent of the total arrests. These data show that the focus on crack was not a function of the relative number of crack transactions.

17. Ibid., p. 435.

18. "Race, Drugs, and Policing: Understanding Disparities in Drug Delivery Arrests," by Katherine Beckett, Kris Nyrop, and Lori Pfingst, *Criminology*, vol. 44, no. 1, 2006, pp. 129–130.

19. Ibid., p. 130.

20. Ibid.

21. "The Police Officer's Dilemma: Using Ethnicity to Disambiguate Potentially Threatening Individuals," by Joshua Correl, Bernadette Park, Charles M. Judd, and Bernd Wittenbrink, *Journal of Personality and Social Psychology*, vol. 83, no. 6, 2002, pp. 1314–1329. See, also, "Seeing Black: Race, Crime, and Visual Processing," by Jennifer Eberhardt, Valerie J. Purdie, Phillip Atiba Goff, and Paul G. Davies, *Journal of Personality and Social Psychology*, vol. 87, no. 6, 2004, pp. 876–893; and "Prejudice and Perception: The Role of Automatic and Controlled Processes in Misperceiving a Weapon," by B. Keith Payne, *Journal of Personality and Social Psychology*, vol. 81, no. 2, 2001, pp. 181–192. For a summary, see *The New Jim Crow*, by Michelle Alexander, pp. 103–105.

22. "Seeing Black: Race, Crime, and Visual Processing," by Jennifer Eberhardt, Valerie J. Purdie, Phillip Atiba Goff, and Paul G. Davies, *Journal of Personality and Social Psychology*, vol. 87, no. 6, 2004, pp. 879–881.

23. "Drug Use and African Americans: Myth Versus Reality," by Betty Watson Burston, Dionne Jones, and Pat Robertson-Saunders, *Journal of Alcohol and Drug Abuse*, vol. 40, winter 1995, p. 19.

24. "Priming Unconscious Racial Stereotypes about Adolescent Offenders," by Sandra Graham and Brian S. Lowery, *Law and Human Behavior*, vol. 28, no. 5, October 2004, pp. 483–504.

25. "Harvesting Implicit Group Attitudes and Beliefs from a Demonstration Web Site," by Brian A. Nosek, Mahzarin R. Banaji, and Anthony G. Greenwald, *Group Dynamics: Theory, Research, and Practice*, vol. 6, no. 1, 2002, especially pp. 102–103; see, also, "The Impact of Anti-Black Racism on Approval of Barack Obama's Job Performance and on Voting in the 2012 Presidential Election," by Josh Pasek, Jon A. Krosnick, and Trevor Tompson, *Unpublished Paper*, October 2012, available at http://comm.stanford.edu/faculty/krosnick/docs/2012/2012%20Voting%20and%20Racism.pdf.

26. *Profiles in Injustice*, by David A. Harris, p. 21.

27. *No Equal Justice*, by David Cole, pp. 47–49.

28. Ibid., p. 47.

29. Ibid., p. 50.

30. Ibid.

31. Ibid.

Chapter 9

1. *The New Jim Crow*, by Michelle Alexander, p. 122.

2. For one detailed analysis of the so-called Broken Windows policing, arguing that there is a lack of empirical evidence supporting its effectiveness, see *Illusion of Order*, by Bernard E. Harcourt.

3. See "Stop-and-Frisk: Fagan Report Summary," *Center for Constitutional Rights*, October 26, 2010, available at, ccrjustice.org/files/Fagan%20Report%20Summary%20Final.pdf.

4. "Injustices of Stop and Frisk," editorial, *The New York Times*, May 13, 2012.

5. See, for example, "In Misdemeanor Cases, Long Waits for Elusive Trials," by William Glaberson, *The New York Times*, April 30, 2013.

6. *Floyd v. City of New York*, 861 F. Supp. 2d 274—Dist. Court, SD.

7. See *Terry v. Ohio*, 392 U.S. 1, 30, 88 S.Ct. 1868, 20 L.Ed.2d 889 (1968).

8. "Stop-and-Frisk: Fagan Report Summary," October 26, 2010, *Center for Constitutional Rights* (CCR).

9. See "Trial Weighs Importance of Arrests in Police Stops," by Joseph Goldstein, *The New York Times*, May 17, 2013.

10. *Floyd v. City of New York*, 861 F. Supp. 2d 274—Dist. Court, SD New York 2012, fn. 160.

11. Ibid., fn. 161.

12. "Recording Points to Race Factors in Stops by New York Police," by Joseph Goldstein, *The New York Times*, March 21, 2013; see *Floyd*

v. City of New York, 861 F. Supp. 2d 274—Dist. Court, SD New York 2012.

13. "Walking While Black in New York," editorial, *The New York Times*, March 22, 2013; and *Floyd v. City of New York*, 861 F. Supp. 2d 274—Dist. Court, SD New York 2012.

14. "'Quotas Exist': Former NYPD Officers Discuss the Data-Driven Department," by Dan Rosenblum, *CAPITAL,* May 4, 2012.

15. "Injustices of Stop and Frisk," editorial, *The New York Times*, May 13, 2012.

16. http://www.nyclu.org/files/releases/Clean_Halls_complaint_3.28.12.pdf.

17. *Ligon v. City of New York*, pp. 35–41. Available at http://www.nyclu.org/files/releases/CleanHallsRuling_1.8.13.pdf.

18. Ibid., p. 36.

19. Ibid., p. 37.

20. Ibid., p. 38.

21. Ibid., p. 38.

22. Ibid., p. 40.

23. Ibid., pp. 41–49.

24. Ibid., p. 46.

25. Ibid., p. 48.

26. Ibid., p. 33.

27. See, for example, *Illusion of Order,* by Bernard E. Harcourt, p. 176.

28. "When Police Violate the Constitution," editorial, *The New York Times*, January 25, 2013; and *Ligon v. City of New York*, pp. 28–29, 32–33.

29. See, for example, "Judge Rejects New York's Stop-and-Frisk Policy," by Joseph Goldstein, *The New York Times*, August 12, 2013.

30. Ibid. See "Judge Scheindlin's Case," by the Editorial Board of *The New York Times*, November 7, 2013; she is appealing the court's decision, and so are 5 retired federal judges and 13 professors of legal ethics. See http://www.nydailynews.com/news/national/judges-legal-pros-back-trial-judge-stop-frisk-ruling-article-1.1521447.

31. Ibid.

32. *Race to Incarcerate*, by Marc Mauer, pp. 160, 164; and *Snitching*, by Alexandra Natapoff, p. 104.

33. "Of 50,000 Arrests in New York City a Year, Most Are Black and Hispanic Men," by Colleen Long and Jennifer Peltz, The Huffington Post, November 13, 2011.

34. Ibid.

35. Response to my question by Francis T. Murphy, retired justice of the Supreme Court of New York; and a conversation with Daryl Atkinson, attorney for the Southern Coalition for Racial Justice.

36. "A Window of Opportunity: Addressing the Complexities of the Relationship between Drug Enforcement and Racial Disparity in Seattle," by Tal Klement and Elizabeth Wiggins, *The Defender Association*, 2001, p. 208.

37. *The Sentencing Project* is a highly respected, nonprofit organization that works for a fair and effective U.S. criminal justice system by promoting reforms in sentencing policy, addressing unjust racial disparities and practices, and advocating for alternatives to incarceration.

38. "Distorted Priorities: Drug Offenders in State Prisons," by Ryan S. King and Marc Mauer, *The Sentencing Project*, September 2002, pp. 4, 10.

39. "Incarceration, Social Capital and Crime: Implications for Social Disorganization Theory," by D. R. Rose and T. R. Clear, *Criminology*, 1998, summarized on pp. 442–443.

40. See, for example, "Snitching and the Code of the Street," by Richard Rosenfeld, Bruce A. Jacobs, and Richard Wright, *British Journal of Criminology*, 2003, p. 306.

41. Search and Destroy: African-American Males in the Criminal Justice System, by J. G. Miller, p. 102; see, also, *Police Informers*, by Rod Settle, p. 200; "The Story of a Snitch," *The Atlantic Monthly*, by Jeremy Kahn, April 2007; "Transparent Policing," by Eric Luna, *Iowa Law Review*, vol. 85, p. 1162; and *Why People Obey the Law*, by Tom R. Tyler, 2006, p. 6.

42. Ibid.

43. "Snitching and the Code of the Street," by Richard Rosenfeld, Bruce A. Jacobs, and Richard Wright, *British Journal of Criminology*, 2003, p. 304.

44. Ibid., p. 296.

45. Ibid.

46. Ibid., pp. 296–297.

47. "Detective Is Found Guilty of Planting Drugs," by Tim Stelloh, *The New York Times*, November 1, 2011.

48. Ibid.

49. "Cops Made Money by Fabricating Drug Charges against Innocent People, Stephen Anderson testifies," by John Marzulli, Rocco Parascandola, and Larry Mcshane, *New York Daily News*, October 14, 2011.

50. "Whither the Criminal Court: Confronting Stops-and-Frisks," by Steven Zeidman, 76 *Albany Law Review* 1187 (2013).

51. Ibid., p. 1198.

52. Ibid., p. 1189.

53. "In Misdemeanor Cases, Long Waits for Elusive Trials," by William Glaberson, *The New York Times*, April 30, 2013; "Stop-and-Frisk Project Reaches 'Appalling' Conclusion: No Right to Misdemeanor Trial in Bronx, NY," by Martha Neil, *ABA Journal*, May 1, 2013; see, also, "No Day in Court," A Report by the Bronx Defenders Fundamental Fairness Project, 2013.

54. Ibid.

55. Ibid.

56. "Stop-and-Frisk Project Reaches 'Appalling' Conclusion: No Right to Misdemeanor Trial in Bronx, NY," by Martha Neil, *ABA Journal*, May 1, 2013.

57. "No Day in Court," by the Bronx Defenders Fundamental Fairness Project, 2013, pp. 19–20.

58. "Why Is the NYPD after Me?" by Nicholas K. Peart, *The New York Times*, Sunday Review, December 17, 2011.

59. Ibid.

60. http://www.nyclu.org/content/stop-and-frisk-data.

61. http://www.medicaljane.com/2014/11/13/new-york-city-mayor -sets-new-marijuana-policy.

62. http://www.nytimes.com/2015/03/10/nyregion/on-marijuana -bratton-and-de-blasio-back-policy-but-still-show-divide.html.

63. http://nypost.com/2015/03/10/de-blasio-insists-he-and-bratton -on-the-same-page-about-pot/.

64. Ibid.

65. http://www.bjs.gov/content/pub/pdf/jagp14.pdf.

66. See "Edward Byrne Memorial Justice Assistance Grant Program: Legislative and Funding History," by Nathan James, *CRS Report to Congress*, January 12, 2007, pp. 2–3.

67. "A Special Report: Hooked on SWAT," by Steven Elbow, *Capital Times*, August 18, 2001; and *Rise of the Warrior Cop*, by Radley Balko, p. 243.

Chapter 10

1. "Secret Justice: Criminal Informants and America's Underground Legal System," by Alexandra Natapoff, *Prison Legal News*, June 15, 2010.

2. Ibid.; see *United States v. Murphy*, 768 F.2d 1518, 1528 (7th Cir. 1985).

3. *Forfeiting Our Property Rights*, by Rep. Henry Hyde, p. 45.

4. Quoted in *Confidential Informants*, by John Madinger, p. 31.

5. See, for example, *Justice without Trial*, 4th ed., by Jerome H. Skolnick, pp. 103–104.

6. *Forfeiting Our Property Rights*, by Rep. Henry Hyde., p. 46; and *Confidential Informant*, by John Madinger, pp. 38–39.

7. See, for example, "Secret Justice: Criminal Informants and America's Underground Legal System," by Alexandra Natapoff, *Prison Legal News,* June 15, 2010; also, *Snitching*, by Alexandra Natapoff, pp. 73–76.

8. "Inside the Informant File," by Dennis G. Fitzgerald, *The Champion*, May 1998.

9. "Vice Isn't Nice: A Look at the Effects of Working Undercover," by Mark R. Pogrebin and Eric D. Poole, *Journal of Criminal Justice*, vol. 21, 1993, p. 385.

10. Cited in *The Ghost Squad*, by John Gosling, p. 19; also, in *Justice without Trial*, 4th ed., by Jerome H. Skolnick, p. 109.

11. "The Federal Bureau of Investigation's Compliance with the Attorney General's Investigative Guideline," (redacted), U.S. Department of Justice, Office of the Inspector General, September 2005, ch. 3, p. 3.

12. *Informants and Undercover Investigations: A Practical Guide to Law, Policy, and Procedure*, by Dennis G. Fitzgerald, 2007, p. 45; also, *Snitching*, by Alexandra Natapoff, p. 19.

13. *Informants and Undercover Investigations: A Practical Guide to Law, Policy, and Procedure*, by Dennis G. Fitzgerald, 2007, p. 57; see also, *Informants: Development and Management*, by Stephen L. Mallory, 2000, p. 23.

14. *Reefer Madness*, by Eric Schlosser, pp. 62–63.

15. "Making Crime Pay: What's the Cost of Using Paid Informers?" by Mark Curriden, *America Bar Association Journal*, vol. 77, June 1991, p. 43.

16. See *Forfeiting Our Property Rights*, by Representative Henry Hyde, p. 46.

17. Ibid., p. 45.

18. See, for example, *Why Our Drug Laws Have Failed and What We Can Do about It*, 2nd ed., by Judge James P. Gray, p. 118; "Guilty before Proven Innocent: How Police Harassment, Jailhouse Snitches, and a Runaway War on Drugs Imprisoned an Innocent Family," by Radley Balko, *Reason*, May 2008; and, "Secret Threat to Justice," by Mark Curridan, *National Law Journal*, February 20, 1995.

19. "The Snitch System: How Snitch Testimony Sent Randy Steidl and Other Innocent Americans to Death Row," by Rob Warden, *Northwestern University Law School's Center on Wrongful Convictions*, 2004.

20. "Exonerations in the United States; 1989 Through 2003," by Samuel R. Gross, Kristen Jacoby, Daniel J. Matheson, Nicholas Montgomery, and Sujata Patil, *Journal of Criminal Law and Criminology*, vol. 95, no. 2, 2005, pp. 543–544.

21. Ibid.

22. *Sourcebook of Criminal Justice Statistics 2010*, Bureau of Justice Statistics, U.S. Department of Justice, table 5.36.

23. "Guilty before Proven Innocent: How Police Harassment, Jailhouse Snitches, and a Runaway War on Drugs Imprisoned an Innocent Family," by Radley Balko, *Reason*, May 2008.

24. "Investigation of the Involvement of Jail House Informants in the Criminal Justice System in Los Angeles County, CA," *Report of the 1989–90 Los Angeles County Grand Jury*.

25. Ibid., pp. 2–6, 10–15, 19.

26. Ibid., pp. 10–15.

27. Ibid., p. 19.

28. Ibid., p .22.

29. Ibid., p. 23.

30. Ibid. pp. 27–30.

31. This section is based mostly on the investigative journalism of Radley Balko, reported in "Guilty before Proven Innocent: How Police Harassment, Jailhouse Snitches, and a Runaway War on Drugs Imprisoned an Innocent Family," by Radley Balko, *Reason*, May 2008; see, also, "Convicted," by Heather Miller, *Independent Weekly*, July 20, 2011.

32. There was one other piece of evidence. In 2001, a local SWAT team broke into Ann's house and found 72 grams of crack cocaine in a guest room dresser. The boyfriend of one of Ann's daughters immediately admitted the drugs were his and turned himself in. He was never charged.

33. To get a more complete account of the Colomb's ordeal, see "Guilty before Proven Innocent: How Police Harassment, Jailhouse Snitches, and a Runaway War on Drugs Imprisoned an Innocent Family," by Radley Balko, *Reason*, May 2008.

34. *Williamson v. U.S.* 311 F.2d 441 (5th Circuit 1962).

35. *America's Longest War*, by Steven B. Duke and Albert C. Gross, pp. 143–144; and *United States v. Cervantes-Pacheco*, 826 F. 2d 310 (5th Circuit 1987).

Chapter 11

1. "Breaking the Law to Enforce It: Undercover Police Participation in Crime," by Elizabeth E. Joh, *Stanford Law Review*, p. 157; and "Under-the-Covers Undercover Investigations: Some Reflections on the

State's Use of Sex and Deception in Law Enforcement," by Gary T. Marx, *Criminal Justice Ethics*, 1992, p. 13.

2. Ibid.

3. "Observations on Police Undercover Work," by George I. Miller, *Criminology*, vol. 25, 1987, p. 34.

4. "Vice Isn't Nice: A Look at the Effects of Working Undercover," by Mark R. Pogrebin and Eric D. Poole, *Journal of Criminal Justice*, vol. 21, 1993, p. 384.

5. "Observations on Police Undercover Work," by George I. Miller, *Criminology*, vol. 25, 1987, p. 33.

6. *Olmstead v. U.S.* 277 U.S. 438, 1928.

7. "United States' policy analysis on undercover operations," by George S. Wagner, *International Journal of Police Science & Management*, vol. 9, no. 4, March 2007, p. 375; "Breaking the Law to Enforce It: Undercover Police Participating in Crime," by Elizabeth E. Joh, *Stanford Law Review*, 2009, p. 174.

8. Ibid.; see *United States v. Murphy*, 768 F.2d 1518, 1528 (7th Cir. 1985).

9. "Observations on Police Undercover Work," by George I. Miller, *Criminology*, vol. 25, 1987, p. 35.

10. *Cops: Their Lives in Their Own Words*, by Mark Baker, p. 136.

11. Ibid., p. 141.

12. *U.S. v. Gamble* 737 F 2d 853 (10th Circuit 1984).

13. *Under Cover*, by Gary T. Marx, p. 149.

14. Ibid.

15. Ibid., p. 236.

16. *US v. Russell*, 411 U.S. 423, 432 (1973); for a discussion, see "Breaking the Law to Enforce It: Undercover Police Participation in Crime," by Elizabeth E. Joh, *Stanford Law Review*, vol. 62, 2009, p. 166.

17. For example. "Breaking the Law to Enforce It: Undercover Police Participation in Crime," by Elizabeth E. Joh, *Stanford Law Review*, vol. 62, 2009, p. 170.

18. *Under Cover*, by Gary T. Marx, p. 66.

19. Ibid.

20. See "Breaking the Law to Enforce It: Undercover Police Participation in Crime," by Elizabeth E. Joh, *Stanford Law Review*, vol. 62, 155, 2009, pp. 171–172; and "The Place of Covert Surveillance in Democratic Societies: A Comparative Study of the United States and Germany," Jacqueline E. Ross, *The American Journal of Comparative Law*, vol. 55, 2007, pp. 571, 576.

21. Ibid.

22. Ibid.; see *People v. Shine*, 590 N.Y.S 2d 965–966 (1992).

23. *Rochin v. California*, 354 U.S. 165 (1952); See "When Nothing Is Shocking: The Ninth Circuit Degrades the Outrageous Government Conduct Defense," by Stephen A. Meister, *Loyola of Los Angeles Law Review*, Vol.22, no. 3 (1989), p. 854.

24. *United States v. Russell*, 459 F. 2d 671–672 (9th Circuit 1972).

25. Ibid.

26. *United States v. Russell*, 411 U.S. 423 (1973); See the discussion of Russell in "When Nothing Is Shocking: The Ninth Circuit Degrades the Outrageous Government Conduct Defense," by Stephen A. Meister, *Loyola of Los Angeles Law Review*, 1989, pp. 859–863; also, "Deception by Police," by Jerome H. Skolnick, in *Moral Issues in Police Work*, edited by Frederick A. Elliston and Michael Feldberg, pp. 81–82.

27. "When Nothing Is Shocking: The Ninth Circuit Degrades the Outrageous Government Conduct Defense," by Stephen A. Meister, *Loyola of Los Angeles Law Review*, 1989, pp. 863–866; See *Hampton v. United States*, 425 U.S. 484 (1976).

28. Ibid., p. 865.

29. "Breaking the Law to Enforce It: Undercover Police Participation in Crime," by Elizabeth E. Joh, *Stanford Law Review*, vol. 62, 155, 2009, p. 175.

30. "Observations on Police Undercover Work," by George I. Miller, *Criminology*, vol. 25, 1987, p. 39.

31. "As Traps Grow, Wary Dealers Force Officers to Take Drugs," by Michael Cooper, *The New York Times*, February 17, 1997.

32. "Observations on Police Undercover Work," by George I. Miller, *Criminology*, vol. 25, no. 1, 1987, p. 39.

33. *Dealing Crack*, by Bruce A. Jacobs, pp. 103–104.

34. Ibid., p. 107.

35. "Strategies to Avoid Arrest: Crack Sellers' Response to Intensified Policing," by Bruce D. Johnson and Mangai Natarajan, *American Journal of Police*, vol. 24, 1995, p. 58.

36. *Dealing Crack*, by Bruce A. Jacobs, p. 109.

37. *Undercover*, by Gary T. Marx, p. 176.

38. Ibid., p. 177.

39. See the discussion in *Undercover* by Gary T. Marx, pp. 160–162; and, "Observations on Police Undercover Work," by George I. Miller, *Criminology*, vol. 25, no. 1, 1987, p. 39.

40. "Ideology and Generations," by D. Ward, PhD dissertation, Yale University, 1981, quoted in *Undercover* by Gary T. Marx. p. 160.

41. *Cops: Their Lives in Their Own Words*, by Mark Baker, p. 160.

42. "Observations on Police Undercover Work," by George I. Miller, *Criminology*, vol. 25, no. 1, 1987, p. 40.

43. "Vice Isn't Nice: A Look at the Effects of Working Undercover," by Mark R. Pogrebin and Eric D. Poole, *Journal of Criminal Justice,* vol. 21, 1993, p. 389.

44. The following account is from *Cops: Their Lives in Their Own Words,* by Mark Baker, pp. 137–140.

45. Ibid.

46. Ibid.

47. "Vice Isn't Nice: A Look at the Effects of Working Undercover," by Mark R. Pogrebin and Eric D. Poole, *Journal of Criminal Justice,* vol. 21, 1993, p. 389.

48. Ibid.

49. "Undercover Police Work: Difficult and Dangerous," by George J. Bryjak, *Adirondack Daily Enterprise,* January 26, 2009.

50. *Police: Streetcorner Politicians,* by William Ker Muir Jr., p. 180.

51. "Ideology and Generations," by D. Ward, PhD dissertation, Yale University, 1981, quoted in *Undercover* by Gary T. Marx. p. 164.

52. "Interview: Robert Leuci," by Andrew Gilman. *Penthouse,* January 1982, p. 80.

53. "Who Really Gets Stung? Some Issues Raised by the New Police Undercover Work," by Gary T. Marx in *Moral Issues in Police Work,* edited by F. A. Elliston and M. Feldberg, pp. 166–167.

54. *Undercover,* by Gary T. Marx, p. 167.

55. Ibid.

56. "Stress in Undercover Policing," by Gary Farkas, in *Psychological Services for Law Enforcement,* edited by J. T. Reese and H. A. Goldstein, 1986; quoted in "Vice Isn't Nice: A Look at the Effects of Working Undercover," by Mark R. Pogrebin and Eric D. Poole, *Journal of Criminal Justice,* vol. 21, 1993, p. 390.

57. Ibid.

58. "Health and Legal Issues in Undercover Narcotics Investigations: Misrepresented Evidence," by Michel Girodo, *Behavioral Sciences & the Law,* vol. 3, no. 3, 1985, pp. 299–308; see, also, research by Pam Fitzgerald available at http://www.wendywestie.com/fitzgerald_undercover.html.

59. "Health and Legal Issues in Undercover Narcotics Investigations: Misrepresented Evidence," by Michel Girodo, *Behavioral Sciences & the Law,* vol. 3, no. 3, 1985, p. 303, especially figure 1.

60. Ibid., p. 304.

61. For a more detailed discussion, see ibid., pp. 304–307.

62. "Observations on Police Undercover Work," by George I. Miller, *Criminology,* vol. 25, no. 1, 1987, pp. 41–42.

63. "Breaking the Law to Enforce it: Undercover Police Participation in Crime," by Elizabeth E. Joh, *Stanford Law Review,* vol. 62, no. 155, 2009, p. 182.

64. See, for example, *Foster v. U.S. Department of Justice,* 933 F.Supp. 687 (1996); and "Transparent Policing," by Eric Luna, *Iowa Law Review,* vol. 85, 1999–2000, p. 1132.

65. "Why Good Cops Go Bad," by Tom Morganthau, in *Newsweek,* December 19, 1994, p. 34, quoted in *Drug War Politics,* by Eva Bertram et al., pp. 48–49.

66. *America's Longest War,* by Steven B. Duke and Albert C. Gross, pp. 113–114; "Police Leaders: Illicit Drug Markets Contribute to Police Corruption," *News Briefs,* July–August 1998, available at http://www.ndsn.org/julaug98/lawenf1.html.

67. *Why Our Drug Laws Have Failed and What We Can Do about It,* 2nd ed., by Judge James P. Gray, p. 77.

68. See www.hrw.org/reports98/police/uspo100.htm, reported in *Beyond the War on Drugs,* by Steven Wisotsky, p. 146.

69. "Police Corruption Witness Makes a Dangerous Friend," by Arnold Markowitz, *Miami Herald,* May 2, 1982, cited in ibid., p. 147.

70. "Corruption in Uniform: The Long View," by Clifford Krauss, *The New York Times,* July 8, 1994, cited in *Drug War Politics,* by Eva Bertram et al., p. 49.

71. *Why Our Drug Laws Have Failed and What We Can Do about It,* 2nd ed., by Judge James P. Gray, p. 80.

72. "Law Enforcement: Information on Drug-Related Police Corruption," Report to the Honorable Charles B. Rangel, House of Representatives, General Accounting Office (Washington, D.C.: USGPO, May 1998), p. 8.

73. "The Thin Blue Lie," by Thomas A. Hagemann, *Los Angeles Daily Journal,* October 27, 1999.

74. "Economic and Social Consequences of Drug Abuse and Illicit Trafficking," United Nations International Drug Control Program, Technical Series Report #6 (New York, NY: UNDCP, 1998), p. 39.

75. *Beyond the War on Drugs,* by Steven Wisotsky, p. 147.

Chapter 12

1. See Criminal Justice Statistics at http://www.albany.edu/sourcebook/tost_6.html#6_b; and *When Prisoners Come Home,* by Joan Petersilia, p. 247.

2. "Prisoners in 2010," by Paul Guerino, Paige M. Harrison, and William J. Sabol, U.S. Department of Justice, Bureau of Justice Statistics, 2011, table 2. The cycling in and out of jails is enormous: From mid-2009 to mid-2010, some 12.9 million people were admitted to local jails, with about 17,000 released in the same period. See, also, http://www.ojp.usdoj.gov/newsroom/pressreleases/2011/BJS11087.htm.

3. See, for example, http://www.sentencingproject.org/template/page .cfm?id=122, where it's estimated that over 60 percent of those in prisons and jails are racial and ethnic minorities.

4. See *But They All Come Back,* by Jeremy Travis, pp. 158–159; and "The Economics of Crime," by Richard Freeman, in *Handbook of Labor Economics*, edited by Orley C. Ashenfelter and David Card, vol. 3C, 1999, ch. 52, p. 355.

5. See *When Prisoners Come Home*, by Joan Petersilia, p. v; and *But They All Come Back*, by Jeremy Travis, pp. 94–95.

6. "Recidivism of Prisoners Released in 1994," by Patrick A. Langan and David Levin, U.S. Department of Justice, Bureau of Justice Statistics, 2002; also presented in *But They All Come Back*, by Jeremy Travis, pp. 94–95.

7. *Criminal Sentences: Law without Order*, by Marvin E. Frankel, p. 7.

8. "Treatment Destruction Techniques," by Michael R. Gottfredson, *Journal of Research in Crime and Delinquency*, vol. 16, no. 1, January 1979, p. 39.

9. For example: "A Meta-Analysis of Corrections-Based Education, Vocation, and Work Programs for Adult Offenders," by David. B. Wilson, Catherine A. Gallagher, and Doris L. Mackenzie, in *Journal of Research in Crime and Delinquency*, vol. 37, no. 4, pp. 347–368; "Assessing Correctional Rehabilitation Policy, Practice, and Prospects," by Francis. T. Cullen and Paul Gendreau, *Criminal Justice, 2000: Policies, Processes, and Decisions of the Criminal Justice System*, vol. 31, edited by J. Horney, U.S. Department of Justice, 2000, pp. 109–176; "Adult Correctional Treatment," by Gerald G. Gates, Timothy J. Flanagan, Laurence Motiuk, and Lynn Stewart, *Crime: Public Policies for Crime Control*, edited by James Q. Wilson and Joan Petersilia, 1999, pp. 361–426; and "Rehabilitation and Treatment Programs," by Francis T. Cullen in *Crime: Public Policies for Crime Control*, edited by James Q. Wilson and Joan Petersilia, 1999, pp. 253–289.

10. "Rehabilitation and Treatment Programs," by Francis T. Cullen in *Crime: Public Policies for Crime Control*, edited by James Q. Wilson and Joan Petersilia, 1999, p. 287.

11. *But They All Come Back*, by Jeremy Travis, p. 156; "Dynamics of Social Capital of Prisoners and Community Reentry: Ties That Bind?"

by Nancy Wolff and Jeffrey Draine, *Journal of Correctional Healthcare*, vol. 10, no. 3, 2003, pp. 457–490; "Collateral Consequences of Imprisonment for Children, Communities, and Prisoners," by John Hagan and Ronit Dinovitzer, vol. 26, of *Crime and Justice*, edited by Michael Tonry and Joan Petersilia, 1999, pp. 121–162; and "Prisoner Reentry in Perspective," by James P. Lynch and William J. Sabol, *Crime Policy Report*, vol. 3, September 2001, The Urban Institute.

12. *When Prisoners Come Home*, by Joan Petersilia, p. 247.

13. "Behind Bars 11: Substance Abuse and America's Prison Population," The National Center on Addiction and Substance Abuse at Columbia University, February 2010, p. 39; see, also, "Mental Health Problems of Prison and Jail Inmates," Bureau of Justice Statistics, Special Report, December 14, 2006.

14. "Behind Bars 11: Substance Abuse and America's Prison Population," The National Center on Addiction and Substance Abuse at Columbia University, February 2010, p. 1.

15. Ibid., p. 52, figure 5A.

16. Ibid., p. 26. "Mental health problems" are defined by having received mental health treatment during the prior 12 months or "experiencing sub-clinical levels of symptoms based on the *DSM-IV*."

17. *When Prisoners Come Home*, by Joan Petersilia, p. 105.

18. The terms "invisible punishment" and "instruments of social exclusion" were coined by Jeremy Travis; see "Invisible Punishment: An Instrument of Social Exclusion," in *Invisible Punishment: The Collateral Consequences of Mass Imprisonment*, edited by Marc Mauer and Meda Chesney-Lind, 2002, pp. 15–16, 23–24, 31.

19. See, for example, "Barred for Life," by Wyatt Olson, in *Miami New Times*, January 16, 2003; and "Lawyering at the Margins: Collateral Civil Penalties at the Entry and Completion of the Criminal Sentence," by Lucian E. Ferster and Santiago Aroca, in *Civil Penalties, Social Consequences*, edited by Christopher Mele and Teresa A. Miller, pp. 214–221.

20. "Disenfranchisement and the Civic Reintegration of Convicted Felons," by Christopher Uggen and Jeff Manza, *Civil Penalties, Social Consequences*, edited by Christopher Mele and Teresa A. Miller, ch. 2; *When Prisoners Come Home*, by Joan Petersilia, pp. 120–126; and *But They All Come Back*, by Jeremy Travis, ch. 9 and pp. 291–292.

Chapter 13

1. "Race, the War on Drugs, and the Collateral Consequences of Criminal Conviction," by Gabriel J. Chin, in *Civil Penalties, Social Consequences*, edited by Christopher Mele and Teresa A. Miller, p. 28.

As Professor Chin explains, "Even if the court or counsel wanted to explain, it would be very difficult to do so because laws imposing collateral consequences are dispersed in various codes, executive orders, and regulations."

2. "Introduction, Proposed Standards on Collateral Sanctions and Administrative Disqualifications of Convicted Persons," by American Bar Association, Task Force on Collateral Sanctions, January 18, 2002; *Marked*, by Devah Pager, pp. 32–35; and *Banished*, by Katherine Beckett and Steve Herbert, pp. 16–22.

3. *But They All Come Back*, by Jeremy Travis, p. 70.

4. Ibid.

5. "After Prison: Roadblocks to Reentry, 2009 Update," A Study by the Legal Action Center, p. 13; "65 Million Need Not Apply: The Case for Reforming Criminal Background Checks for Employment," by Michelle Natividad Rodriquez and Maurice Ensellem, *National Employment Law Project*, March 2011, pp. 3, 27; "Internet Lets a Criminal Past Catch Up Quicker," by Erica Goode, *The New York Times*, April 28, 2011; and "Use and Management of Criminal History Record Information: A Comprehensive Report, 2001 Update," Bureau of Justice Statistics, U.S. Department of Justice, which estimated the number of Americans with a criminal history at more than 59 million in 1999.

6. *When Prisoners Come Home*, by Joan Petersilia, pp. 108–109, and table 6.2 on p. 110.

7. "Faulty Criminal Background Checks," editorial, *The New York Times*, July 25, 2012.

8. Ibid.

9. "After Prison: Roadblocks to Reentry, 2009 Update," A Study by the Legal Action Center, p. 7.

10. Ibid., p. 10. The states that prohibit all employers and occupational licensing agencies from using data on arrests without conviction for hiring decisions are: CA, UT, WI, IL, MI, OH, NY, MA, and RI. The states that allow limited use of this type of information are: NM, AR, and NH. See also "After Prison: Roadblocks to Reentry," A Study by the Legal Action Center, 2004, map on p. 11.

11. "Unequal Protection: Comparing Former Felons' Challenges to Disenfranchisement and Employment Discrimination," by Elena Saxonhouse, *Stanford Law Review*, vol. 56, no. 6, 2004, pp. 1597, 1611–1612; and "Walking a Tightrope: Balancing Competing Public Interests in the Employment of Criminal Offenders," by Jennifer Leavitt, *Connecticut Law Revue* 24, 2002, pp. 1301–1306.

12. *What Employers Want: Job Prospects for Less-Educated Workers*, by Harry J. Holzer, Russell Sage Foundation, 1996, p. 59.

13. "Can Employers Play a More Positive Role in Prisoner Reentry?" by Harry J. Holzer, Steven Raphael, and Michael Stoll, in *Prisoner Reentry and the Institutions of Civil Society: Bridges and Barriers to Successful Reintegration*, The Urban Institute, March 2002, p. 10.

14. Ibid., p. 3.

15. *"Getting Paid": Youth Crime and Work in the Inner City*, by Mercer L. Sullivan, p. 69.

16. *The Minds of Marginalized Black Men: Making Sense of Mobility, Opportunity, and Future Life Chances*, by Alford A. Young, 2003, p. 95.

17. *Punishment and Inequality in America*, by Bruce Western, ch. 5; "Crime and the Employment of Disadvantaged Youths," by Richard B. Freeman, *NBER Working Paper 3875*, 1991; "How Unregulated Is the U.S. Labor Market? The Penal System as a Labor Market Institution," by Bruce Western and Katherine Beckett, *American Journal of Sociology*, vol. 104, no. 4, 1999, pp. 1030–1060; "Incarceration and Racial Inequality in Men's Employment," by Bruce Western and Becky Pettit, *Industrial and Labor Relations Review*, vol. 54, no. 3, pp. 3–16.

18. *Punishment and Inequality in America*, by Bruce Western, pp. 126–127, and table 5.3. The lifetime income loss for Hispanics is 2.1 percent.

19. Ibid., p. 129.

20. See *Marked*, by Devah Pager, ch. 4.

21. Ibid., pp. 59–62.

22. Ibid. See figure 4.3 on p. 67 and figure 4.4 on p. 70.

23. Ibid., p. 71.

24. See, for example, "Unequal Protection: Comparing Former Felons' Challenges to Disenfranchisement and Employment Discrimination," by Elena Saxonhouse, *Stanford Law Review*, vol. 56, no. 6, 2004, pp. 1597, 1610–1611; "The Character Component of Occupational Licensing Laws: A Continuing Barrier to the Ex-felon's Employment Opportunities," by Bruce E. May, *North Dakota Law Review*, vol. 71, 1995, pp. 188–189; "A Meta-Analysis of Corrections-Based Education, Vocation, and Work Programs for Adult Offenders," by David B. Wilson, Catherine Gallagher, and Doris L. Mackenzie, in *Journal of Research in Crime and Delinquency*, vol. 37, 2000, pp. 347–368; "Work as a Turning Point in the Life Course of Prisoners," by Chris Uggen, *American Sociological Review*, vol. 65, no. 4, 2000, pp. 529–546; and "Government Personnel Policies Impacting the Hiring of Ex-Offenders," by Matthews and Amanda Casarjian, *Safer Foundation*, 2002, p. 54.

25. "The Impact of Local Labor Market Conditions on the Likelihood That Parolees Are Returned to Custody," by Steven Raphael and David F. Weiman, in *Barriers to Reentry: The Labor Market for Released Prisoners in Post-Industrial America*, edited by Shawn Bushway, Michael A. Stoll, and David F. Weiman, Russell Sage Foundation, 2007, pp. 304–332.

26. *Crime in the Making: Pathways and Turning Points through Life*, by Robert Sampson and John H. Laub, 1993, p. 162.

27. "The Mark of Cain," by Webb Hubbell, *Criminal Justice*, fall 2001, p. 33.

28. "Labor Markets and Crime," by Shawn Bushway and Peter Reuter, in *Crime*, edited by James Q. Wilson and Joan Petersilia, p. 221.

29. *National Advisory Commission on Criminal Justice Standards and Goals*, p. 431.

30. *It's about Time: America's Imprisonment Binge*, 3rd ed., by James Austin and John Irwin, 1994, p. 129.

31. See *Marked*, by Devah Pager, p. 25; and, *When Prisoners Come Home*, by Joan Petersilia, p. 105.

32. *Marked*, by Devah Pager, p. 25.

33. Ibid.; and "Estimates from Preventing Parolee Failure Program: An Evaluation," California Department of Corrections, 1997.

34. See, for example, *When Prisoners Come Home*, by Joan Petersilia, p. 105.

35. Ibid., p. 114; and "Unequal Protection: Comparing Former Felons' Challenges to Disenfranchisement and Employment Discrimination," by Elena Saxonhouse, *Stanford Law Review*, vol. 56, no. 6, 2004, pp. 1597, 1613.

36. "After Prison: Roadblocks to Reentry, 2009 Update," Legal Action Center, p. 9.

37. "Give Ex-Offenders a Chance to Renew," by W. Wilson Goode Sr., *Philadelphia Inquirer*, October 21, 2002.

38. "Unequal Protection: Comparing Former Felons' Challenges to Disenfranchisement and Employment Discrimination," by Elena Saxonhouse, *Stanford Law Review*, vol. 56, no. 6, 2004, pp. 1597, 1613; and, *Marked*, by Devah Pager, 2007, pp. 32–35.

39. Ibid.

40. See *When Prisoners Come Home*, by Joan Petersilia, 2003, pp. 113–114; and *American Corrections*, 9th ed., by Todd R. Clear and George F. Cole, 2011, p. 454.

41. "Paying a Price, Long after the Crime," by Alfred Blumstein and Kiminori Nakamura, *The New York Times*, January 9, 2012.

42. "Chicago Metropolis 2020: 2006 Crime and Justice Index," by Donald G. Lubin et al., Pew Center on the States, 2006, p. 35.

43. "After Prison: Roadblocks to Reentry, 2009 Update," Legal Action Center, p. 9; see, also, "Invisible Punishment: An Instrument of Social Exclusion," in *Invisible Punishment: The Collateral Consequences of Mass Imprisonment*, edited by Marc Mauer and Meda Chesney-Lind, p. 24; *When Prisoners Come Home*, by Joan Petersilia, p. 115; and *But They All Come Back*, by Jeremy Travis, p. 69.

44. "Texas Ex-Offenders Are Denied Job Licenses," by Eric Dexheimer, *Statesman*, April 11, 2011.

45. See, for example, "Welfare and Housing—Denial of Benefits to Drug Offenders," by Gwen Rubinstein and Debbie Mukamal, in *Invisible Punishment*, edited by Marc Mauer and Meda Chesney-Lind, pp. 37–38; "No Place Like Home: Housing and the Ex-Prisoner," by Katharine H. Bradley, R. B. Michael Oliver, Noel C. Richardson, and Elspeth M. Slayter, Boston: Community Resources for Justice, November, 2001, p. 1; "Homeless Shelter Use and Reincarceration following Prison Release," by Stephen Metraux, and Dennis P. Culhane, *Criminology and Public Policy*, vol. 3, no. 2, March 2004, pp. 139–160.

46. "Returning Home: Understanding the Challenges of Prisoner Reentry: Maryland Pilot Study: Findings from Baltimore," by Christy Visher, Nancy LaVigne, and Jeremy Travis, *Urban Institute: Justice Policy Center*, January 2004, pp. 164–165.

47. "Housing Strategies to Strengthen Welfare Policy and Support Working Families," by Barbara Sard and Margy Waller, Center on Urban and Metropolitan Policy and the Center on Budget and Policy Priorities—Research Brief, The Brookings Institution, 2002, p. 3.

48. *When Prisoners Come Home*, by Joan Petersilia, pp. 120–121.

49. "Ex-Offender Needs versus Community Opportunity in Seattle, Washington," by Jacqueline Helfgott, *Federal Probation*, 1997, pp. 14–19.

50. Ibid.

51. Federal spending on low-income housing dropped from 7 percent of the federal budget in 1978 to 0.7 percent in 1988, and continues at a depressed level: "Changing Priorities: The Federal Budget and Housing Assistance, 1976–2005," by C. N. Djolbeare, I. B. Saraf, and S. Crowley, National Low Income Housing Coalition, 2004; cited in *Banished*, by Katherine Beckett and Steve Herbert, p. 29.

52. *When Prisoners Come Home*, by Joan Petersilia, p. 121.

53. For citations of the studies on returning prisoners becoming homeless, see *But They All Come Back*, by Jeremy Travis, pp. 239–240;

and "Incarceration and Homelessness," by Stephen Metraux, Caterina G. Roman, and Richard S. Cho, 2007 National Symposium on Homelessness Research.

54. See "Called 'Out' at Home: The One Strike Eviction Policy and Juvenile Court," by Wendy J. Kaplan and David Rossman, *Duke Forum for Law & Social Change*, vol. 3, 2011, p. 115.

55. See, for example, ibid., p. 122; *But They All Come Back*, by Jeremy Travis, p. 232; and "Welfare and Housing—Denial of Benefits to Drug Offenders," by Gwen Rubinstein and Debbie Mukamal, in *Invisible Punishment*, edited by Marc Mauer and Meda Chesney-Lind, pp. 46–47.

56. *But They All Come Back*, by Jeremy Travis, p. 231; 42 U.S.C. § 1437d : US Code—Section 1437d (1) (7); see 24 CFR 966.4 (1) (5) (3) (iii); also, "Every Door Closed: Barriers Facing Parents with Criminal Records," by Amy E. Hirsch et al., Center for Law and Social Policy and Community Legal Services, Inc., 2002, p. 50.

57. "Called 'Out' at Home: The One Strike Eviction Policy and Juvenile Court," by Wendy J. Kaplan and David Rossman, *Duke Forum for Law & Social Change*, 2011, p. 119.

58. See, for example, "No Place Like Home: Housing and the Ex-prisoner," by Katharine H. Bradley, R. B. Michael Oliver, Noel C. Richardson, and Elspeth M. Slayter, *Community Resources for Justice*, 2001, p. 3.

59. "Every Door Closed: Barriers Facing Parents with Criminal Records," by Amy E. Hirsch et al., Center for Law and Social Policy and Community Legal Services, Inc., 2002, p. 41; available at http://www.clasp.org/admin/site/publications_archive/files/0092.pdf.

60. Ibid., p. 45.

61. Ibid., p. 46.

62. Under the Section 8 program, the offense would have to have occurred "on or near" the premises; this program authorizes the payment of rental housing assistance to private landlords on behalf of low-income households.

63. For a description of the cases, see *Department of Housing and Urban Development v. Rucker*; opinion of the Court by Justice Rehnquist, available at http://www.law.cornell.edu/supct/html/00-1770.ZO.html; and *But They All Come Back*, by Jeremy Travis, p. 233.
6442. U.S.C. § 1437d(l)(6)

65. *Department of Housing and Urban Development v. Rucker*; opinion of the Court by Justice Rehnquist, March 26, 2002. For section 8 voucher housing, the same rules apply except that the drug-related criminal activity must be "on or near" the premises, not "on or off."

66. "Despite High Court Ruling, Three of Four Oakland Eviction Tenants to Stay," editorial, *San Mateo Daily Journal*, April 6, 2002.

67. See http://www.legalmomentum.org/assets/pdfs/martinez4-16-021tr .pdf.

68. See http://www.hud.gov/offices/pih/programs/ph/rhiip/phguidebook new.pdf.

69. See, for example, "Litigating around the Long Shadow of *Department of Housing and Urban Development v. Rucker*: The Availability of Abuse of Discretion and Implied Duty of Good Faith Affirmative Defenses in Public Housing Criminal Evictions," by Robert Hornstein, *University of Toledo Law Review,* vol. 43, no. 1, 2011–2012, pp. 11–12.

70. Ibid., pp. 2–3.

71. See "Called 'Out' at Home: The One Strike Eviction Policy and Juvenile Court," by Wendy J. Kaplan and David Rossman, *Duke Forum for Law & Social Change,* vol. 3, 2011.

72. Ibid., pp. 121–122.

73. Ibid., p. 117.

74. Ibid., p. 120.

75. "Back on Track: Supporting Youth Reentry from Out-of-Home Placement to the Community," by Ashley Nellis and Richard Hooks Wayman, National Alliance to End Homelessness and The Sentencing Project, fall 2009; also, ibid., p. 133.

76. See "Overview of Young Adult Homelessness in Minnesota," *Amherst H. Wilder Foundation: Wilder Research*, by Gregg Owen et al., June 2008; and, ibid.

77. Ibid.

78. "Homeless Shelter Use and Reincarceration following Prison Release: Assessing the Risk," by Stephen Metraux and Dennis P. Culhane, *Criminology and Public Policy*, 2004, p. 139.

79. See http://aspe.hhs.gov/hsp/homelessness/symposium07/metraux, Introduction, p. 1.

80. "Health Care for Homeless Persons," by Bruce. D. Levy and James. J. O'Connell, *New England Journal of Medicine,* vol. 350, June 3, 2004, pp. 2329–2332; also, *Banished*, by Katherine Beckett and Steve Herbert, ch. 1.

81. For the relevant citations, see "Homeless Shelter Use and Reincarceration following Prison Release: Assessing the Risk," by Stephen Metraux and Dennis P. Culhane, *Criminology and Public Policy*, 2004, p. 141.

82. See, for example, "Mental Health and Treatment of Inmates and Probationers," by Paula M. Ditton, U.S. Dept. of Justice, Bureau of Justice Statistics, 1999.

83. See "Revolving Doors: Imprisonment among the Homeless and Marginally Housed Population," by B. Margot et al., *American Journal of Public Health*, vol. 95, no. 10, October 2005, p. 1747.

84. See "Incarceration and Homelessness," by Stephen Metraux, Caterina G. Roman, and Richard S. Cho, *National Symposium on Homelessness Research*, 2007, pp. 9–11 for relevant citations.

85. "Revolving Doors: Imprisonment among the Homeless and Marginally Housed Population," by B. Margot et al., *American Journal of Public Health*, vol. 95, no. 10, October 2005, p. 1751.

86. See *Banished*, by Katherine Beckett and Steve Herbert, pp. 105–106.

87. Ibid., p. 110.

88. See http://www.desc.org/.

89. *Banished*, by Katherine Beckett and Steve Herbert, pp. 114–115.

90. *Street Lives*, by Steven VanderStaay, p. 14.

91. See, for example, *The Body Economic: Why Austerity Kills*, by David Stuckler and Sanjay Basu, ch. 8, especially pp. 125–126.

92. The law was called Personal Responsibility and Work Opportunity Reconciliation Act. See, for example, "Welfare and Housing— Denial of Benefits to Drug Offenders," by Gwen Rubinstein and Debbie Mukamal, in *Invisible Punishment*, edited by Marc Mauer and Meda Chesney-Lind, pp. 40–41; and *When Prisoners Come Home*, by Joan Petersilia, pp. 124–126.

93. Public Law No. 104–193, paragraph 115.

94. "Welfare and Housing—Denial of Benefits to Drug Offenders," by Gwen Rubinstein and Debbie Mukamal, in *Invisible Punishment*, edited by Marc Mauer and Meda Chesney-Lind, pp. 40–41; *When Prisoners Come Home*, by Joan Petersilia, pp. 124–126; and, *But They All Come Back*, by Jeremy Travis, pp. 291–292.

95. "After Prison: Roadblocks to Entry," report by the Legal Action Center: 2009 Update, pp. 11–12. For the law in every state including the District of Columbia, see http://www.lac.org/roadblocks-to-reentry/main.php?view=law.

96. "Race, the War on Drugs, and the Collateral Consequences of Criminal Conviction," by Gabriel J. Chin, in *Civil Penalties, Social Consequences*, edited by Christopher Mele and Teresa A. Miller, 2005, p. 37.

97. See *U.S. v. Hester* (1998); and ibid.

98. Ibid.

99. Ibid., p. 38. See *U.S. v. Hernandez-Avalos* (2001); and *U.S. v. Restrepo-Aguilar* (1996).

100. "Welfare and Housing—Denial of Benefits to Drug Offenders," by Gwen Rubinstein and Debbie Mukamal, in *Invisible Punishment*, edited by Marc Mauer and Meda Chesney-Lind, pp. 42–43; and "Making Welfare Reform Work Better: Improving TANF Program Results for Recipients with Alcohol and Drug Problems," by Gwen Rubinstein, Legal Action Center, September 2000, pp. 2–4.

101. Ibid.

102. "Does Federal Financial Aid Affect College Enrollment? Evidence from Drug Offenders and the Higher Education Act of 1998," by Michael F. Lovenheim and Emily G. Owens, *NBER Working Paper*, no. 18749, February 2013, p. 3; and *Why Our Drug Laws Have Failed and What We Can Do about It*, 2nd ed., by Judge James P. Gray, pp. 27, 166.

103. https://nces.ed.gov/programs/digest/d13/tables/dt13_331.90.asp.

104. "Does Federal Financial Aid Affect College Enrollment? Evidence from Drug Offenders and the Higher Education Act of 1998," by Michael F. Lovenheim and Emily G. Owens, *NBER Working Paper*, no. 18749, February 2013, pp. 23–24.

105. Ibid., p. 24.

106. "Mass Imprisonment and the Disappearing Voters," by Marc Mauer, in *Invisible Punishment*, edited by Marc Mauer and Meda Chesney-Lind, p. 50.

107. "Democratic Contraction? Political Consequences of Felon Disenfranchisement in the United States," by Christopher Uggen and Jeff Manza, *American Sociological Review*, vol. 67, no. 6, December 2002, table 4a, p. 793.

108. Ibid.

109. "State-Level Estimates of Felon Disenfranchisement in the United States, 2010," by Christopher Uggen, Sarah Shannon, and Jeff Manza, *The Sentencing Project*, July 2012, pp. 1–3; see table 1, p. 3.

110. Ibid., p. 15.

111. In Nebraska, the ban is only for two years, and, in Arizona, it applies only to recidivists. The remaining states are AL, DE, FL, KY, MS, NV, TN, VA, and WY.

112. Ibid.

113. States that have in recent years liberalized disenfranchisement provisions for ex-felons are Delaware (2000), Maryland (2003), Nebraska (2005), Nevada (2003), New Mexico (2001), and Texas (1997). States that have restricted voting laws are Utah (1998), Massachusetts (2000), and Kansas (2002); see, also, "Disenfranchisement and the Civic Reintegration of Convicted Felons," by Chistopher Uggen and Jeff Manza,

in *Civil Penalties, Social Consequences*, edited by Christopher Mele and Teresa A. Miller, pp. 73–74.

114. Ibid., pp. 72–73.

115. "Why Deny Prisoners the Vote?" by Martin Kettle, *The Guardian*, January 21, 2011.

116. See, for example, "Gilding the Cage: Prisoners Get Better Rights in Unexpected Places," *The Economist*, August 17, 2013; "Prisoners' Right to Vote: Q&A," by Alan Travis, *The Guardian*, February 10, 2011; and http://www.cbc.ca/archives/categories/politics/rights-freedoms/voting -in-canada-how-a-privilege-became-a-right/all-inmates-can-vote.html. Other countries that allow prisoners to vote are: Australia, New Zealand, Austria, Albania, Croatia, the Czech Republic, Denmark, Finland, Germany, Iceland, France, Japan, Lithuania, Kenya, Macedonia, Montenegro, Netherlands, Norway, Peru, Ireland, Poland, Romania, Serbia, Sweden, and Switzerland. (A few of these countries do not allow criminals who commit fraud or extreme crimes of violence to vote.) Source for this list is: "Let Inmates Keep the Right to Vote," by Lynne Winfield, *The Royal Gazette Online*, December 20, 2012.

116. "Prisoners' Right to Vote: Q&A," by Alan Travis, *The Guardian*, February 10, 2011.

117. "Damage to Family Relationships as a Collateral Consequence of Parental Incarceration," by Philip M. Genty, *Fordham Urban Law Journal*, vol. 30, 2002–2003, pp. 1671, 1678; and *When Prisoners Come Home*, by Joan Petersilia, p. 43.

118. See "Effects of Parental Incarceration on Young Children," by Ross D. Parke and K. Alison Clarke-Stewart, pp. 5–6, in *From Prison to Home: The Effect of Incarceration and Reentry on Children, Families and Communities*, a conference report presented at the National Policy Conference of the Urban Institute and the U.S. Department of Health and Human Services, December 2001.

119. "Parents in Prison and Their Minor Children," by Lauren E. Glaze and Laura M. Maruschak, *Bureau of Justice Statistics: Special Report*, August 2008, p. 22, appendix table 17.

120. "Prisoners in 2013," by Ann E. Carson, U.S. Dept. of Justice Bureau of Justice Statistics, September 2014, NCJ247282, federal data, p. 16; state data, p. 15.

121. "Incarcerated Parents and Their Children," by Laura M. Maruschak, Lauren E. Glaze, and Christopher J. Mumola, in *Children of Incarcerated Parents*, edited by J. Mark Eddy and Julie Poehlmann, 2010.

122. For example, "Procedural Due Process Rights of Incarcerated Parents in Termination of Parental Rights Proceedings: A Fifty State

Analysis," by Philip M. Genty, *Journal of Family Law*, vol. 30, 1991–1992, pp. 757, 759; see, also, *But They All Come Back*, by Jeremy Travis, pp. 126–144.

123. U.S. Sentencing Commission, 2008–2012, datafiles, USSCFY08—USSCF.

124. *But They All Come Back*, by Jeremy Travis, p. 132.

125. See *All Alone in the World: Children of the Incarcerated*, by Nell Bernstein, p. 78.

126. See, for example, "11 US Senators Question Shutting of Danbury Women's Prison," by Grace Merritt, *The CT Mirror*, August 2, 2013; and "For Women, a Second Sentence," by Piper Kerman, *The New York Times*, August 13, 2013.

127. "11 US Senators Question Shutting of Danbury Women's Prison," by Grace Merritt, *The CT Mirror*, August 2, 2013.

128. "For Women, a Second Sentence," by Piper Kerman, *The New York Times*, August 13, 2013; see, also, "Damage to Family Relationships as a Collateral Consequence of Parental Incarceration," by Philip M. Genty, *Fordham Urban Law Journal*, vol. 30, 2002–2003, pp. 1673–1674. For citations on research documenting the importance for children of regular communication with parents, see footnote 23 on p. 1674.

129. "Parents in Prison and Their Minor Children," by Lauren E. Glaze and Laura M. Maruschak, *Bureau of Justice Statistics: Special Report*, August 2008, p. 18, appendix table 10.

130. "A Woman's Journey Home: Challenges for Female Offenders and Their Children," by Stephanie Covington, in *From Prison to Home: The Effect of Incarceration and Reentry on Children, Families and Communities*, conference paper presented at the National Policy Conference of the Urban Institute and the U.S. Department of Health and Human Services, December 2001, p. 9.

131. *All Alone in the World: Children of the Incarcerated*, by Nell Bernstein, p. 81.

132. *When Prisoners Come Home*, by Joan Petersilia, p. 44

133. *All Alone in the World: Children of the Incarcerated*, by Nell Bernstein, p. 80.

134. "Families and Incarceration," by Donald Braman, in *Invisible Punishment*, edited by Marc Mauer and Meda Chesney-Lind, pp. 118–122.

135. Ibid., p. 120.

136. Ibid.

137. Ibid., pp. 120–121.

138. "Why Does It Cost so Much for Prisoners to Keep in Touch with Their Families?" *The Economist*, May 25, 2013; *But They All Come*

Back, by Jeremy Travis, pp. 135–136; and *When Prisoners Come Home*, by Joan Petersilia, pp. 45–46.

139. *Going Up the River*, by Joseph T. Hallinan, p. xiv.

140. "Costly Phone Calls for Inmates," editorial, *The New York Times*, September 23, 2012; and "Why Does It Cost so Much for Prisoners to Keep in Touch with Their Families?" *The Economist*, May 25, 2013.

141. "Costly Phone Calls for Inmates," editorial, *The New York Times*, September 23, 2012.

142. "Unfair Phone Charges for Inmates," editorial, *The New York Times*, January 6, 2014.

143. See, for example, "Criminal Convictions, Incarceration, and Child Welfare: Ex-Offenders Lose Their Children," by Peter D. Schneider, in *Every Door Closed: Barriers Facing Parents with Criminal Records*, ch. 4, report from Center for Law and Social Policy and Community Legal Services, Inc., 2002, p. 54.

144. See, for example, "A Daily Disaster for Children," by Jody Adams, *The New York Times*, February 19, 2001.

145. "Children's Interests in a Familial Context: Poverty, Foster Care, and Adoption," by Naomi R. Cahn, *Ohio State Law Journal*, vol. 60, 1999, pp. 1189, 1198–1199; see, also, "When Welfare Ends: Removing Children from the Home for Poverty Alone," by Dan Braveman and Sarah Ramsey, *Temple Law Review*, vol. 70, 1997.

146. "Assessing the Consequences of Welfare Reform for Child Welfare," by Kristin Shook, *Poverty Research News,* vol. 2, no. 1, winter 1998, pp. 8–12, cited in "Children's Interests in a Familial Context: Poverty, Foster Care, and Adoption," by Naomi R. Cahn, *Ohio State Law Journal*, vol. 60, 1999, pp. 1198–1199.

147. "Children's Interests in a Familial Context: Poverty, Foster Care, and Adoption," by Naomi R. Cahn, *Ohio State Law Journal*, vol. 60, 1999, p. 1191, 1199; also, "Foster Parent Adoption: The Legal Framework," by Andre P. Derdeyn, in *The Psychology of Adoption*, edited by David M. Brodzinsky and Marshall D. Schechter, 1990, pp. 332, 336–337.

148. *The Welfare of Children*, by Duncan Lindsey, p. 155.

149. *Shattered Bonds*, by Dorothy Roberts, p. 34.

150. "President Clinton's Budget Proposal for New Funding for Child Welfare Services Targeted for Family Support and Preservation Services," testimony of Peter Digre, *Committee on Ways and Means, Subcommittee on Human Resources, U.S. House of Representatives*, April 21, 1993, pp. 87–88; see, also, "Assessing the Influence of Welfare Reform on Child Welfare Systems," by Kristen Shook Slack, *Focus,* vol. 22, no. 1, 2002, pp. 102–103, table 1.

151. The following statement is in *Stanley v. Illinois*, 405 U.S. 645 (1972).

152. *Meyer v. Nebraska*, 262 U.S. 390, 262 U.S. 399 (1923).

153. *Skinner v. Oklahoma*, 316 U.S. 535, 316 U.S. 541 (1942).

154. *May v. Anderson*, 345 U.S. 528, 345 U.S. 533 (1953).

155. See, for example, "Children's Interests in a Familial Context: Poverty, Foster Care, and Adoption," by Naomi R. Cahn, *Ohio State Law Journal*, vol. 60, 1999, pp. 1197–1198; and *When Prisoners Come Home*, by Joan Petersilia, pp. 126–127.

156. Ibid.

157. See "Truth in Sentencing in State Prisons," by Paula M. Ditton and Doris James Wilson, *Special Report: Bureau of Justice Statistics*, January 1999, table 7.

158. See the U.S. Government Accounting Office, 1999.

159. "Children's Interests in a Familial Context: Poverty, Foster Care, and Adoption," by Naomi R. Cahn, *Ohio State Law Journal*, vol. 60, 1999, p. 1205.

160. "Criminal Convictions, Incarceration, and Child Welfare: Ex-Offenders Lose Their Children," by Peter D. Schneider, in *Every Door Closed: Barriers Facing Parents with Criminal Records*, ch. 4, report from Center for Law and Social Policy and Community Legal Services, Inc., 2002, pp. 60–61, 64–65; also, *Shattered Bonds*, by Dorothy E. Roberts, p. 116.

161. "Protecting the Ties That Bind from Behind Bars; A Call for Equal Opportunities for Incarcerated Fathers and Their Children to Maintain the Parent–Child Relationship," by Elise Zealand, *Columbia Journal of Law and Social Problems*, vol. 31, 1998, pp. 247, 255–256; and, "Criminal Convictions, Incarceration, and Child Welfare: Ex-Offenders Lose Their Children," by Peter D. Schneider, in *Every Door Closed: Barriers Facing Parents with Criminal Records*, ch. 4, report from Center for Law and Social Policy and Community Legal Services, Inc., 2002, p. 64.

162. *When Prisoners Come Home*, by Joan Petersilia, p. 127.

163. "Protecting the Ties That Bind from Behind Bars; A Call for Equal Opportunities for Incarcerated Fathers and Their Children to Maintain the Parent–Child Relationship," by Elise Zealand, *Columbia Journal of Law and Social Problems*, vol. 31, 1998, p. 260.

164. *But They All Come Back*, by Jeremy Travis, p. 128; the data are from "Damage to Family Relationships as a Collateral Consequence of Parental Incarceration," by Philip M. Genty, *Fordham Urban Law Journal*, vol. 30, 2002–2003, p. 1678.

165. "Child Protection and Child Outcomes: Measuring the Effects of Foster Care," by Joseph J. Doyle Jr., *American Economic Review*, December 2007, pp. 1583–1584; and "Child Protection and Adult Crime: Using Investigator Assignment to Estimate Causal Effects of Foster Care," by Joseph J. Doyle Jr., *Journal of Political Economy*, August 2008, pp. 747–748.

166. Ibid.

167. Ibid.

168. "The Impact of Foster Care on Development," by Catherine R. Lawrence, Elizabeth A. Carlson, and Byron Egeland, *Development and Psychopathology*, vol. 18, 2006, pp. 57–76.

169. "Re-entry and Reintegration: The Road to Public Safety, Report and Recommendations of the Special Committee on Collateral Consequences of Criminal Proceedings," *New York State Bar Association*, 2006, p. 163.

170. "Changing Fortunes or Changing Attitudes? Sentencing and Corrections Reforms in 2003," by Jon Wool and Don Stemen, *Vera Institute of Justice*, 2004, see p. 4 for a list of states that have increased or implemented a variety of fees and fines, even for misdemeanors; "Economic Sanctions in Criminal Justice: Purposes, Effects and Implications," by Mark H. Bergstrom and R. Barry Ruback, *Criminal Justice & Behavior*, vol. 33, 2006, see the list of county fees and costs in Pennsylvania on p. 254; and, "Making the 'Bad Guy' Pay: Growing Use of Cost Shifting as Economic Sanction," by Kirsten D. Levingston, in *Prison Profiteers*, 2007, edited by Tara Herivel and Paul Wright, pp. 59–61.

171. "Economic Sanctions in Criminal Justice: Purposes, Effects and Implications," by Mark H. Bergstrom and R. Barry Ruback, *Criminal Justice & Behavior*, vol. 33, 2006, pp. 242, 260.

172. "Debt to Society Is Least of Costs for Ex-Convicts," by Adam Liptak, *The New York Times*, February 23, 2006.

173. "Out of Prison and Deep in Debt," editorial, *The New York Times*, October 6, 2007.

174. Ibid; and *Repaying Debts*, by Rachel L. McLean and Michael D. Thompson, Bureau of Justice Assistance and Council of State Governments Justice Center, 2007.

175. "Making the 'Bad Guy' Pay: Growing Use of Cost Shifting as Economic Sanction," by Kirsten D. Levingston, in *Prison Profiteers*, 2007, edited by Tara Herivel and Paul Wright, pp. 71–74.

176. The War on Marijuana in Black and White, report by the ACLU, June 2013, pp. 24–26.

177. See "Debt to Society Is Least of Costs for Ex-Convicts," by Adam Liptak, *The New York Times*, February 23, 2006.

178. "Poverty Keeps Woman Jailed, Lawsuit Says," by Carlos Campos, *Atlanta Journal-Constitution*, September 19, 2006.

179. "Fees for Probation Services," by S. Christopher Baird, Douglas A. Holien, and Audrey J. Bakke, *National Council on Crime and Delinquency*, January 1986, p. viii.

180. "Making the 'Bad Guy' Pay: Growing Use of Cost Shifting as Economic Sanction," by Kirsten D. Levingston, in *Prison Profiteers*, 2007, edited by Tara Herivel and Paul Wright, p. 54.

181. "2010 Annual Report," Corrections Corporation of America, TN 2011.

182. The quote is from: "Rights at United States Borders," by Jon Adams, *BYU Journal of Public Law*, 2004, pp. 356–357; see also, *Profiles in Injustice*, by David A. Harris, pp. 214–215; *America's Longest War*, by Steven B. Duke and Albert C. Gross, pp. 123–124; and "Protecting the US Perimeter: Border Searches under the Fourth Amendment," by Yule Kim, *Congressional Research Service*, June 29, 2009, p. 9.

183. U.S. Constitution, article 1, par. 8, cl. 3; and see "Rights at United States Borders," by Jon Adams, *BYU Journal of Public Law*, 2004, pp. 354–357.

184. *Profiles in Injustice*, by David A. Harris, p. 214.

185. Ibid.

186. "Protecting Our Perimeter: 'Border Searches' under the Fourth Amendment," by Stephen R. Vina, *CRS Report for Congress*, 2006, p. 4; and "Protecting the U.S. Perimeter: Border Searches under the Fourth Amendment," by Yule Kim, *CRS Report for Congress*, June 29, 2009, p. 4.

187. "Protecting Our Perimeter: 'Border Searches' under the Fourth Amendment," by Stephen R. Vina, *CRS Report for Congress*, 2006, p. 15.

188. "Protecting the U.S. Perimeter: 'Border Searches' under the Fourth Amendment," by Yule Kim, *CRS Report for Congress*, June 29, 2009, p. 16.

189. *United States v. Montoya de Hernandez*, 473 U.S. 531, 541 (1985).

190. Ibid.; and "Rights at United States Borders," by Jon Adams, *BYU Journal of Public Law*, 2004, p. 359.

191. *United States v. Montoya de Hernandez*, 473 U.S. 531, 541 (1985).

192. "Rights at United States Borders," by Jon Adams, *BYU Journal of Public Law*, 2004, pp. 364–365.

193. Ibid., p. 11; "Protecting Our Perimeter: 'Border Searches' Under the Fourth Amendment," by Stephen R. Vina, *CRS Report for Congress*, 2006, p. 15, and fn. 66.

194. *United States v. Montoya de Hernandez*, 473 U.S. (1985).

195. Ibid., pp. 531, 538; see, also, *America's Longest War*, by Steven B. Duke and Albert C. Gross, p. 124.

196. *Profiles in Injustice*, by David A. Harris, p. 215.

197. Ibid., p. 208; see, also, pp. 208–213.

198. Ibid.

199. "Protecting Our Perimeter: 'Border Searches' under the Fourth Amendment," by Stephen R. Vina, *CRS Report to Congress*, 2006, pp. 21–23, quote on p. 23; and "Protecting the US Perimeter: 'Border Searches' under the Fourth Amendment," by Yule Kim, *Congressional Research Service*, June 29, 2009, pp. 22–24.

Chapter 14

1. "Historical Legal Basis for Drug Testing," by Paul Armentano and Donna Shea, *DocumentNORML*, February 15, 2012.

2. "Relationship between Student Illicit Drug Use and School Drug-Testing Policies," by Ryoko Yamaguchi, Lloyd D. Johnston, and Patrick M. O'Malley, *Journal of School Health*, vol. 73, no. 4, April 2003, p. 1.

3. See, for example, http://www.aclu.org/features/f083000a.html; "Court Rulings Signal a Shift on Random Drug Tests in Schools," by Jodi Wilgoren, *The New York Times*, March 25, 2001; http://www.edweek.org/ew/vol-17/20drug.h17; and, http://supct.law.cornell.edu/supct/html/94-590.ZO.html.

4. *Vernonia Sch. Dist. 47J v. Acton* (94–590), 515 U.S. p. 646 (1995).

5. *New Jersey v. T.L.O.*

6. Ibid.

7. *Todd v. Rush County Schools* (1998).

8. *Board of Education of Independent School District No. 92 of Pottawatomie County et al. v. Earls et al.* (2002).

9. Ibid.

10. Ibid.

11. "Public School Students' Fourth Amendment Rights after Vernonia and Earls: Why Limits Must Be Set on Suspicionless Drug Screening in the Public Schools," by Christopher A. Gorman, *Vermont Law Review*, vol. 29, 2004.

12. Ibid., pp. 168–169.

13. See, for example, "Strip Search Review Tests Limits of School Drug Policy," by Joan Biskupic, *USA TODAY*, April 16, 2009.

14. *Board of Education of Independent School District No. 92 of Pottawatomie County et al. v. Earls et al.* (2002).

15. *What You Need to Know about Testing in Schools*, Office of National Drug Control Policy, 2002, p. 5.

16. CNN/USA Today Gallup Poll, June 21–23, 2002.

17. "Poll Finds Backing for Drug Tests: One Quarter Report Abuse in Workplace," by Cindy Skzycki, *The Washington Post*, December 14, 1989.

18. "The Effectiveness of Mandatory Random Student Drug Testing," by Susanne James-Burdumy et al., *U.S. Department of Education*, July 2010, p. xix.

19. Ibid., p. xxi, and table 1.

20. Ibid.

21. "Drug Testing in Schools: Policies, Practices, and Association with Student Drug Use," by Ryoko Yamaguchi, Lloyd D. Johnston, and Patrick M. O'Malley, Youth, Education, and Society Occasional Paper 2. Ann Arbor, MI: *Institute for Social Research*, University of Michigan, 2003. This occasional paper extends the analysis of the following article by adding another year of data: "Relationship between Student Illicit Drug Use and School Drug-Testing Policies," by Ryoko Yamaguchi, Lloyd D. Johnston, and Patrick M. O'Malley, *Journal of School Health*, vol. 73, no. 4, 2003, pp. 159–164.

22. "Drug Testing in Schools: Policies, Practices, and Association with Student Drug Use," by Ryoko Yamaguchi, Lloyd D. Johnston, and Patrick M. O'Malley, Youth, Education, and Society Occasional Paper 2. Ann Arbor, MI: *Institute for Social Research*, University of Michigan, 2003, p. 7.

23. Ibid., pp. 14–15.

24. "An Assessment of the Scientific Support Underlying the FY 2011 Budget Priorities of the Office of National Drug Control Policy," by Rosalie Liccardo Pacula, testimony presented before the *House Oversight and Government Reform Committee, Subcommittee on Domestic Policy*, April 14, 2010.

25. "Testing for Drugs of Abuse in Children and Adolescents: Addendum—Testing in Schools and at Home," by the Committee on Substance Abuse and Council on School Health, *Pediatrics*, vol. 119, no. 3, March 1, 2007, p. 628.

26. Ibid.

27. Ibid., pp. 628–629.

28. "Drug Testing in General Medical Clinics, in School and at Home: Physician Attitudes and Practices," by Sharon Levy et al., *Journal of Adolescent Health*, vol. 38, no. 4, April 2006, pp. 336–342.

Chapter 15

1. Drug-Free Workplace Act of 1988.

2. See *National Treasury Employees Union v. Von Raab* (1989) and *Skinner v. Railway Labor Executives' Association* (1989).

3. Omnibus Transportation Employee Testing Act, Pub. L. No. 102–143 (1991).

4. "Drug Testing," ACLU, available at http://www.aclu.org/criminal-law-reform/drug-testing.

5. "Drug Testing Poses Quandary for Employers," by Katie Zezima and Abby Goodnough, *The New York Times*, October 24, 2010.

6. Ibid.

7. "Drug Testing Poses Quandary for Employers," by Katie Zezima and Abby Goodnough, *The New York Times*, October 24, 2010.

8. Ibid.

9. http://landrumhrblog.com/2012/10/09/what-can-you-do-when-an-employee-seems-unfit-for-duty. The exceptions are for those in public-safety jobs, such as police, pilots, firefighters, and bus and truck drivers, who can be required to self-report prescription drugs that could impair their ability to do their job.

10. http://www.ca6.uscourts.gov/opinions.pdf/14a0206p-06.pdf.

11. "Workplace Injuries and Illnesses—2011," Bureau of Labor Statistics, October 25, 2012, p. 1.

12. "Traumatic Occupational Injuries," Centers for Disease Control and Prevention, 2012.

13. "The Effects of Substance Use on Workplace Injuries," by Rajeev Ramchand, Amanda Pomeroy, and Jeremy Arkes, *RAND Center for Health and Safety in the Workplace*, 2009, pp. 26–29.

14. Ibid., pp. 37–41.

15. Ibid., pp. 3–4. See the studies referred to on these pages.

16. Ibid.

17. "Testing Drugs versus Testing for Drug Use: Private Risk Management in the Shadow of Criminal Law," by Robert J. MacCoun, *Depaul Law Review*, vol. 56, no. 507, 2006–2007, p. 514.

18. Ibid., p. 513.

19. "Drug Testing in the Workplace: Summary Conclusions of the Independent Inquiry into Drug Testing at Work," *The Joseph Rowntree Foundation*, June 2004.

20. Ibid., p. 2.

21. Ibid.

22. Ibid.

23. Ibid.

24. Ibid.

25. Ibid.

26. Ibid.

27. "Prevalence and Factors Related to Canadian Workplace Health Programs," by Scott Macdonald, Richard Csiernik, Pierre Durand, Margaret Rylett, and T. Cameron Wild, *Canadian Journal of Public Health*, March–April 2006.

28. Ibid., p. 124.

29. Ibid.

30. "Canadian Human Rights Commission Policy on Alcohol and Drug Testing," *Canadian Human Rights Commission*, June 2002, pp. 1–16.

31. Ibid., p. 1.

32. Ibid., p. 2.

33. Ibid., p. 4.

34. For example, in a 2011 Rasmussen telephone poll of likely voters, 53 percent believed that welfare recipients should automatically be drug tested before they can receive benefits. An additional 13 percent favored random drug testing of applicants, while 29 percent believed they should be tested only if there is reasonable suspicion. See http://www.rasmussenreports.com/public_content/politics/general_politics/july_2011/53_support_automatic_drug_testing_for_welfare_applicants.

35. http://www.stripes.com/gates-as-vp-memoir-is-full-of-interesting-tidbits-1.261813.

Chapter 16

1. "Majority Now Supports Legalizing Marijuana," *Pew Research*, April 4, 2013.

2. Ibid., and http://www.gallup.com/poll/165539/first-time-americans-favor-legalizing-marijuana.aspx.

3. http://www.nytimes.com/2013/08/13/nyregion/stop-and-frisk-practice-violated-rights-judge-rules.html?_r=0.

4. See "Memorandum to the United States Attorneys and Assistant Attorney General from the Criminal Division," *The Attorney General*, August 12, 2013.

5. See "US Moves to Curb Long, Mandatory Drug Sentences," by Dan Levine and David Ingram, *Reuters*, August 12, 2013.

6. Ibid.

7. http://sentencing.typepad.com/sentencing_law_and_policy/mandatory_minimum_sentencing_statutes/.

8. "Memorandum to the United States Attorneys and Assistant Attorney General for the Criminal Division," *The Attorney General*, August 12, 2013; and http://news.uscourts.gov/sites/default/files/Judge-Bell-Chairman-Leahy-mandatory-minimums.pdf.

9. http://www.justice.gov/iso/opa/resources/3052013829132756857467.pdf.

10. The Controlled Substances Act of 1970. The quote is the guidance that Congress has provided the Justice Department as to how to enforce the law.

11. http://www.justice.gov/iso/opa/resources/3052013829132756857467.pdf.

12. "Marijuana Milestone," *The Economist*, November 8, 2014.

13. "Q&A: Legal Marijuana in Colorado and Washington," by John Walsh, The Brookings Institution, May 21, 2013.

14. See "Answers Sought for When Marijuana Laws Collide," by Ashley Southall, *The New York Times*, September 10, 2013.

15. Ibid.

16. See "Marijuana Legalization: Toker's Delight," *The Economist*, September 21, 2013.

17. See the Comprehensive Crime Control Act of 1984.

18. See the statements by Bill Johnson, executive director of the National Association of Police Organizations, and John W. Thompson, interim executive director of the National Sheriffs' Association, in: "Holder Limits Seized-Asset Sharing Process That Splits Billions with Local, State Police," by Robert O'Harrow Jr., Sari Horwitz, and Steven Rich, *Washington Post*, January 16, 2015.

Chapter 17

1. See http://www.whitehouse.gov/sites/default/files/ondcp/policy-and-research/fy_2014_drug_control_budget_highlights_3.pdf. In FY 2013, the federal government spent $9.4 billion on domestic drug law enforcement, $3.9 billion on interdicting drugs, and $1.9 billion on drug law enforcement in foreign countries. The government also spent $9.4 billion on prevention and treatment. See figure 1, p. 2, and tables 1–3 on pp. 12–14.

2. See, for example, Corrections Corporation of America, a for-profit company that owns and manages prisons; it was incorporated in 1983.

3. See Chapter 10.

4. http://articles.latimes.com/1990-09-06/news/mn-983_1_casual -drug-users.

5. http://www.ropercenter.uconn.edu/data_access/tag/illegal_drugs .html.

6. See the October 22, 2013, *Gallup* poll, and the August 20, 2013, *Rasmussen* poll.

7. *Dreams from My Father*, by Barack Obama, pp. 93–94.

8. http://www.nytimes.com/2006/10/24/world/americas/24iht -dems.3272493.html?_r=0&pagewanted=print.

9. See "Bummer," by Jacob Sullum, *Reason*, September 12, 2011.

10. For a review of the scientific evidence on the dangers of marijuana, see, for example, *Drugs: America's Holy War*, by Arthur Benavie, pp. 51–54, and ch. 10.

11. See, for example, "Obama's War on Pot," by Tim Dickinson, *Rolling Stone*, February 16, 2012; and "Obama's Drug War: After Medical Marijuana Mess, Feds Face Big Decision on Pot," by Ryan Grim and Ryan J. Reilly, The Huffington Post, January 26, 2013.

12. See Obama's remarks to *Mail Tribune* on March 22, 2008.

13. "Majority of Parents Support Medical Marijuana Legalization, Says Survey by Partnership at drugfree.org," by Robin Wilkey, The Huffington Post, July 17, 2013; see, also, "Poll: Public Supports Medical Marijuana, but Not Full Pot Legalization," by Fred Backus, *CBS News*, November 18, 2011.

14. Ibid.

15. Ibid.

16. Ibid.

17. See "Barack, the Unmerciful Drug Warrior?: Why Doesn't Obama Pardon More Drug Offenders?" by Jacob Sullum, *Forbes*, August 15, 2013; and "Obama Has Granted Clemency More Rarely Than Any Modern President," by Dafna Linzer, *ProPublica*, November 2, 2012.

18. Ibid.

19. "Despite New Pardons, Obama's Clemency Rate Is Still Lowest in Recent History," by Cora Currier, *ProPublica*, March 5, 2013; and "Crime and Punishment and Obama," by Bill Keller, *The New York Times*, February 24, 2014.

20. "White House Czar Calls for End to 'War on Drugs,'" by Gary Fields, *The Wall Street Journal*, May 14, 2009.

21. http://www.recovery.gov/Accountability/inspectors/Documents /Edward%20Byrne%20Memorial%20Justice%20Assistance%20 Grants%20and%20Byrne%20Competitive%20Grants.pdf.

22. See "Bummer: Barack Obama Turns Out to Be Just Another Drug Warrior," by Jacob Sullum, *Reason*, October 2011; and "7 Ways the Obama Administration Has Accelerated Police Militarization," by Radley Balko, The Huffington Post, July 10, 2013.

23. See "7 Ways the Obama Administration Has Accelerated Police Militarization," by Radley Balko, The Huffington Post, July 10, 2013; and *Rise of the Warrior Cop*, by Radley Balko, p. 301.

24. Ibid.

25. See "Bummer: Barack Obama Turns Out to Be Just Another Drug Warrior," by Jacob Sullum, *Reason*, October 2011; and "7 Ways the Obama Administration Has Accelerated Police Militarization," by Radley Balko, The Huffington Post, July 10, 2013.

Chapter 18

1. See, for example, *Smoke and Mirrors*, by Dan Baum, p. 177.

2. For documentation on the corruption of public officials as a result of the drug war, see Chapter 11: Undercover Police; also, *Drugs: America's Holy War*, by Arthur Benavie, pp. 69–71; and *Beyond the War on Drugs*, by Steven Wisotsky, p. 147.

3. "Has the Drug War Created an Officer Liars' Club?" by Joseph D. McNamara, *Los Angeles Times* (Orange County edition), February 11, 1996.

4. See Chapter 10: Criminal Informants.

5. "Crime in the United States, 2010," U.S. Department of Justice—Federal Bureau of Investigation, released September 2011; and, SAMHSA, Center for Behavioral Health Statistics and Quality (formerly the Office of Applied Studies), *National Survey on Drug Use and Health*, 2009 and 2010.

6. http://www.bjs.gov/content/pub/pdf/aus9010.pdf.

7. http://www.drugwarfacts.org/cms/Drug_Usage#Lifetime.

8. http://www.sentencingproject.org/template/page.cfm?id=128; and http://www.bjs.gov/content/pub/pdf/ppus11.pdf, tables 2, 3, 4, and 6.

9. "Introduction, Proposed Standards on Collateral Sanctions and Administrative Disqualifications of Convicted Persons," by American Bar Association, Task Force on Collateral Sanctions, January 18, 2002. See, also, *Marked*, by Devah Pager, pp. 32–35, and *Banished*, by Katherine Beckett and Steve Herbert, pp. 16–22.

10. For documentation, see *Drugs: America's Holy War*, by Arthur Benavie, p. 36.

11. Ibid., p. 44.

Chapter 19

1. http://www.justice.gov/dea/docs/factsheet.pdf.

2. See "National Drug Control Strategy, Data Supplement 2012," by Gil Kerlikowske, director, Office of National Drug Control Policy, tables 62, 63, and 64. The price for heroin dropped from $1,896 to $408 over the same period; for crack, the price declined from $450 in 1986 to $64 in 2011; and for methamphetamine the price fell from $437 in 1981 to $123 in 2011. These number are for purchases of 2 grams or less for cocaine, 1 gram or less for heroin and crack, and 10 grams or less for methamphetamine. The price trends for larger amounts purchased are similar.

3. Ibid., table 65; see also *Drug War Heresies*, by Robert J. MacCoun and Peter Reuter, pp. 30–31.

4. http://www.monitoringthefuture.org/data/12data/pr12t14.pdf, and ibid., p. 32.

5. "Police Crackdowns: Initial and Residual Deterrence," by Lawrence W. Sherman, in *Criminal Justice Review Annual*, edited by Michael Tonry and Norval Morris, 1990, pp. 18–25; See also, *Reckoning*, by Elliot Currie, p. 105.

6. "Policing Drugs: The Cultural Transformation of a Victimless Crime," by Jerome H. Skolnick, Jurisprudence and Social Policy Program, University of California, Berkeley, 1986, pp. 47–49; See, also, *Reckoning*, by Elliot Currie, p. 206.

7. *The Fix*, by Michael Massing, p. 71.

8. ODALE stands for Office for Drug Abuse Law Enforcement.

9. "A view from the front lines of the drug war," by Volney V. Brown, *Orange County Register*, September 10, 1996.

10. See *Drug War Heresies*, by Robert J. MacCoun and Peter Reuter, pp. 96–98, 256–257; and *America's Longest War*, by Steven B. Duke and Albert C. Gross, p. 242.

11. *Drug War Heresies*, by Robert J. MacCoun and Peter Reuter, pp. 256–257.

12. Personal possession and use are still legally prohibited, but violations are administrative matters, not criminal. Trafficking remains a criminal offense. Experts believe the decline in diseases is a result of people being less afraid to get medical help.

13. "Drug Decriminalization in Portugal: Lessons for Creating Fair and Successful Drug Policies," by Glenn Greenwald, CATO Institute, April 2, 2000; and "5 Years After: Portugal's Drug Decriminalization Policy Shows Positive Results," by Brian Vastag, *Scientific American*, April 7, 2009.

14. "Toward a Global View of Alcohol, Tobacco, Cannabis, and Cocaine Use: Findings from the WHO World Mental Health Surveys," by Louisa Degenhardt et al., July 1, 2008, available at http://journals.plos.org/plosmedicine/article?id=10.1371/journal.pmed.0050141. The countries were Colombia, Mexico, United States, Belgium, France, Germany, Italy, Netherlands, Spain, Ukraine, Israel, Lebanon, Nigeria, South Africa, Japan, People's Republic of China, and New Zealand. In addition, per capita cannabis use in the United States and New Zealand were by far the highest of any other country; and the United States was an outlier in the use of cocaine.

15. Statement by Edward Ellison in the *London Daily Mail*, March 10, 1998.

16. See *Crack in America*, edited by Craig Reinarman and Harry G. Levine, p. 348.

17. *Busted*, edited by Mike Gray, p. 206.

18. "Ending the 'War on Drugs': The Fierce Urgency of . . . When?" by Norm Stamper, The Huffington Post, February 26, 2009.

19. "18th Annual National Survey Results of Police Chiefs and Sheriffs," *National Association of Chiefs of Police*, 2005.

20. Ibid.

21. http://medicalmarijuana.procon.org/view.additional-resource.php?resourceID=000149.

22. *Drug War Heresies*, by Robert J. MacCoun and Peter Reuter, p. 1.

23. "Task Force Report from ASC to Attorney General Janet Reno," 1995, quoted in *Crack in America*, by Craig Reinarman and Harry G. Levine, p. 249.

24. "A Communication to Judge James P. Gray," in *Why Our Drug Laws Have Failed and What We Can Do about It*, 2nd ed., p. 103.

25. *Busted*, edited by Mike Gray, p. 210.

26. http://www.foxnews.com/world/2010/05/13/ap-impact-years-trillion-war-drugs-failed-meet-goals/.

27. *The Budgetary Impact of Ending Drug Prohibition*, by Jeffrey A. Miron and Katherine Waldock, see p. 12, table 7.

Selected Bibliography

Alexander, Michelle. *The New Jim Crow*. New York: The New Press, 2010.

Ashenfelter, Orley C., and David Card, eds. *Handbook of Labor Economics*. Netherlands: Elsevier B.V, vol. 3C, 1999.

Austin, James, and John Irwin. *It's About Time: America's Imprisonment Binge*, 3rd ed. Belmont, CA: Wadsworth Publishing, 1994.

Baker, Mark. *Cops*. New York: Simon & Schuster, 1985.

Balko, Radley. *Rise of the Warrior Cop*. New York: Public Affairs, 2013.

Baum, Dan. *Smoke and Mirrors*. Boston: Little, Brown and Company, 1996.

Beckett, Katherine, and Steve Herbert. *Banished*. New York: Oxford University Press, 2009.

Benavie, Arthur. *Drugs: America's Holy War*. New York and London: Routledge, 2009.

Bernstein, Nell. *All Alone in the World: Children of the Incarcerated*. New York: The New Press, 2007.

Bertram, Eva, Morris Blachman, Kenneth Sharpe, and Peter Andreas. *Drug War Politics*. Berkeley: University of California Press, 1996.

Brodzinsky, David M., and Marshall D. Schechter, eds. *The Psychology of Adoption*, rev. ed. New York: Oxford University Press, 1993.

Brown, Michael K., and Martin Carnoy. *Whitewashing Race: The Myth of a Color Blind Society*. Oakland: University of California Press, 2005.

Chemerinsky, Erwin. *The Case against the Supreme Court*. New York: Viking, 2014.

Cole, David. *No Equal Justice*. New York: The New Press, 1999.

Currie, Elliot. *Reckoning*, 1st ed. New York: Hill and Wang, 1993.

Duke, Steven B., and Albert C. Gross. *America's Longest War*. New York: G. P. Putnam's Sons, 1994.

Eddy, Mark J., and Julie Poehlmann, eds. *Children of Incarcerated Parents*, 1st ed. Washington, D.C.: Urban Institute Press, 2010.

Elliston, Frederick A., and Michael Feldberg, eds. *Moral Issues in Police Work*. Washington, D.C.: Rowman & Littlefield Publishers, 1985.

Frankel, Marvin E. *Criminal Sentences: Law without Order*. New York: Hill and Wang, 1973.

Gray, James P. *Why Our Drug Laws Have Failed and What We Can Do about It*, 2nd ed. Philadelphia: Temple University Press, 2012.

Gray, Mike, ed. *Busted*. New York: Nation Books, 2002.

Haldeman, H. R. *The Haldeman Diaries*. New York: G. P. Putnam's Sons, 1994.

Hallinan, Joseph T. *Going Up the River*. New York: Random House, 2003.

Harcourt, Bernard E. *Illusion of Order*. Cambridge, MA: Harvard University Press, 2001.

Harris, David A. *Profiles in Injustice*. New York: The New Press, 2002.

Herivel, Tara, and Paul Wright, eds. *Prison Profiteers*. New York: The New Press, 2007.

Hyde, Henry. *Forfeiting Our Property Rights*. Washington, D.C.: CATO Institute, 1995.

Jacobs, Bruce A. *Dealing Crack*, 1st ed. Boston, MA: Northeastern University Press, 1999.

Levy, Leonard W. *A License to Steal*. Chapel Hill: The University of North Carolina Press, 1996.

Lindsey, Duncan. *The Welfare of Children*. New York: Oxford University Press, 2003.

MacCoun, Robert J., and Peter Reuter. *Drug War Heresies*. New York: Cambridge University Press, 2001.

Madinger, John. *Confidential Informant*. New York: CRC Press, 1999.

Marx, Gary T. *Under Cover*. Berkeley: University of California Press, 1988.

Massing, Michael. *The Fix*, 1st paperback printing. Berkeley: University of California Press, 2000.

Mauer, Marc. *Race to Incarcerate*. New York: The New Press, 2006.

Mauer, Marc, and Meda Chesney-Lind, eds. *Invisible Punishment*. New York: The New Press, 2002.

Mele, Christopher, and Teresa A. Miller, eds. *Civil Penalties, Social Consequences*. New York: Routledge, 2005.

Miron, Jeffrey A. *Drug War Harms*. Oakland: The Independent Institute, 2004.

Muir, William Ker, Jr. *Police: Streetcorner Politicians*. Chicago: University of Chicago Press, 1979.

Natapoff, Alexandra. *Snitching*. New York and London: New York University Press, 2009.

Obama, Barack. *Dreams from My Father*, repr. New York: Broadway Books, 2007.

Pager, Devah. *Marked*. Chicago: The University of Chicago Press, 2007.

Petersilia, Joan. *When Prisoners Come Home*. New York: Oxford University Press, 2003.

Provine, Doris Marie. *Unequal under Law*. Chicago: The University of Chicago Press, 2007.

Reinarman, Craig, and Harry G. Levine, eds. *Crack in America*. Berkeley: University of California Press, 1997.

Roberts, Dorothy. *Shattered Bonds*. New York: Basic Civitas Books, 2002.

Sampson, Robert, and John H. Laub. *Crime in the Making: Pathways and Turning Points through Life*. New York: Oxford University Press, 1995.

Schlosser, Eric. *Reefer Madness*. Boston: Houghton Mifflin Company, 2003.

Settle, Rod. *Police Informers: Negotiation and Power*. Sydney, Australia: Federation Press, 1995.

Skolnick, Jerome H. *Justice without Trial*, 4th ed. New Orleans: Quid Pro Books, 2013.

Smelser, Neil, William Julius Wilson, and Faith Mitchell Page, eds. *America Becoming: Racial Trends and Their Consequences*, vol. 2. Washington, D.C.: National Academies Press, 2001.

Stuckler, David, and Sanjay Basu. *The Body Economic: Why Austerity Kills*. New York: Basic Books, 2013.

Sullivan, Mercer L. *"Getting Paid": Youth Crime and Work in the Inner City*, 1st ed. Ithaca, NY: Cornell University Press, 1989.

Tonry, Michael. *Malign Neglect*. New York: Oxford University Press, 1995.

Travis, Jeremy. *But They All Come Back*. Washington, D.C.: The Urban Institute Press, 2005.

Western, Bruce. *Punishment Inequality in America*. New York: Russell Sage Foundation, 2006.

Wilson, James Q., and Joan Petersilia, eds. *Crime: Public Policies for Crime Control*. New York: Oxford University Press, 1999.

Wisotsky, Steven. *Beyond the War on Drugs*. Buffalo, NY: Prometheus Books, 1990.

Young, Alford A., Jr. *The Minds of Marginalized Black Men: Making Sense of Mobility, Opportunity, and Future Life Chances*. Princeton, NJ: Princeton University Press, 2011.

Index

About the Author

ARTHUR BENAVIE, PhD, is emeritus professor of economics at the University of North Carolina at Chapel Hill, NC. He is the author of several books, including *Deficit Hysteria*, *Social Security under the Gun*, and *Drugs: America's Holy War*. He has won several awards for excellence in undergraduate teaching, as well as the University of Michigan's Fred M. Taylor Award in Economic Theory.